CLARENDON LAW SERIES

Edited by
PAUL CRAIG

CLARENDON LAW SERIES

LAND LAW

SECOND EDITION

By
ELIZABETH COOKE

University of Reading

OXFORD
UNIVERSITY PRESS

OXFORD
UNIVERSITY PRESS

Great Clarendon Street, Oxford, OX2 6DP,
United Kingdom

Oxford University Press is a department of the University of Oxford.
It furthers the University's objective of excellence in research, scholarship,
and education by publishing worldwide. Oxford is a registered trade mark of
Oxford University Press in the UK and in certain other countries

© E. Cooke, 2012

The moral rights of the author have been asserted

First Edition published in 2006
Second Edition published in 2012

Impression: 1

British Library Cataloguing in Publication Data
Data available

Library of Congress Cataloging in Publication Data
Library of Congress Control Number: 2012935409

ISBN 978–0–19–965322–5
ISBN 978–0–19–965323–2 (pbk)

Printed in Great Britain by
CPI Group (UK) Ltd, Croydon, CR0 4YY

'Leaf and branch, water and stone; we put the thought of all that we love into all that we make.'
J. R. R. Tolkien

PREFACE TO THE SECOND EDITION

This book is about the structure of land law and the way that land lawyers think; much of it therefore remains unchanged. But the law has developed, in the last few years, far enough to warrant a second edition. We have new material to come to terms with in the law of common intention constructive trusts and of proprietary estoppel; and the jurisprudence of human rights has continued to mature. My own perspective has changed too; since the summer of 2008 I have been serving as a Law Commissioner for England and Wales, and have had tremendous fun helping to bring the Commission's project on easements and covenants to a conclusion. I hope that what I have written may have conveyed some of that fun to those who read this book; to all of you, thank you for reading.

Lizzie Cooke
January 2012

PREFACE TO THE FIRST EDITION

I have written this book because Peter Birks asked me to.

Peter's vision for the Clarendon series was that they should be accessible and useful to three audiences: to students; to judges, academics, and other lawyers; and to folk who are not lawyers but would like to know what the law is about. A tall order indeed. I have had all three in mind. I would be particularly pleased if I could pass on to a student readership some of my love for this subject, with its ancient roots and modern blossoming, its structure, and its messiness.

To the student: this is not an exposition of the law designed to enable you to solve problems. It is intended to be useful as an introduction before you begin detailed study, and again when you have finished that analysis, to draw together the threads, to show you the bigger picture, and to show you where it is all going. There is much more to land law than a set of rules about land transfers. The subject goes to the heart of social policy and plays a part in determining what sort of society we live in.

I have had a lot of help. Parts of the draft have been read by two lawyers and two physicists: I am so grateful to Martin Dixon, Sarah Worthington, Jonathan Gregory, and Phil Wolf, who have given their time and their comments generously, and have helped me to see more clearly what I am trying to do. Each has made a difference to the book in its final form. The bad bits are all my own work. I should like to thank Michael Croker, Registrar at the Land Registry's Stevenage Office, for information and enlightenment. The conventions of the Clarendon series prevent my giving proper acknowledgment in the text to all the writers whose work is central to my thinking about land law. To all of them, my thanks for all they have taught me; to borrow Sarah's words from the preface of her wonderful Clarendon, they will recognize their footprints in what I have written. My dear husband, John, has read the whole manuscript at a late stage, and has made a lot of important points; he, Gillian, and Dominic have kept me sane and jolly.

I have endeavoured to state the law as it stands in mid-March 2006, and a few days after the House of Lords delivered its judgment in *Kay and others v London Borough of Lambeth, Leeds City Council v Price and others* [2006] UKHL 10. There has therefore not been a great deal of time to reflect on that decision. Nor do we know the outcome of the UK's application for leave to appeal to the Grand Chamber the decision of the European Court of Human Rights in Application No. 44302/02 *Pye v UK* (2005). Interesting times.

Lizzie Cooke
March 2006

CONTENTS

TABLE OF CASES

TABLES OF STATUTES

1

WHAT IS LAND LAW?

We belong to the earth. We are made of it; we are tied to it by gravity; indirectly, we eat it. Without it, there is no human race. In the end, we return to it: dust to dust, ashes to ashes.

Until then, the earth belongs to us. Or so we say. English land law has grown from our deeply entrenched habit of saying 'mine!', a word that all toddlers learn quickly and shout often. We say it not only of our toys and our food and our houses, but also about bits of the earth. English land law is the product of people who say they *own* land. Some communities do not have this habit of thought. But we have, and our land law is shaped by that fact. A while after we learn to say 'mine!', we learn to share; and we have to do that with the earth too. The Englishman's house is his castle, but no man is an island; he is more like a spider diagram or a complex road junction. Land is so rich and complex, and so helpfully permanent (usually), that owning it is not like owning a piano. 'My' land is a home and a source of income for me, a pathway for my neighbour, a sort of hostage for the bank, a place to stay for my lodger, and an investment for my landlord.

Land law is about the connections between people and land. It is also about the relationships between people, jostling for space and allocating resources. It is as fascinating as people themselves, and as dynamic. As people change, so do the ways they use and think about land, and land law today looks different, even on this one small island, from how it did fifty years ago, and in another generation's time it will have changed again.

The land law in this book is the law of part of a small island. It is the law of England and Wales; not Northern Ireland, which has adopted some but not all of English land law; nor Scotland, which has inherited the Roman law of property, in common with most of Europe and in contrast with England and Wales. English land law is based on the 'common law', developed here after the island was invaded and conquered in 1066 and to some

extent separated from the continental legal heritage. Today that
separation seems more disturbing than it did in the days before
the European Union; it is no longer possible to write a book like
this without at least glancing at the civil law systems across the
channel.

But the land law in this book is also the law of a significant
part of the world. As a colonial power, up until the mid-
twentieth century, we exported English law to the nations we
conquered. It was often an inappropriate gift. But the result is
that nowadays, absent the British Empire, we can identify a
'common law world' with which we share a legal tradition.
Much of what is found in this book would not be especially
foreign to a lawyer in Australia, New Zealand, parts of North
America or of Africa; and developments in the law of those
jurisdictions are nowadays enriching our understanding of the
assumptions underlying English land law.

So what is land law? A great deal of law that involves or
regulates land and its use—planning law, environmental law, the
law of construction contracts, and many others—is not part of
the core discipline with which we are concerned here. Land law
is the law concerning property rights in land, also known as the
law of real property. So what are property rights? What is real
property? What is land?

WHAT ARE PROPERTY RIGHTS?

'Property' in everyday language has a range of meanings. Think
of 'the property of a gentleman'; 'the properties of carbon
dioxide'; or the description of God in the *Book of Common
Prayer*, 'whose property is always to have mercy'. Property for
a lawyer means rights—rights that people have in, or over,
things, tangible or otherwise. A very wide range of things can
be the subject of property rights—everything from socks to
shares, from ideas to animals. Things that belong are important
to me in monetary terms, or because I like or enjoy them, and
even in terms of my identity, my status, and my relationship
with other people. There are a few things in which the law states
that there cannot be property rights, for a range of reasons.
Among them are people, for moral reasons; so we do not have

slaves, and 'my' children are not mine in any proprietary sense. The fresh air we breathe cannot be property, because for a thing to be property it must be in some sense scarce. There is no point in having property rights in something that everyone has more than enough of. Contrast bottled oxygen. The view from my window cannot be my property in this jurisdiction, even though it is unique. The reason for that may be convenience; a view is something that English law does not want people to litigate about.

There are many different property rights. There is ownership, the most important and extensive property right; ownership enables you to say 'this is mine'. There are lesser rights which we can call non-ownership rights. They are sometimes called third party rights, because when land is bought, the former owner transfers it to the new owners (two parties to a deal) and there may be third parties who hold non-ownership rights in the land such as rights of way, or a mortgage or a tenancy. Such rights are property rights—or, as we say, they are proprietary[1]—even though they are not ownership rights.

All these property rights can be thought of as bundles, or collections of abilities. The bundle known as ownership is the most extensive. Think of something of yours: a potted plant or a bicycle. You can do a lot with it; 'can' in the sense not merely that you are physically able to, but also that you are entitled to. You can use it; hide it; care for it; neglect it; destroy it; lend it to someone; give it away; sell it. There is a problem if you try to do any of these things with my property. You will find either that you physically can (use it, destroy it etc), but will be in trouble for infringing my rights; or that however hard you try (to lend it, give it away, sell it) you will not succeed.

Is there a core to the ownership bundle, one essential ingredient? One suggestion is alienability, meaning that if something is mine, I have the power, legally, to make it yours. This seems to be almost always true; although there are counter-examples. Much of the nation's heritage property belongs to the National Trust, which is able to acquire land and then to declare it

---

[1] The word 'proprietary' is here used interchangeably with the adjective 'property'.

inalienable. It is property nonetheless. A more truly core concept is the power to exclude others. My piano is mine, and
therefore I am entitled to stop you playing it; my land is mine,
and so I can keep you out. There are counter-examples:
I cannot keep you out, for example, if you are a policeman
with a search warrant. But outside those exceptions, I can keep
you out because I have the key; more importantly, I can
keep you out because I am entitled to do so. The law gives
me 'trespassory protection'.

The lesser property rights are also bundles, though smaller
ones. If I am the tenant, rather than the owner, of a house, there
are things I can do with it. I can invite guests in. I can, in most
tenancies, choose what to plant in the garden. I can sell my
tenancy. I can close the door on anyone, the landlord included,
during the term of the tenancy. And of course there are lots of
things I cannot do, such as demolish the house. The holder of a
right of way can walk along it (or drive, or whatever are the
terms of the easement), and the courts will help him prevent
anyone, including the owner, from interfering with his right.
But his right of way does not authorize him to dig up the track,
or to build on it.

Notice the complexity being described here. Land is so useful
and flexible that lots of people can have different sets of rights in
it; land may be 'mine', while other people may have property
rights in it. Indeed, land law does not always make a rigid
distinction between ownership and non-ownership rights; if
I grant you a 999-year lease of my land, that lease is an ownership right (both of us can reasonably say that the land is 'mine'),
and it is also a non-ownership right held by you in *my* land.

We have to think about the strength, or enforceability, of
these bundles of rights as well as their content. Being legal rights,
property rights are enforced by society, or the state, and ultimately by force. And property rights, by contrast with personal
rights, are special because they are good against everyone. Personal rights, by contrast, are only good against one person or a
few individuals. It works like this. Rights involve other people.
If I have a right to do something, you have an obligation not to
prevent me; if I have a right to payment for something you have
bought from me, then you have an obligation to pay me but no

one else has. Property rights are much stronger. This is my lap-top, and it remains my lap-top whoever steals it from me. I can demand it from anyone who has it. By contrast, I have a contractual right to a salary from the University of Reading; that is only a personal right because I cannot demand it from anyone else. There can be personal rights over land: I have a personal right to spend time in my office, and that right arises from my contract of employment. If Reading University sells its land, including my office, I will no longer have a right to spend time in my office. My right to be on/in this bit of land is a personal one, known as a licence. A licence may be contractual, or it may be gratuitous, such as you give to a guest when you invite him in. A lease or tenancy, by contrast, is a property right; it gives exclusive possession of land, usually in return for a money payment to the freehold owner. My lease of a flat gives me a right to be there and to shut everyone else out. I have that right vis-à-vis my landlord, who owns the freehold of the building (these terms will be explained later; they are used here on the basis that most of us have at least a colloquial understanding of them). And if my landlord sells his freehold I will still have that right against any future owner of the building, for as long as the lease lasts. The traditional lodger, living in part of a house with its owner, paying for lodging and perhaps food but without the right to shut the front door on his landlord, has a personal, contractual right to be in the house—a contractual licence—and not a proprietary right.

WHAT IS REAL PROPERTY?

Land law is a department of property law, known technically as 'real property'—the term is less familiar than 'real estate', which is derived from it. Why the term (are pianos unreal?), and why does this form of property require a special area of law?

The term 'real' is easy. It derives from the medieval law of remedies. The law of property protects our rights to exclude, and therefore provides a remedy when property has been taken away from us. At a fairly early stage a division of remedies was evolved; the courts came to the view that for most things, money was an adequate remedy, but not for land. If I took away your falcon or your suit of armour and disposed of it, I would be ordered to pay you damages; but if I deprived you of your land, the uniqueness of that land would demand that the land itself be returned to you. 'Real' derives from the Latin *res*, a thing; for land, the remedy is the thing itself.

All property that is not real is personal. There is an unpleasant overlap of terminology here. The law enforces personal rights and property rights; within the law relating to property rights, the law distinguishes personal property and real property. The distinction between real and personal property used to be vital, because it determined which rules of inheritance would be applied to the property. The heir of one's real property might be different from the heir of one's personal estate. Now there is no difference so far as inheritance is concerned. And the law of remedies, the origin of the distinction, is today much more flexible, so that there is no firm rule that real property attracts real rather than monetary remedies. Nevertheless the term 'real property' is still used, partly out of lawyers' habit, as a convenient way of delineating land law from the law relating to other types of property.

Historically, the law of real property was special. Why? The answer is a mix of both current and outmoded concepts. To some extent it arose from the special value of land, in a bygone era when nothing else was so valuable or so significant to the individual. That is now no longer the case; one's pension, perhaps, or other investments may have taken over that importance. What remains is the other reason: the public aspect of land ownership. The state has an interest in the protection of all forms of property (this used to be the province of the legal philosophers, but is now expressed more visibly in the Human Rights Act 1998); arguably, if rights in land become chaotic the resulting social disruption is greater than if other forms of ownership are threatened. The state has a role in ensuring the certainty and the publicity of land ownership, for everyone's sake. The flip side of that particular coin is taxation. Land is a source of revenue, and many of the fluctuations in English land law have happened when the state has felt the need to assert or increase its ability to cream off some of the value of land.

At any rate, real property continues to be governed by rules different from those that apply to cushions or copyrights. Perhaps the most convincing reason for this today is complexity. In land, but not in most items of personal property, it is possible to have numerous different bundles of rights—numerous interests, as we say—organized amongst themselves according to importance, and also across time. Some rights in land can be exercised now, while others can only be used later, like a theatre ticket bought now for a performance next week. We have to say more about this later.

WHAT IS LAND?

Land law is about property rights in land; and we have to say what 'land' means, for it refers not merely to the earth. Land is defined in section 205(1)(ix) of the Law of Property Act 1925:

'Land' includes land of any tenure, and mines and minerals, whether or not held apart from the surface, buildings or parts of buildings (whether the division is horizontal, vertical or made in any other way) and other corporeal hereditaments; also a manor, an advowson, and a rent and other incorporeal hereditaments, and an easement, right, privilege, or benefit in, over, or derived from land; . . . and 'mines and minerals' include any strata or seam of minerals or substances in or under any land, and powers of working and getting the same, . . . and 'manor' includes a lordship, and reputed manor or lordship . . . [2]

This is wordy and off-putting. It is also an unhelpful mix of things and rights. The important points to take from it at this stage are, first, that land includes the buildings on it; and it includes buildings separated from the earth, so that the owner of the top-storey flat is still a landowner. Second, that 'land' also includes intangible things: 'incorporeal hereditaments' are rights, such as rights of way. The owner of a typical English mid-terrace house needs access to his garden from the street. As

[2] Some words have been omitted here: some no longer appear in the statute because they have been repealed, and are represented there by dots; others remain in the statute but are not quoted here because they are obsolete but have not yet been repealed.

well as owning his house and garden, therefore, he is likely to have a right of way across his neighbours' gardens from the end of the terrace. That right of way is land. It is a right that relates to a different piece of land from the house and garden itself; and it cannot be exercised by anyone who does not own that house and garden. It can be thought of as an item of intangible property, attached to physical property. Third, land includes some rights that are not attached to physical land. An advowson is the right to choose a priest to be rector of a church; we shall not be saying any more about that. The lordship of a manor is a medieval survival, a collection of rights stripped of any useful content and likely to be meaningless or irrelevant now.

It is a peculiarity of English land law that easements (useful rights over another's land, such as a right of way) come into the second category rather than this third one; they have to be linked with physical land, and cannot be enjoyed as stand-alone rights. By contrast, a public right of way, over a street or a footpath, is not regarded as a property right and does not fall within this definition of land. This is difficult to explain, because the public right of way is certainly a right to do something on land; but it is easy to see that my right to walk down the pavement does not increase my personal wealth because everyone else has it too. It has no scarcity value. The law will defend my use of it; but it does not give me the power to prevent others from doing the same. There is no trespassory protection which, as we have seen, is an essential element of ownership and is important in some form for the non-ownership rights.

The statute does not give a complete answer to 'What is land?', and the courts have filled in some detail. Ownership of land includes, unless the contrary is stipulated, most of what can be found on it. Most importantly, buildings and everything fixed permanently to them, and crops and plants growing on it. It includes anything buried in the ground; but Roman coins and other historical items buried in or found on the land count as treasure trove and must be surrendered to the state. The rule is 'finders keepers' for anything found on land, rather than buried in it, whether the finder is the landowner or his visitor (but not a trespasser). Buildings themselves are ambiguous; what about the garden shed, wired up and perhaps plumbed in? What about the fixed but removable features of the building, such as the fitted kitchen or the light bulbs? The law has sorted things out as they have arisen, looking at the extent to which these potential 'fixtures' are actually fixed to the building, and the purpose of their being fixed. Were they intended to be taken away again? Were they intended to make the house a better house, or were they nailed up, as a picture might be, simply as a secure place to put something which was not meant to form part of the house.

There is a collection of rather dry rules here. They should never be needed at all when land is sold because a properly written contract will leave nothing to litigate about. They may become relevant in a dispute about inheritance (does 'my house' include my pictures?). One of the leading modern cases about the nature of land was about a mobile home,[3] and its purpose was not to determine ownership but to decide whether or not the building fell within the limits of rent control regulation. It could only do so if it was part of the land; and the court held that it was. In doing so, the court solved one small practical problem for one individual, and as a by-product added a paragraph to explanations of what land is.

TENSIONS AND THEMES IN LAND LAW

Land law is the battle ground for a struggle between competing categories of rights and competing values. Is the law to respond to complexity by simplifying, so as to make land as marketable as possible; or is it to respond by preserving as many rights as possible, at the expense, if necessary, of marketability? Do we safeguard the interests of those wanting to buy land or do we safeguard those who already have rights in it? A shorthand for this set of questions is to ask: is land law to tend towards dynamic security, or static security?

The trend, for a couple of centuries or more, has been to move towards dynamic security. Much of this book is devoted to the story of that trend. Major steps have been taken, sometimes by Parliament and sometimes by the courts, to simplify

---

[3] *Elitestone Ltd v Morris* [1977] 1 WLR 687, HL.

title to land—'title' meaning here the whole complex of rights owned by different people in one piece of land. This is done not by taking rights away but by adjusting their enforceability. So although property rights are in principle distinguishable from personal rights in land by their universal enforceability, that principle has been tweaked, particularly in the last century and a half. Today, property rights vary in their enforceability, and the most important tool used to achieve this has been the registration of title to land.

Registration creates a public record of ownership and of third party rights. It also exerts control over those rights by making the fact, or the form, of registration the crucial element in enforceability. Unregistered rights may have no, or very little, proprietary effect. This has happened even though, at the same time, the law is constantly adapting to provide new protection for those for whom formally created and publicly registered rights are unavailable or unsuitable. The latter trend has become increasingly important as home ownership has become more widespread, and as family relationships have become more complex and informal. So we have seen over the last century something of a tug of war between static and dynamic security, between protection and marketability. Dynamic security has tended to win. We have to ask, and we shall have to keep asking, whether that position is likely to change now that human rights, including the right to protection for our home and our possessions, are becoming part of the way we think about land law.

PROPERTY RIGHTS AND
HUMAN RIGHTS

The Human Rights Act 1998 brought into our domestic law the European Convention on Human Rights and Fundamental Freedoms. It introduced new ways of enforcing human rights: reinterpreting legislation so as to be compatible with the Convention rights, where possible, and declaring legislation to be incompatible with the Convention as a last resort. It therefore brought into new prominence the need to consider all aspects of law in the light of human rights, including property law.

The Convention is not, in the main, about property. But Article 1 of the First Protocol provides:

Every natural or legal person is entitled to the peaceful enjoyment of his possessions. No one shall be deprived of his possessions except in the public interest and subject to the conditions provided for by the law and by the general principles of international law.

The preceding provisions shall not, however, in any way impair the right of a State to enforce such laws as it deems necessary to control the use of property in accordance with the general interest or to secure the payment of taxes or other contributions or penalties.

Article 8 of the Convention provides:

1. Everyone has the right to respect for private and family life, his home and his correspondence.

2. There shall be no interference by a public authority with the exercise of this right except such as is in accordance with the law and is necessary in a democratic society in the interests of national security, for public safety or the economic well-being of the country, for the prevention of disorder or crime, for the protection of health or morals, or for the protection of the rights and freedoms of others.

The human rights affirmed by the Convention are not themselves property rights; they do not, by themselves, give anyone a right over a particular piece of land. Having property is not, under this Convention, a human right. By contrast the South African Constitution, for example, gives all its citizens the right to a home (although it has not yet been possible to make that right a reality). The European Convention gives you the right not to be deprived of a possession or of your home only if you already have one in the first place. As to possessions, Article 1 of the First Protocol to the Convention distinguishes deprivation of possessions from control of their use. The latter is readily justifiable where compensation is paid (an everyday example is the obligation of a landowner to have conduits for utilities passing over or under his land if required); but deprivation is more serious, and the European Court of Human Rights has looked particularly at issues of 'proportionality', asking whether the deprivation in question is a proportionate and reasonable means of attaining the public purpose that it is supposed to serve.

The issue for land law is whether or not the Convention rights force a re-examination of the property rights we already recognize. When a landlord has a statutory right to evict a tenant from the landlord's property purely because the tenancy has come to an end and without giving any other reason, is that compatible with the tenant's human rights to respect for his home and to peaceful enjoyment of his possessions? When the law has given a long leaseholder the right to 'enfranchise', that is, to buy the freehold of his leasehold property at a price that reflects the value of the ground but not of the buildings, is that a justifiable interference with the freeholder's right to enjoy his possessions? When a bank repossesses a house because mortgage repayments have not been kept up, is that an infringement of human rights? Where a landowner has lost his title to a squatter, who has gained ownership of the land by treating it as his own for a number of years, is that compatible with the landowner's human rights?

Putting that dilemma more generally: does the Human Rights Act 1998 force us to re-examine established property rights on the basis that they might *not* be in the public interest or that, if they are, the means taken to enforce them might not be proportionate to the interest protected? If for example the law states that you must leave your home because it is someone else's property and that you have no proprietary or contractual right to be there, can you complain that your human rights have been violated? Until a few years ago the answer given by the courts was 'no, never'. Today, the answer is 'possibly', when the landowner is a public authority. On the other hand, the issue about the squatter's title has now been the subject of a decision in Strasbourg, and the answer given is surprisingly comfortable for the common law tradition, as is the answer about leasehold enfranchisement.

So there is no question of a general dismantling, or even threatening, of our property law in the face of human rights. Nevertheless, the impact of human rights is becoming a pervasive issue as litigants and the courts take on board the fact that rights and remedies in land law are, at least, open to challenge on the basis of human rights. A number of well-established principles will continue to be re-examined over the years.

Those, then, are the concepts necessary to an understanding of land law. In the next chapter we look at the way property rights in land have been developed over centuries in order to reach the position we see today.

BIBLIOGRAPHY

P. Birks, 'Before We Begin: Five Keys to Land Law' in S. Bright and J. Dewar, eds, *Land Law: Themes and Perspectives* (Oxford, Oxford University Press, 1998) 457.

S. Bright, 'Of Estates and Interests: a Tale of Ownership and Property Rights' in S. Bright and J. Dewar (eds), *Land Law: Themes and Perspectives* (Oxford, Oxford University Press, 1998) 529.

K. Gray and S. Francis Gray, *Elements of Land Law* (Oxford, Oxford University Press, 5th edn, 2008) 86–114.

2

PROPERTY RIGHTS IN LAND

The first chapter of this book explained some of the central concepts of land law. This chapter introduces the more specific ideas that form the building blocks of land law, namely property rights in land, and explains how they evolved by a mixture of design and accident. It is in four parts. The first is about ownership rights. The second introduces the systems of law and equity and the contrast between legal and equitable ownership rights. The third considers the range of non-ownership rights, both legal and equitable. The result is a heap of rights which may all be found in one piece of land. The fourth part of this chapter explains a little about the enforceability of the different elements of this heap. How the heap is organized, and enforceability managed, is the subject of Chapter 3.

OWNERSHIP OF LAND

Tenure: how is land held?

English law differs from the civil law tradition found in Europe, in that it expresses ownership rights as relationships. Ownership may be freehold or leasehold; these labels can be seen in estate agents' windows. Both forms of ownership imply a connection; for the freehold owner, with the Crown, and for the lease-holder, with a landlord. Both forms are known as 'tenure', that is, ways of holding land, because they were not originally ownership rights. Both evolved, more or less directly, from the landholding system of the Middle Ages, known as the feudal system, in which the king allowed his subjects to hold or control land in return for services rendered to him.

There is a case for ignoring the feudal system. Most English landowners go through life in ignorance of it, and their land-owning activities are unaffected by it. But it remains part of the English land lawyer's mental furniture; it retains some practical effect; and the consolidation of the feudal system under the Norman kings is the first stage in the story that has to be told in order to explain where we are today.

The feudal system was a feature of medieval life. It was a network of relationships, whereby the powerful gave protection, in the form of material assistance and the use of land, to the weaker, who gave their service in return. The system seems to have existed before 1066, both in Anglo-Saxon society and in continental Europe. It has been claimed that the French developed it as a way of strengthening their defence against the Viking invaders, who nevertheless settled and put down strong roots in Normandy in the tenth and eleventh centuries. When one of those Vikings, William of Normandy, won the throne of England, he needed a way to control his conquered country, and the feudal system was one of the means he used. His genius may have been in adapting what had in essence been a series of local networks and converting it into a nationwide system of governance; or it may be that the picture we have today, and the story we tell, is in part the result of the success of the propaganda of later monarchs, in particular of Henry VIII.

The story goes like this. When William took the crown, he took the whole of England; he became, as contemporary legal documents describe him, *Dominus Rex*—'*dominus*' is the Latin term for an owner as well as a master. Then, while remaining owner of the whole of the country, he parcelled out the land and bestowed it on his followers, not as a gift but as something to make use of. One of his followers might be given, for example, a manor near Reading to have and to hold. 'Manor' in that context means simply an area of land; the word has come to mean land with feudal rights attached to it. He is described as a tenant (from the Latin *tenere*, one who holds), and was obliged to provide a service for the king in return. The service was defined as a particular activity. If it was knight service, then the tenant would be obliged to provide a specified number of knights for the king to command in each campaigning season. If the service demanded was religious, known as *frankalmoyn*, then the tenant was obliged to provide prayers for the king's soul (a reasonable arrangement if the tenant was the abbot of a monastery: Battle Abbey near Hastings, founded in order to give thanks for the king's victory, is an obvious example).

This left the tenant with a great deal of land and a weighty obligation. In order to meet it, he would do the same again: he would grant part of the land he held—he would *subinfeudate*—to someone else to hold it in return for services, not to the king but to him. The service would be knight service, but whereas the tenant-in-chief holding the land directly from the king (or 'of the king' as it is usually put) might owe the king 50 knights each summer, *his* tenant might owe *him* five knights. And of course he parcelled his land out to a number of individuals on these terms, in order to fulfil his own obligation. But *these* men would, again, subinfeudate, and so on. Further down the feudal pyramid, the service was less likely to be knight service and more likely to be agricultural; and at the bottom layer of the pyramid was the villein, who held land in return for agricultural service on his own lord's land, and who was not free. He could not leave that land, and he had very few rights.

William did not wipe out all pre-conquest land ownership and impose a feudal structure from the top down, even though the story has often been presented in that way. Such an upheaval would have been neither practical nor necessary. It is likely that the lower rungs of the existing Anglo-Saxon feudal ladders would have been left intact (being occupied by people too insignificant to trouble the new king and his henchmen), with the conqueror's friends slotted into the higher levels. The structure was unified by the king's rank as ultimate lord, and made visible in the ceremony of homage, in which the tenant had to do homage to his lord—he had to kneel, to give his hands to his lord and express loyalty and dependence. Here lie the seeds of many a later war. Would the king of England do homage to the king of France for his cross-channel holdings (as William the Conqueror himself did)?

Although the structure of the feudal system is easy to grasp, the detail of its operation is more subtle. There were far more services than are mentioned here. It is an entertainment to go through them—grand serjeanty, petty serjeanty, socage, gavelkind, copyhold—many of them expressed in the law-French that remained the language of the courts until the sixteenth century; but we get no more from it now than historical diversion. While they lasted there was a wonderfully colourful range of relationships, generating an immense amount of law.

But the feudal system slowly imploded after the enactment of a statute called *Quia Emptores* (simply the first two words of its long title in Latin: 'Because buyers [of land] . . .') in 1290, which forbade further subinfeudation. Thus when a lineage died out, the internal rungs of the feudal ladder disappeared. The end result of the process, all these centuries later, is that with a very few exceptions there is only one remaining layer of feudal tenancy, held directly from the Crown. Therefore all land in the United Kingdom is either held by one feudal tenant directly from the Crown, or retained by the Crown as Crown land. The Crown land we have all seen is the beach; most of the foreshore of England and Wales is still held by the Crown, but there are other areas too.

The feudal services themselves have lost their colour and variety. A series of statutory provisions, from the seventeenth century to 1925, abolished them or converted them into money payments, which rapidly became valueless because of inflation. Today all freehold owners remain feudal tenants, but almost all hold on socage tenure—in theory a form of agricultural service, in practice a nullity. A handful of very distinguished folk who hold their land by statute do something more interesting; the Duke of Marlborough, for instance, holds the Blenheim estate in return for the presentation of a fleur-de-lys flag at Windsor once a year. For the rest of us, the practical significance of the feudal system is very limited indeed. Our land reverts to the Crown if the tenant dies without heirs or a will; and if a tenant becomes bankrupt (or insolvent, in the case of corporate land-owners) the land will ultimately pass to the Crown by a process known as escheat. There remain large areas of Crown land, of course, that have not been granted to feudal landholders.

Over the border, in Scotland, feudalism has only just died. The Abolition of Feudal Tenure etc (Scotland) Act 2002 took effect in 2004 and removes the Crown's position as *dominus*, or ultimate lord of the land. It also removes a whole system of conveyancing and landholding relationships; for the Scots had no *Quia Emptores* and therefore have been free to subinfeudate—and have kept on doing so. Thus land ownership remained in the feudal, ladder-like pattern, with numbers of intermediate tenants receiving feudal services, invariably in monetary form. That pattern has now been wiped out, with compensation where necessary; and with no sign, so far, of any challenge from a human rights point of view despite the fact that, technically, it could be seen as an expropriation of property. The reason multi-layered feudalism survived for so long in Scotland was that it had become a form of planning control; if land was subinfeudated rather than sold outright, the feudal superior could impose services that effectively controlled how the land was used. These obligations have been reorganized as a consequence of the abolition of the feudal system, and the important ones preserved as obligations attached to land, sometimes for the benefit of the former feudal superior and in some cases for the benefit of neighbouring properties.

Further out in the common law world, feudalism remains a live and crucial issue. The processes of settlement and conquest led to the export of English land law; sometimes by agreement, as in New Zealand, more often by imposition, as in Australia. The result was that the land of the colonized jurisdiction vested in the Crown, as surely as it did here in 1066, and the Crown was free to make grants of land—which it did, not in large parcels to military cronies, but in little marketable/farmable/mortgageable/mineable lots to settlers. A modern New Zealander may well be able to trace his title (that is, a chain of ownership) back to a named grantee in the nineteenth century; scarcely anyone in England can trace their title back to the military henchman of 1066. So the colonies took on a fresh, although one-layered, feudalism that independence has not always changed. In Australia and New Zealand, for example (though not in America), land is still held from the Crown.

One of the wonderful developments in land law worldwide in the twentieth and twenty-first centuries has been a re-examination of the position of those who were deprived of land in the process of colonization. Aboriginal title is an important issue now in the common law world, and various different methods have been found of giving, or giving back, or recognizing land rights. And this has led to a fresh look at feudalism. One of the routes to the restoration of land rights in Australia has been the re-examination of what actually happened when land vested in the Crown, and a re-think of the traditional theory. The principal stimulus for this was a case brought by aboriginal Australians living on land which had never been the subject of a feudal grant.[1] It was one of those rare and happy instances where circumstances conspired to produce a test case where the issue in question was clear and isolated. The upshot of this and other cases in Australia was a new view—that the Crown is not literally the owner of ungranted land; it has the right to make feudal grants, and meanwhile the Crown's role pertains more to taking care of the land than to having dominion over it. It has responsibility rather than ownership. Therefore, in these quite unusual circumstances, aboriginal title survived colonization; and legislation followed the decision in *Mabo* to give a marginally better deal to aboriginals. The consequences of these decisions for Australia, in constitutional law even more than in land law, are still being worked out; and we may see reflections of the Australian developments in English land law when steps are taken, as is surely likely, to abolish feudalism here.

Estate: for how long is land held?

In land law, then, the feudal relationship is always there, quietly in the background. Tenure is one aspect of the feudal system: it tells us how (ie from whom, and for what service) land is held, as discussed above. A landowner is said to be a tenant[2] who holds land on, or for, a particular tenure. But there is another aspect; the tenant is also said to have an 'estate'. 'Estate' here means a right that is limited in time. A tenant's estate tells us how long his land is held for, because in the feudal system landholding is not supposed to be permanent. When the king and his cronies granted land to those lower down the feudal ladder (or, as discussed, imposed the relationship of their choice on conquered subjects without actually changing the occupation of

---

[1] *Mabo v Queensland (No 2)* (1992) 175 CLR 1.
[2] We are still using the word in the ancient sense of one who holds land, not in the modern sense to denote a leaseholder.

the land), they granted the land for a particular length of time. Why part with it forever? Why not grant land just for the lifetime of a particular tenant, so that when he dies, his immediate lord retrieves the land and can grant it afresh to someone else. He can then choose whether to grant it to the current tenant's son, or to someone who, at the relevant time, might be more useful to him; he can review the services for which it is held; he can perhaps extract a price for the grant. If that was the lord's preference, he would grant a life estate. A more magnanimous approach was to grant the land for an estate not just for life, but 'in tail': the term comes from Norman French, *taillé*, meaning limited. Such an estate (called a fee tail or an entail—the word 'fee' denotes something that can be inherited) lasts for the lifetime of the current tenant and the lives of his direct descendants: thus it can pass from the tenant to his son, to his son's son, etc; but it reverts to the lord when the lineage fails. Much more secure for the tenant was the fee simple estate. This was an estate in fee, again, but the fee was simple: anyone could inherit it. It could pass to the heirs of the tenant, or to anyone else to whom he chose to bequeath it. It was possible for the tenant to prevent it ever passing back to the lord or, ultimately, to the Crown, although it might do so if the tenant had no family and failed to make a will.

As may be imagined, complications arose when the heir was female; also when the heir was a minor, in which case he became the ward (almost the property) of the feudal lord until his majority: there, rather surprisingly, lies the origin of the courts' modern powers in their wardship jurisdiction to protect children. In any event, the lord was usually able to extract a price at the point when the estate changed hands on the death of a tenant.

That sort of thing is long gone, but the different estates remain. Today, virtually all land is held in common socage tenure from the Crown for an estate in fee simple. But in some cases the different estates coexist; and we can say that another difference between English land law and the civil law tradition found in the rest of Europe is that English law is comfortable with the idea that there may be more than one different ownership right coexisting in one piece of land.

Imagine a will made by Ham, leaving his home to his second wife Pam for her lifetime (she therefore takes a life estate), and leaving the fee simple to the son of his first marriage, Sam—a not unusual arrangement. During Pam's lifetime, she holds an estate *in possession*, while Sam's estate is held *in remainder*; both she and Sam have an item of property that they can give away or sell (there is a market in life estates—the property purchased lasts just as long as the original holder lives), although only Pam is entitled to make use of the land right now. When Pam dies, her estate disappears and Sam's fee simple becomes an estate in possession.

Estates can be rather more complex than just described. For example, they can be subject to termination on the happening of specified events, either automatically or at the grantor's option. There is of course a huge volume of law as to which is which, and, in any event, as to what sort of condition is legally acceptable. What is the effect, for example, of a gift of land in fee simple to X provided she never marries? (The answer in that particular instance is that the gift is made unconditional, and the proviso has no effect; but some other clauses aiming to control lives through land have been effective). A fee tail can be limited to the estate owner's male heirs, or his female heirs, or his heirs born of a particular wife, and so the land may pass from one branch of a family to another. Such is the background to Jane Austen's *Pride and Prejudice*. Then there are rules about the characteristics of the estates, and the behaviour of those who hold them. Given the possibility of 'owning' land, if we can call it that, for one's lifetime only, there have to be rules about what one is allowed to do with the land during that time. This is known as the law of waste. Given that these limited estates are nevertheless items of property, there have to be rules about whether, and under what conditions, they can be marketed. Readers of Victorian novels are referred to *Felix Holt* (and, for a modern twist, to Charles Paliser's *Quincunx*); an estate that will last until the death of the last of A's descendants *can* be sold to B, but it will still come to an end on the death of the last of A's descendants, and the potential for that as a narrative device in fiction is delightful, however inconvenient the real-life practicalities.

the two court systems, we have retained the two forms of property right because they have different characteristics.

But the explanation based on the court systems begs a rather longer story. Again we have to go back to the Middle Ages; the classic version of the story involves a knight going away on a crusade, unsure of his return, concerned for the safety of his family and his property in his absence. To secure both he conveys his lands to his friend, to keep for him. He might also hand over his jewellery and his spare horse; but the land cannot just be handed over, and so the knight carries out all the formalities of transfer of legal ownership, so that his friend can truly hold the property for him.

On his return, his friend refuses to re-transfer the land to him. The knight therefore seeks justice from the king, but the judge in the king's court will not assist him; his 'friend' holds the legal title to the land, and the judge does not have the power to go beyond that. However, by the fourteenth century the king has begun to delegate some judicial functions to the Lord Chancellor, and *his* courts, known as the courts of chancery, are an alternative recourse for our deprived knight. The Lord Chancellor holds ecclesiastical office, and his view of things is rather different. His concern is for matters of conscience, and he is prepared to look past the legal title and to order the friend to return the property, for in reality—in conscience, in equity—it belongs to the knight. The dating of all this is obscure, but it seems to have been established by the early fifteenth century.

Once all this has evolved, ownership of land looks different depending upon which court is dealing with a dispute. 'At law' in the king's courts, it belongs to the transferee; 'in equity' it belongs to the knight who transferred it to be held on his behalf or, as the language of the time had it, 'to his use'. The earliest label for what we now call a trust was a 'use', and here is the distinctive feature of common law landholding.

Another question had to be resolved by the courts of equity; what if the friend had sold the land during the knight's absence? The purchaser might not know anything about the knight; should the knight be able to claim it back from him? The courts of equity evolved a rule for this; they took the view that the purchaser should not have to give the land back to the knight unless his conscience was touched by the knight's claim; and his conscience was affected if he knew about that claim. In other words, although legal rights bind all the world, the knight's equitable ownership was enforceable against all except a bona fide purchaser (that is, a purchaser in good faith) of the legal estate for value without notice. There is the rule mentioned earlier; while contemplating it in this chapter it is helpful to bear in mind that it is no longer accurate today because of the effect of title registration, to be explained below and in Chapter 3.

The trust was remarkably useful, and not only for long absences. Friars, debarred by their vows from holding property, had no problem occupying and taking the profits of land held for their use. Feudal tenants anxious to avoid the problems of wardship—whereby the feudal overlord will hold land while an heir is a minor, and then receive a fee for transferring it back to him when he reaches his majority—would transfer land to an adult friend to hold until the child came of age. Restrictions on the ability to pass on one's land by will could be evaded by making the desired arrangement behind a trust, known at that date as a 'use' because it involved land being transferred to X 'for the use of' Y. We now call X the trustee and Y the beneficiary; Y's equitable ownership of the land is also known as a beneficial interest. Henry VIII, anxious to reap all the profits of his feudal overlordship, did his best to wipe out that particular device by a law called the 'Statute of Uses' but it was nowhere near sufficiently tightly drafted, and lawyers soon found ways round it by contorted conveyancing devices. The trust was now well-established as a way of organizing entitlement to land.

The development of the trust

The need to keep the reality of land ownership away from feudalism and its associated liabilities died away along with feudalism itself. But other uses were found for the trust, more comprehensible to us now even if remote from most of our experience. The landed gentry, who until the twentieth century owned most of the land in this country, adopted the trust as a structuring device in order to control the ownership of land for future generations. Combine the trust mechanism, whereby land or money can be held by one or more individuals with responsibility to look after it for the benefit of family members, with the potential of the doctrine of estates for the planning of ownership over time, and it is possible to create a structure (known as a 'settlement') in which land is held on trust for some generations. The terms might be that Ed shall own it for his lifetime, then Fred for his lifetime; then it is to pass to Ted and his male heirs; failing those heirs, Samantha is to have a fee simple. Ed gets the land now; he has an estate in possession. Ted knows now that he will get the land later; he has an estate in reversion, which he already owns, although it will not become an estate in possession until Ed's death. Samantha has an estate in remainder; again, that is something she owns now. (The usual analogy is with a theatre ticket, which is now your property, although you cannot enter the theatre until the night of the performance.) Note that normally we are talking about vast tracts of land, most of it tenanted; so the organization of ownership into time-slices was a way of organizing, not so much who lived in the family home/mansion (several generations might live there, irrespective of ownership) but who took the income from the land.

Trusts were also useful as ways of managing the property of married women, who could not hold a legal estate in land until 1882 (a problem for the rich but not for the poor), but could have land held on trust for them. Trusts could also be used, and still are, to enable land to be managed on behalf of an irresponsible beneficiary. This all generated a vast amount of law. What, for example, were the rights of the beneficiaries of the land among themselves and vis-à-vis the trustees? Could the beneficiaries deal with their equitable property rights, or interests? If so, how? Could they sell them? Could they mortgage them? And what of the public interest? The settlement was designed, in large measure, to ensure that land stayed in the family, whereas the industrial revolution demanded a market in land. How might the government ease the aristocracy's stranglehold on the countryside? This problem was to some extent managed by a device called the rule against perpetuities, which states that land may not be settled too far into the future; but death duties proved a far more effective way of getting land out of the hands of the gentry.

The aristocracy and the vast estates have largely gone now, and trusts are important in other areas of life, such as wealth management, investment vehicles, and pensions, rather than family landholdings. Trusts may be set up when the intention is, explicitly, that one person (or, for technical reasons to be explained, more usually two people) shall look after and manage property, such as a pension fund or a nominee shareholding, for another or others. And there will be a trust of land, whether or not the people involved intend it or are even aware of it, in a number of situations. It may happen deliberately, where it is intended that one or more trustees look after land for the benefit of one or more others. There is a trust (whether intended or not) whenever the ownership of land is structured over time. Ham's will, discussed at p 22, creates a trust, whereby the house is held for Pam for her lifetime and then passed on to Sam. During Pam's lifetime, the legal fee simple must be held by trustees for Pam and Sam's benefit. This is because the freehold estates other than the fee simple can only now be equitable. There are no legal life estates. Where there is a life estate, *someone* must hold the legal fee simple, and he will hold it as a trustee. In this case, Ham may appoint trustees in his will, but if he fails to do so his executors will find that they have a continuing role as trustees of the house. Finally, and very importantly, there is a trust whenever land is owned jointly, by two or more people at the same time, for reasons to be discussed.

Why there is a trust in all these cases, and why the trust is so vital to land law, will become clearer when the legislation of 1925 is understood. For now, note that whenever there is a trust, there is a split in ownership, so that one or more trustees hold the legal fee simple, and one or more beneficiaries hold equitable owner-ship rights. Equally, whenever legal and equitable (or 'beneficial') ownership is split between different people, there is a trust.

NON–OWNERSHIP RIGHTS

The possibilities

Whether land is freehold or leasehold, the owner is likely to be subject to the rights of others; these are the legal, rather than physical, limits of ownership. The most important one is likely to be a mortgage.

The major change in patterns of home ownership during the twentieth century has been the rise of owner-occupation. This has been referred to as the property-owning democracy; or, more realistically, as the property-mortgaged-to-a-building-society-owning democracy. For we cannot afford the capital value of our homes, any more than most people could 150 years ago; but what has changed is the availability of finance. It is now normal in this country—far more so than in most of Europe—for the homeowner to be a freeholder or long leaseholder, having borrowed the money for the purchase from a financial institution, and therefore subject to the obligation to repay that loan. Obligations are easily broken, and can be lost forever when the borrower goes bankrupt; a mortgage is a security right which attaches the loan to land. If the loan is not repaid by the borrower, the lender can take the land itself and can sell it and have first call on the sale proceeds to repay his loan. If the land is sold by the borrower and the loan is not repaid, the mortgage (if properly created) sticks to the land, and the lender keeps his rights no matter who the owner is. Thus the mortgage is a non-ownership right in land to which most landowners, whether domestic or commercial, are subject at some stage.

Land is more than just a place in which to live or work; like all other items of property it is an asset, a piece of wealth with a market value. And it is a source of credit. A mortgage may enable the acquisition of the home or business premises; a mortgage of a home already owned may secure a loan for the improvement of that home, or for the financing of the home-owner's business. Once in place, it imposes restrictions on the owner's powers to deal as he wishes with his property. And when these arrangements go wrong, the law must regulate the competing claims of the homeowner, one or more mortgagees, the homeowner's other creditors if any, and her family.

There may well be other non-ownership rights attached to land, apart from those of the mortgagee. Neighbouring land-owners may have rights, either to use the property (eg a right of way) or to restrict the owner's use (eg to ensure that he does not carry on a business from his home). This is the law of easements and covenants, which other jurisdictions call land obligations. Easements and covenants are property rights. As indicated above, one of the big issues to which they give rise is the potential for them to stick to the land when it is sold. They are property rights, but they exist as attachments to other land. They can be transferred from one person to another, but only where those people are the successive owners of the land to which they are attached. They can be thought of as pieces of string, tied at one end to the burdened land and at the other end to the benefited land.

A further external constraint lies in the law of town and country planning. Any development or change of use of land requires, in principle, the permission of the local planning authority. This is potentially far more restrictive than any constraints arising from the private law of land obligations. It is not discussed in detail in this book because it is not part of the law of real property, for the technical reason that the planning authority does not have property rights in our land; but it is a significant and inescapable aspect of land ownership.

Legal and equitable non-ownership rights

We have already seen that equity gives proprietary force to the rights of the beneficiaries of trusts. Our deprived knight found that his moral ownership right was enforced by the courts of equity. He has an equitable ownership right, which is not as strong as a legal ownership right because some purchasers will not be bound by it. Equity also recognizes a whole range of non-ownership rights, giving them proprietary force (albeit not as strong as that of legal rights) in circumstances where they did not qualify as legal rights.

Easements (ie rights of way and other third party rights over land), leases, and mortgages were originally recognized and enforced by the courts of law. But the courts of equity would also recognize them, and would do so on less stringent conditions than those imposed by the courts of law. To be recognized by the law—to be legal—a mortgage must be created by deed (an especially formal piece of paper); but the courts of equity would enforce one created in writing or by an oral agreement, and such a transaction was therefore an equitable mortgage. Similarly with easements and leases. Historically, the courts of equity were kinder than those of law; they would recognize arrangements which *ought* to be enforced, even though formalities had been missed. A key concept of equity is unconscionability: a claimant's informally granted lease, say, would be upheld because it would be unconscionable for the landlord to deny the deal. In modern times there are strict limits to the level of informality that will be tolerated even for an equitable property right to be created, on which more later.[4] Today, of course, equity is no longer operated in separate courts; but the courts will enforce both law and equity, and will recognize both forms of property right.

In addition, there are some non-ownership rights over land recognized only by the courts of equity and not at all at law, and therefore existing today as equitable rather than legal interests. The two most significant examples are the estate contract and the restrictive covenant (the genetics of the two are closely similar, as both are forms of contract).

Estate contracts

I make an enforceable agreement with you, that I will buy your land, say, in a month's time. What are my rights, if any, meanwhile? If you sell the land to C before the month is up, I can get damages from you for breach of contract; but can I instead enforce the contract against C, and therefore get the land? If I die before the month is up, can my right under the contract be inherited? The answer to that is as follows: the courts of equity were prepared to enforce contracts for the purchase of land (outright, or for the purchase of some interest in it such as an easement) by an order for specific performance, ie an order that the contract be performed, rather than merely an award of damages. From that fact there follow a number of steps, although with not entirely watertight logic. Because he could obtain specific performance, the courts of equity regarded the purchaser as in some sense the owner of the land before the

---

[4] See Chapter 5.

contract was completed. So he was, to some extent, an equitable owner; and therefore the seller held on trust for him until completion of the contract. And from that it follows that the answers to the two questions above are 'yes' and 'yes'; the purchaser's pre-completion rights can be inherited; and, like any other equitable interest in land, they can be enforced against a purchaser with notice of them.

This is important not merely for straight sale-and-purchase contracts, but also for other contractual arrangements: for example options to buy (I can buy the land at my option, ie if I choose to do so, for a certain period), or rights of pre-emption (I have first refusal if you choose to sell). These are useful devices for structuring transactions and their finance; and they are robust devices because equity has turned these contractual rights into property rights.

Restrictive covenants

A covenant is a promise in a deed. It is common, when selling part of one's land (to someone who is therefore going to become one's neighbour) to require the buyer to make promises in the deed that transfers the land to him. Nowadays, he might be asked to promise not to use the land for anything other than a private residence. In the nineteenth century, before statutory planning control, and in an era where large areas of land were being sold to provide urban housing, covenants were vital.[5] They would typically include covenants not to build a house in front of a line on a plan (so as to create a pleasant street with front gardens); not to build a house of less than a certain value; not to build more than a certain number of houses; not to use the land for business purposes, etc. I have sold my land to you and you have made these promises. You now sell the land to someone else (or perhaps in small pieces to lots of people); can I enforce those promises against the subsequent owners? If not, they are valueless. At law, the promises generate only personal, contractual obligations. But again, equity rides to the rescue, regarding them as far more substantial:[6] substantial enough to

---

[5] It will be recalled that this was achieved in a different way in Scotland, by the use of feudal obligations.

[6] *Tulk v Moxhay* (1848) 2 Ph 744.

cling to the land, so that subsequent buyers who have notice of them must also observe them. Where title to the land is registered, they can be recorded on the register so as to make them enforceable against purchasers.[7]

Equity's capacity to rescue the covenant was limited by one factor: the covenant must be negative. Positive covenants—those which, however worded, involve a promise to do something rather than to refrain from doing something—do not cling to freehold land.[8] If you promise to maintain the fence between your property and mine, and then sell your land, I cannot make my new neighbour keep your promise. We have already referred to this problem as the reason why flats, and other interdependent properties, are generally leasehold but may now be commonhold.[9]

THE ENFORCEABILITY OF LEGAL AND EQUITABLE PROPERTY RIGHTS

Most property rights in land, then, can be legal or equitable; just a few can only ever be equitable. We began the second section of this chapter by saying that legal and equitable rights in land are of different strengths. What does it mean to say that legal rights are stronger than equitable ones? We saw the answer to this when we looked at the deprived knight and the early form of trust. It involves a modification of what was said in Chapter 1 about the nature of property rights; we said there that while a personal right is good only against the one person with the corresponding obligation (to repay a debt, for example), property rights are good against the whole world. My car is my car, and no one is exempt from that fact. And the same was originally true of legal property rights in land. If I held a legal easement over your garden, I would continue to hold it no matter who

---

[7] See p 37.
[8] *Rhone v Stephens* [1994] 2 AC 310, HL, affirming the law as understood since *Tulk v Moxhay* (see n 6). Positive covenants in leases are different, as we shall see.
[9] See further in Chapter 7.

bought the land. But that was not quite true of equitable interests. The courts of equity, when they began in the Middle Ages to enforce, as property rights, claims which the courts of law would not recognize, had to decide how far they should go. We have seen the conclusion they came to: that equitable rights would not be effective against—would not bind, as the jargon puts it—all the world, but only some people; namely, those who knew about them, or should have known about them, or who took the land without giving value for it (eg someone to whom the land is given). They would bind all except the bona fide purchaser of the legal estate for value without notice.

Thus if I held an equitable easement over your garden, and you then sold the land, the buyer would only be bound by my easement (ie would have to let me keep on using the pathway, or whatever it was) if he knew about it, or if he did not know but should have known (eg because there was an obvious path leading from my garden across yours to the road). Only if he bought the legal estate in the land in good faith, completely innocent of any rights I might have, would he be able safely to ignore my easement in the future, and I would lose my right. If you give the land away, the new owner is not protected from my right; only a purchaser, who gives value for the land, is protected. Legal rights bind all the world; but equitable interests bind all except the bona fide purchaser of a legal estate in the land, for value, without notice of the right claimed. The term 'purchaser' is a wide one and is used of anyone taking any interest in land, whether ownership or a lesser right such as a mortgage, in exchange for something of value, usually money, but not necessarily a market price.

Such was the original distinction between legal and equitable rights; they are good against different classes of people, the equitable ones against a smaller class. The distinction depended upon the operation of the rules about notice, which dictated who knew, and who did not know but should have known and therefore is deemed to know. This is constructive notice: what you should have known about if you had not put the telescope to your blind eye, and if you had made the proper enquiries that any purchaser must make. And that itself became much less simple than it sounds, so that it was terribly easy for a purchaser of land to be caught by equitable interests that he really did not know about and could not, practically, have expected even though legally he was deemed to know about them. It was largely as a result of this difficulty and complexity that land law was thoroughly reformed in 1925.

Following that reform, the distinction between legal and equitable rights survives in its historical form only in the context of land that is not registered. Where land is registered—or, to put it correctly, where title to land (ie ownership of land) is registered—the distinction has become a different one. The modern significance of the legal/equitable distinction is still concerned with enforceability, but is closely linked with registration: legal estates and interests are registrable and are given the full protection of registration, in that registration makes them both valid and enforceable. Equitable interests may have their priority protected by registration, so that they are enforceable against the whole world, but their validity is not guaranteed by the registration system. What this means is that the distinction is in some ways less important than it was; the registration system can make equitable rights just as robust as legal rights, provided they are valid and actually appear on the register.

Now we need to examine how we moved from the old world, in which equitable property rights were enforceable against all except a specially favoured class of purchaser, to the new, where enforceability is determined by registration.

BIBLIOGRAPHY

S. Anderson, *Lawyers and the Making of English Land Law 1832–1940* (Oxford, Clarendon Press, 1992).

George Elliot, *Felix Holt, the Radical* (Oxford, Oxford University Press, 1988).

C. Palliser, *The Quincunx* (London, Penguin Books, 1990).

K. G. Reid, *The Abolition of Feudal Tenure in Scotland* (Edinburgh, LexisNexis, 2003).

A. W. B. Simpson, *A History of the Land Law* (Oxford, Clarendon Press, 1986).

3

LAND LAW AND
REGISTRATION TODAY

This chapter endeavours to give a portrait of land law today, in the light of the 1925 reforms and of the developments of the last 80 years. It is the central pivot of the book, describing the way in which the title registration system governs and structures the enforceability of property rights in land.

This chapter explores the heart of land law. It is in four parts. The first explains how the reforms of 1925 addressed the problem of complexity by redefining legal and equitable estates and interests. The second shows how the 1925 legislation managed the enforceability of property rights in land, particularly by registration. The third elaborates on this by showing how the law has managed the problem of hidden, undocumented ownership rights in land. The final part completes the picture by exploring the reliability of registered title to land, otherwise known as 'indefeasibility'.

1925 AND THE MANAGEMENT
OF COMPLEXITY

The background to 1925

Chapter 2 gave an impression of the complexity of the rights that can be attached to any piece of land. Picture an office block, a house, or a farm. There will always be someone with an ownership right, and there may be more than one. Someone will hold a fee simple (unless this is Crown land); there may also be one or more people with an ownership right that is limited in time—either a freehold estate (a life estate, for example) or a lease (long or short), so that the fee simple owner's right to use the property is suspended for a while. There may also be people who do not own the land, but have more restricted rights over it: a mortgage or a right of way. These rights will be a mix of legal and equitable ones A word for all this is fragmentation. Fragmentation can be a weakness and a strength. It is a strength because it means that many people can have rights, of varying degrees of permanence, in land; fragmentation is therefore something to be embraced and developed rather than something that grew up by historical accident. But it is a weakness because it brings complexity. Complexity is a problem if there is no reliable source of information about the rights in a piece of land. The problem is compounded if the system for enforceability is unreliable so that rights may be unexpectedly unenforceable (a problem for the right-holder) or unexpectedly enforceable (a problem for a purchaser of the land).

Complexity is particularly problematic for those who hold rights in land if the enforceability of their rights depends upon the purchaser knowing about them. How can they be sure that a potential purchaser will find out about them? Equally, potential purchasers are at risk; if there are too many interests in land, the purchaser may simply be unable to find out about, let alone physically find, all the people he needs to settle with in order to buy it. If he misses someone, and buys the land or a property right over it, he may find that what he bought is worthless because someone else's right trumps it, particularly if this was a right that the law deemed him to know about even though he did not.

Penny the purchaser buys land from Simon the seller. Before she buys, she (or, more likely, her conveyancer) looks carefully through the title deeds and checks whether or not Simon or his predecessors have granted any rights over the land. Is it mortgaged, for instance? If it is, she will not hand over the purchase price without ensuring that it is first applied in payment of the mortgage debt; otherwise, the land will still be mortgaged after her purchase.[1] She also inspects the property for signs of other interests in the land—someone else living there, perhaps, or a track across the garden from a neighbouring property to the

---

[1] This is done by obtaining an undertaking from the seller's solicitor that the money will be so used; the procedure remains the same today. Undertakings are super-enforceable promises, in that the solicitor will be subject to professional disciplinary action if he breaks one.

road. Note that the law assumes that Penny will inspect, whether or not in practice she does so. Having checked in this way as much as she can, Penny buys the land. Then a stranger claims to have an interest in the land. If the right claimed is a legal one, perhaps a legal easement, Penny is bound by it in any event, even if the deed that created it was lost—ignorance is irrelevant. If the right is equitable, perhaps a mortgage created informally, it will not be apparent from the deeds, and the purchaser is bound only if she had notice of it, but it *may* be—depending on the circumstances—that the law deems her to have known, because she should have known. It may be that the evidence was available but she missed it. In that event the interest is enforceable against her. This is disastrous. Simon should have paid off such claimants, but he did not, and he has now disappeared.

This scenario was the nightmare of the nineteenth-century conveyancer; if the risk of it occurring did not actually make land unsafe to buy, it certainly made conveyancing very expensive. The problem was so great that one of the proposals in the nineteenth century was to reduce all equitable interests in land to the status of personal rights, so that they could not bind a purchaser. It is unsurprising that that idea did not get off the ground, given the wealth tied up at that time in land of which ownership was structured over time in complex family trusts. The fact that such a dramatic solution was mooted shows how serious the problem was. If land cannot safely be bought or used as security for money, or if the costs of a safe transaction are too high, the value of land falls. The eventual reform package, originally enacted in 1922 and now found in the statutes of 1925, did not explicitly make equitable property rights into personal rights; but it limited the proprietary effect of equitable ownership rights (ie their enforceability) so that in most cases a purchaser would be safe from them, even if he knew about them. In Chapter 1 we mentioned the tension between static security (the protection of existing interests in land) and dynamic security (the protection of a purchaser); in the management of enforceability in the 1925 reforms we see a huge preference for dynamic security.

The shape of land law today, and the way we manage the problems of information and enforceability arising from the complexity of rights in land, depends upon the changes made in 1925. To English lawyers they seem so essential to land law that we tend to forget that the rest of the common law world live happy and useful lives without at least some of them. The 1925 reforms were not the only possible ways to solve the problems of complexity.

Six property statutes were enacted in 1925.[2] By now, they are much amended and to some extent replaced, but the Law of Property Act 1925 remains fundamental to our land law. It is not an easy Act to read, as it is not a code, not a fresh start, but presupposes a great deal of very elderly law; and the 1925 legislation as a whole is difficult to summarize. The most fundamental steps taken in the management of English land law are as follows. First, a hierarchy was created of legal and equitable interests in land which severely cut down the number of estates in land that could exist as legal estates. Second, existing legislation for title registration was improved, and preparations were made for the extension of the system. That extension is now nearly completed; and it is through title registration that the law now organizes information and enforceability. Third, the 1925 legislation established the use of the trust to structure joint ownership and to complete the management of enforceability through the doctrine of 'over-reaching'. This was intended to be a reliable method of safe-guarding purchasers from unexpected equitable ownership rights. It has not worked as intended, because of social changes that the 1925 reformers could not have predicted, but convey-ancing techniques have supplied the necessary additional pro-tection, reinforcing dynamic security. The result is a system of land law that provides robust protection for purchasers of land and that therefore helps maintain the value of land. It needs only a little knowledge of Western society to see how impor-tant this is to us.

[2] Law of Property Act 1925, Settled Land Act 1925, Administration of Estates Act 1925, Trustee Act 1925, Land Charges Act 1925, and Land Registration Act 1925. Of these, the latter two have been repealed by later Acts of the same names.

Legal and equitable interests in land: the 1925 hierarchy

Section 1 of the Law of Property Act 1925 is a defining moment of English land law. It sets up an organization, or hierarchy, of three ideas: legal estates, legal interests, and equitable interests. This is actually the nearest we get to a distinction between ownership rights and non-ownership rights, though there is no one-to-one correspondence with those terms. The aim is to limit the number of legal rights that a purchaser has to think about, so as to make land safer to purchase. The trade-off is that certain rights can only be equitable, or second-class, so that those who hold them are less secure because their rights are less widely enforceable.

Section 1 states that there are just two legal estates: the 'fee simple absolute in possession' and the 'term of years absolute'. The fee simple is the freehold estate described at the beginning of this chapter: and it must be absolute, that is, not subject to conditions which make it liable to disappear, and it must be in possession rather than in remainder or in reversion. The term of years absolute is a lease; but despite the reference to years, it means a lease of any length, even the humble weekly tenancy. Thus, a number of rights were demoted in 1925: it is no longer possible to have a legal life interest.[3]

Next, section 1 defines legal interests. Parts of it have been repealed, and for practical purposes now the legal interests are mortgages, easements, and rentcharges. The first two we have met, and are pervasive; the latter we shall say very little about. A rentcharge is a payment imposed on a freeholder, used now very rarely and only as a way of enforcing some forms of covenant. These two groups—the legal estates and legal interests—correspond approximately to ownership rights and non-ownership rights (not exactly, because leases can be both).

Section 1 ensures that a purchaser, checking for the legal rights in land—that is, for the ones most likely to be enforceable against him—need check only for a limited number of different

---

[3] There were transitional provisions to ensure that legal interests actually in existence on 1 January 1926 remained enforceable as if they were legal interests even if demoted by the statute.

kinds of right. Another provision of the same statute[4] ensures that no more than four people can hold a legal estate in land—again, for simplicity's sake. So if a farm is bought by the ten trustees of a charity, say, or by a business partnership of six, or is bequeathed to ten brothers and they decide to keep it rather than sell it, only four of them can hold the legal fee simple and be registered as owners at the Land Registry (the first four named in the transfer if it lists more than four), but all of them hold an equitable fee simple in the land.

The third part of section 1 states that everything else—any other property right in land—is an equitable interest. This includes everything from the restrictive covenant—that is, an obligation not to do something on the land, for example not to run a business on it—to an ownership right that is less than a fee simple absolute in possession, such as a life interest.

Section 1 therefore simplifies legal and equitable ownership in a rather basic and numerical way. It does not create anything new, but sets the filing cabinet in order and makes a decision as to what goes in each drawer, enabling us to categorize any interest in land that we may meet. But that alone does not, of course, sort out complexity; for the real problems of complexity are information and enforceability and (therefore, as explained above) the safety of the market. For that, we must look to registration.

REGISTRATION AND THE MANAGEMENT OF ENFORCEABILITY

What is title registration?

Now we come to the second of the 1925 changes; the management of the enforceability of property rights in land. From today's perspective, the central plank of the management plan is title registration, although it would not have looked that way in 1925.

In order to explain how title registration works, we have to digress a little and explain the word 'title'. It has two legal

---

[4] Section 34.

meanings. Lawyers use them without explaining, relying on the context to show which is intended. First, it means the whole collection of property rights in a piece of land. The title to my house comprises, typically, the fee simple ownership, burdened by the rights of a mortgagee and perhaps those of a neighbour who has an easement over the back yard. It can be paraphrased as 'entitlement'. Its second, subsidiary meaning is the *evidence* of title. If I am asked to show my title to my land, I am going to point to the register of title held at the Land Registry. The register displays a portrait of the property rights in my land, and also *is* my title in the sense that it proves my ownership.

This is a change. Read any novel, ask most folk, and you will be told that the way to prove ownership of land is to produce your deeds; and that your deeds are precious, to be kept in the bank or in a deeds box. Traditionally this was true; 'my deeds', or 'the deeds' of the house, would comprise a stack of documents, of which the top one was the conveyance to me, the one underneath that was the conveyance to my predecessor, and so on, going back a couple of generations or so and demonstrating my right to the land by telling the story of its ownership. But the advent of title registration means that this story is no longer needed to prove entitlement, because title registration replaces deeds.

If registration is a way of tackling complexity, there are a number of ways of doing it. One way is simply to create a public record of deeds. It is possible to make an official copy of every deed connected with a piece of land, so that it does not matter if the original gets lost. That is a start. In addition, there can be a sanction for not registering a deed. The system can decree that unregistered deeds are ineffective. Or it can state that unregistered deeds are effective between the people who made them but do not have priority, so that they do not affect anyone buying the land later. Either of these measures will protect purchasers by ensuring that they are unaffected by anything they cannot see on the register. Equally, the holders of non-ownership rights are protected against later owners of the land, provided they register the deed that created their right. Such a system is called deeds registration; it operates very successfully in South Africa and in all the American states, for example. In order to work well, it needs an efficient indexing system so that deeds can be readily found; some sort of insurance system against mistakes in the register; and clear rules as to the effect of deeds which are not registered, but which a purchaser knows about. Middlesex and Yorkshire had deeds registries from the early eighteenth century. The system was never extended nation-wide; new registrations ceased after 1925 and the deeds registries closed in 1976. Deeds registration is worth mentioning here in order to make clear what title registration is not: it is *not* merely a record of what the deeds to a property say.

Deeds registration has two weaknesses, both linked closely to complexity; first, it does not take away the work of examining a title. The buyer of land must still find and read all the deeds to a property and work out what their effect is (although the register makes them easy to find). Second, it does not protect a purchaser against rights that were not created by deed. The latter is important in a system which recognizes equitable property rights in land: equitable interests do not need to be created by deed (often they are equitable just because a deed was not used). So the problem of purchasers being tripped up by unexpected equitable interests is not eliminated by deeds registration.[5] Enter title registration, which does something different.

Title registration is a central record of title to land. It wipes out the work of examining deeds; it also controls the validity of registrable interests. It is the latter that is fundamentally different from the concept of deeds registration.

First, then, title registration transforms the record of title. This in itself was revolutionary when title registration was first devised. Instead of copying the deeds, the register sets out their effect in a single document. When a transaction takes place the deed or other document is sent to the registrar who reads it, interprets it, and records its effect. The deed itself is thrown away. The vision is that the purchaser should be able to find out all he wants about the property rights in a piece of land just by looking up the property in the register, making land transfer as simple as is the transfer of shares in a company.

---

[5] In America, the risks are managed through a pervasive commercial system of title insurance.

Title registration can be thought of as a collection of cards in a filing cabinet (as it originally was), or of electronic documents (as it now is). Each document represents, not a piece of land, but a legal estate in land (a fee simple or a lease for more than seven years);[6] so there can be more than one document for a given piece of land. Each document, known as an individual register, describes the estate, and tells us about any non-ownership rights over other land (such as easements) that are attached to this estate; it states who owns it, and occasionally gives a little more information about the owner, in particular any restriction of his ability to deal with the land; finally, it sets out rights to which the estate is subject, such as rights of way and mortgages. The individual register is not as simple as a share certificate; but it is at least a translation of that idea into a representation of land ownership. The purchaser no longer has to look back at the history of ownership, whether through a stack of deeds or through the folios of a deeds register—indeed he is not allowed to look at history. Title is all in the present tense.

Registration of title was devised in the middle of the nineteenth century, by Sir Robert Torrens in South Australia. Similar registration statutes were enacted throughout the common law world and are now known as the 'Torrens systems'. English title registration began in 1862, just four years after the South Australian statute (the Real Property Act 1858) and, in contrast to its Australian counterpart, worked very badly. So it was not a concept for which all lawyers were enthusiastic in 1925. Today, after the replacement of the rather nervous Land Registration Act 1925 by the confident and assertive Land Registration Act 2002, it is central to land law and is unchallengeable as the way in which information and enforceability are controlled.

In 1925 about 300,000 titles were registered. Today, over nineteen million titles are registered. It is not known what proportion of registrable titles are registered, but the Land Registry's current estimate of the proportion of land in England and Wales that is registered, by area, is approximately 73 per cent. The extension of registration was achieved gradually,

---

[6] Some other estates, listed in s 2 of the Land Registration Act 2002, generate an individual register; they are ancient, unusual, and not discussed here.

by bringing new areas into the system every few years and
providing that, in areas of compulsory registration, certain transactions triggered an obligation to register. The principal triggering events today are sales, first legal mortgages, the transmission
of land on death, the appointment of new trustees of land, and
the creation or sale of leases longer than the seven-year registration threshold. Today, the whole of England and Wales is an
area of compulsory registration; and it is hoped that at some
stage the register will be complete. The range of 'triggering
events' is now so wide that almost all land will become compul-
sorily registrable at some point. The 2002 Act has also sought to
encourage voluntary registration by making registered title more
attractive than unregistered, so as to encourage voluntary registration; the Act has made it almost impossible for title to be
acquired against a registered owner by adverse possession—
squatters' rights, or squatters' title, as it is known.[7] There are
signs that this is working, as a number of local authorities have
registered their landholdings. The 2002 Act also makes it possible for Crown land to be registered, by the rather strange device
of enabling the Crown to grant to itself a fee simple, which can
then be registered. This is because only estates in land can be
registered, and the Crown, as the feudal overlord, is the one
person who does not have an *estate* in land.[8]

Once title is registered, any transactions involving that legal
estate or any legal interests derived from it are ineffective until
registration has taken place (with the exception of leases for
seven years or less).[9] A deed must be executed in order to
transfer a legal estate or create a legal interest, but the registration
system has taken away the power of the deed. In cases where a
deed is necessary, it is no longer sufficient. When that deed is
sent to the registry and the register is updated, a legal estate or
interest is transferred or created, depending on the nature of the
transaction. Where necessary, a new individual register, with a

---

[7] Discussed in Chapter 9.

[8] The real difficulty for the prospect of universal registration may be those
areas of land whose ownership is long forgotten; the ownership of grass verges
beside roads, for example, is notoriously difficult to trace.

[9] Discussed in Chapter 4 at p 82.

fresh title number, is created, for example on the grant of a lease of more than seven years. It is therefore useful to refer to legal estates and interests as the 'registrable estates'. And the landowner does not have an estate created or transferred by deed, but a registered estate, emanating from the fact of registration. This is the second revolutionary aspect of title registration, referred to above. Even where the deed transferring land from Ned to Ted, say, is void because of fraud or mistake, registration of the deed makes Ted the owner of the land. This is startling and we shall have to explore more of its implications later.[10] For now, note that registration involves a guarantee of title. Registered estates are guaranteed valid and enforceable, and if there is a mistake on the register which causes loss to an innocent party, the latter will be compensated. Equally, someone who has a registered estate and loses it because of the correction of a mistake in the register will be compensated. Again, more of this later.

The register has thus taken control of title. Registration is said to operate on the mirror principle, namely that the register is a mirror of the title. This is true provided we understand that what the register is mirroring is not a stack of deeds, but the truth about a title to a piece of land. The deeds are irrelevant except for that short period between what the estate agents call completion, when signed documents are handed over, and their registration.[11]

Title registration takes a big swipe at complexity by not only centralizing and safeguarding information, but also reducing the number of documents, and the amount of interpretation, involved in examining title. The examining and summarizing is all done by the registrar, and all irrelevant bits of history are swept away. As well as keeping information safe, it makes it

---

[10] Section 58 of the Land Registration Act 2002; see p 65 ff.

[11] The Land Registration Act 2002 was drafted with the intention that there would in due course be a move to a system of electronic conveyancing, so that the parties' own act of completing the transaction would update the register. That would remove the 'registration gap' entirely. However, plans for a comprehensive system of electronic conveyancing are not now being developed, according to the Land Registry's *Annual Report for 2011*; see further Chapter 4.

succinct and eliminates all or most of the work of examining title. However, it also goes one step further: it defines very closely what interests can bind a purchaser of land.

The mechanism for enforceability

The Land Registration Act 1925 provided a list of those interests that are to have priority over the purchaser—that is, the interests that are enforceable against him—when a disposition is registered. The Land Registration Act 2002 does the same, in section 29.[12] The idea is that a prospective purchaser can check down this list and see all the types of interests that will burden the land when he owns it. The old rules, that a legal estate binds all the world and an equitable interest binds by notice, no longer apply.

The list contains three items. Taking them out of order: first, if the title is leasehold, the purchaser takes the land subject to any obligations laid upon the tenant by the lease itself. This is easy and uncontroversial. So is the second item, namely anything appearing on the register. This refers in particular to burdens on the registered title, that is, non-ownership rights which have been protected by being entered on the register. We know that any legal interests in the land to which the title is registered (eg legal easements or mortgages) can only be created by registration, so they simply cannot exist unless they appear on the register. Moreover, most equitable interests—but not beneficial interests under trusts, for reasons to be explained—may be, but do not have to be, entered on the register. This form of registration is optional, and is known as recording rather than registration. It does not guarantee validity, but it does guarantee priority. The holder of an equitable easement, or of the benefit of a restrictive covenant, must record his right against the owner's title if he wants his rights to be effective after the owner sells on. (He *must*, because the old rules of notice are disapplied by the registration statute, so there is no other form of protection for him.)

---

[12] Section 30 contains the same list adapted for use when what is being transferred is a mortgage rather than an ownership right; see Chapter 6, p 150, n 5.

Why can trust interests not be entered on the register as other equitable interests can? Quite simply because the 1925 reformers intended them to be ineffective against purchasers. They sought to operate a 'curtain', whereby trusts could not be seen on the register and were irrelevant to conveyancing. There is more to be said about the protection of purchasers from trust interests, as we shall see.

Back to the list: the third item is 'interests that override a registered disposition', listed in a schedule to the statute. And here we have a big disappointment, because overriding interests are ones which bind a purchaser even though they are not on the register. The mirror tells the truth, but not the whole truth.

Consider the good reasons for allowing some such interests to be enforceable. First, there are some transactions which are so short-lived that the legislature considered them unsuitable for registration. At present, almost all leases for seven years or less are not registrable. A tenant under a six-year lease cannot point to a register which shows his title; he can only display his lease, and the transfer of the lease to him if he is not the first tenant to hold that lease, and so on. But his lease is an overriding interest vis-à-vis his landlord's title; if his landlord (be he a freeholder or a leaseholder) sells the land the tenant's lease survives and is enforceable against the buyer. Second, some legal interests can arise without any formality at all. Leases for three years or less (including, therefore, a periodic tenancy) can be created without using a deed and without even putting anything in writing; equally, in some circumstances legal easements can be created without documentation.[13] In these cases there is no document to register; but the legal interests created are enforceable against the title they depend upon. Third, there are some transactions which the legislature wished to privilege; in particular, interests of the state. So a local land charge (an obligation imposed by a local authority, such as a compulsory purchase order or a tree preservation order) is enforceable against the land (ie against anyone who owns it) without the authority having to register it.

[13] See Chapter 8, p 217 ff.

A further policy concern is seen in what is now the most significant of the overriding interests:

An interest belonging at the time of the disposition to a person in actual occupation, so far as relating to the land of which he is in actual occupation, except for—

(c) an interest—
(i) which belongs to a person whose occupation would not have been obvious on a reasonably careful inspection of the land at the time of the disposition, and

(ii) of which the person to whom the disposition is made does not have actual knowledge at that time . . . [14]

This category is listed as paragraph 2 of Schedule 3 to the Land Registration Act 2002; but all the significant case law on it was pre-2002, and so refers to section 70(1)(g) of the Land Registration Act 1925. Its aim was to protect the rights of those who lived in a property, even if it did not belong to them, and even if their rights were not registered. The provision means that an equitable lease, even though unrecorded,[15] is enforceable against a purchaser if the landlord sells, provided that the tenant is actually living or working at the property. Similarly, someone who lives at the property and happens to have an option to purchase it will find that his option is enforceable against a future owner of the land. The policy operating here is the protection of the home. And if someone is in actual occupation as described in the Schedule, a purchaser who goes to look at the land (generally buyers do but mortgagees do not) cannot claim to have been taken by surprise; the right is only enforceable if the occupation is obvious. The 2002 statute states this; the 1925 one did not, but the draftsman's intention was probably the same.

So there are good reasons for allowing some unregistered rights to be enforceable, and the list of such rights was designed

---

[14] There is more to this paragraph, but these are the parts relevant to this discussion.

[15] Recall that this is not a legal interest and so not a registrable estate, so it cannot be registered but may be recorded; the difference is that validity is not guaranteed.

so as to be harmless to purchasers. Of the examples we have given so far, all but short legal leases are going to be pretty rare in any event. However, the overriding interest for those in actual occupation—paragraph 2 of Schedule 3—has turned out to be a minefield. For reasons to be explained, the 1925 legislators did not anticipate that beneficial interests under trusts could be overriding interests in this category. They were right about that in 1925, but a major decision of the House of Lords early in the 1980s effected a fundamental change. There is more to tell of the story of actual occupation interests, and we shall do so below, in the context of the enforceability of beneficial interests in land.

Section 29 and the register's negative warranty

Section 29 of the Land Registration Act 2002 is part of the register's guarantee of title; writers on the Torrens system have called it (or rather its equivalents in other statutes) the 'negative warranty' of registration: the promise that there are no other interests in the land that could affect a purchaser. So how watertight is section 29? Are these three categories the *only* interests that can possibly bind a purchaser? In particular, what of the old conundrum, the unregistered interest that the purchaser knows about? The old deeds registration systems had to address this, and came up with more than one answer. It is actually extremely difficult for a court to hold that a purchaser is unaffected by an interest about which he knew, but which happens to be unregistered. Knowledge is very persuasive, which is why the courts of equity came up with the old rules of notice. But part of the point of title registration is to disapply those rules because they involve so many pitfalls for the purchaser. In fact, one decision under the Land Registration Act 1925 did hold that a purchaser was bound by notice—in effect, though not in so many words.[16] The decision was made possible by an unintended quirk in the drafting of the 1925 statute. A definition of a 'purchaser' required him to be 'in good faith', which enabled the court to find that, since he knew

---

[16] *Peffer v Rigg* [1977] 1 WLR 285.

about the unregistered interest, he could not *in good faith* seek to escape from it. But the case is widely agreed to have been wrongly decided, and the definitions used in the 2002 statute make it impossible for it to be replicated under the new statute.

Section 29 is therefore designed to be truly watertight. However, consistent with that is one further possibility. This is that a purchaser might, by his own conduct, make himself liable to a third party who had an interest in the land immediately before the disposition. This is a fresh liability arising, in effect, after section 27 has done its work, and not a burden passed on from the former proprietor through the filter of section 27. The one case where this is agreed to have happened is *Lyus v Prowsa*.[17] Mr and Mrs Lyus contracted to purchase a house on a housing development, and protected their contract by recording it on the register. However, the site was already mortgaged to a bank. The developer went into liquidation and the bank sold the development. A mortgagee sells the title as it stood at the date of the mortgage, and is not bound by an option registered at a later date. So the bank's purchaser took free from the option in accordance with the then equivalent of section 29. However, the transfer stated that the purchaser took the land 'subject to' the option insofar as it was enforceable—a step taken out of caution by the bank—and, significantly, the purchaser paid a reduced price because it was believed that the option would be binding. Accordingly, it was found that the purchaser held the land on constructive trust for the prospective buyer of the plot, who could therefore exercise the option. The decision is the subject of some scepticism. Comments made in the Court of Appeal in *Ashburn Anstalt v Arnold*[18] confirm the authority of the decision, but stress that its application will be very narrow indeed. But the principle is in line with much more developed case law on the point in most Torrens registration systems, where it is known as the *in personam* exception to the guarantee of title that the register gives. '*In personam*' means 'against the individual', because it is the enforcement of a liability against an individual, by making him a trustee. It has to be regarded as a

---

[17] [1982] 1 WLR 1044.   [18] [1988] 2 All ER 147.

concept that could be operated in extreme circumstances, where otherwise section 29 would produce too grave an injustice for the courts to swallow. A deliberate plan by a seller and buyer to defeat a third party's interest would probably be an example.

Land charges registration: the dying alternative

Before we go on to explore the enforceability of beneficial interests in land under the land registration statutes, we have to mention the management of enforceability of interests in land, the title to which is not registered. This accounts for a small proportion of titles today, but in 1925 most titles were unregistered. For these, the legislation introduced a new form of registration designed to manage the enforceability only of non-ownership rights in land: land charges registration. It is not yet obsolete but should one day become so if ever title registration becomes universal. Where the title to land is *not* registered at the Land Registry, some but not all non-ownership rights may by registered on the Land Charges Register. If not registered, they are void against very nearly, but not quite, all forms of purchasers for value.

Investigation of the title to unregistered land therefore involves two jobs: the purchaser must examine the deeds, to discover the legal ownership of the land and most legal interests in it; he must also search the Land Charges Register to discover the interests listed in the Act (some legal, most equitable; for example some types of mortgage, contractual interests, and equitable easements). Some interests, in particular those of beneficiaries of trusts, will not be found either in the deeds or on the Land Charges Register; they bind the purchaser by notice in the usual way unless the conditions for overreaching are met, as described below. Land charges registration is not a good system and none will weep when/if it finally becomes obsolete. In 1925, the intention was that ten years later there would be a review of the two systems: registered title on the one hand, and on the other the Land Charges Register, to see which was working better. At the time, many would have placed their bets on land charges registration and unregistered title. The review never took place, and title registration has gradually become pervasive as more and more titles became registered. Today, every Land Charges Register search done by a purchaser of unregistered land is the last; once the purchase is completed, the purchaser's title must be registered. So land charges registration is alive, but dying. Whether or not it will ever become decisively and properly dead depends upon whether or not title registration is eventually completed in England and Wales.

THE ENFORCEABILITY OF BENEFICIAL INTERESTS IN LAND

Trusts

Equitable ownership rights, or beneficial interests, were a major concern of the reformers. One of the risks that prompted reform was the danger for purchasers of being bound by constructive notice of beneficial interests. And the 1925 reforms actually proliferated trusts, making the management of enforceability all the more urgent.

How did the 1925 legislation proliferate trusts, and how was enforceability controlled?

Section 1 of the Law of Property Act 1925 reduced the number of legal estates in land. The corresponding increase in equitable ownership rights meant more trusts, because whenever there are equitable ownership rights in land there must also be someone holding the legal estate, which is held in trust for the equitable owner(s). That is not a necessary truth, but it is one of the principles upon which English land law happens to operate. So by making limited ownership rights equitable, section 1 proliferated trusts.

But there is more. The 1925 legislation ensured that there is a trust of land in every case where there is joint ownership of land, concurrent as well as successive.

A trust arises where the equitable owners outnumber the permitted legal owners; if ten brothers own a farm, the first four are trustees of the land for all ten (themselves included). It is easy to see the point of trusteeship in such a case; the four legal owners must have a responsibility to use their ownership powers for the benefit of all ten, and must not be permitted to take advantage of their position. The real surprise is that *all* cases of concurrent co-ownership involve a trust. When a commercial partnership of four accountants, say, buys an office, or a couple buys a house, the land is automatically held on trust, the joint owners being both trustees and beneficiaries. Most couples buying a home will probably never know this.

Whatever is the point of having a trust in such cases? Where land is held for Pam for life with remainder to Sam in fee simple, the beneficiaries actually have competing interests (short-term enjoyment versus capital value), and trustees have an obvious management and decision-making role. But where trustees and beneficiaries are identical and the position and powers of both/all are equal, trusteeship is not going to solve any problems if there is a dispute. Most of the common law world does not use a trust structure for ordinary joint owner-ship like this; so why does English law do so? The central role of the trust in land law seems to have been a response to two concerns, neither of which makes the use of trusts inevitable although that is how English law deals with them. One was a concern about proliferation of interests. Cases where legal and equitable ownership match may cease to be such, because equitable ownership may diversify over time. The accountancy partnership may grow; one of the couple may die and leave her share in the property to two children. But if the legal estate is held on trust, it can stay simple, even where equitable owner-ship diversifies. And the caring/management function of trus-tees becomes necessary and useful in that sort of case, as does the court's power to intervene in cases where trustees and/or beneficiaries are in dispute.[19] The other concern was about enforceability. A major reason why trusts seemed such a safe device to the 1925 reformers was the availability of a device known as 'overreaching' to control the enforceability of bene-ficial interests.

---

[19] Sections 14 and 15 of the Trusts of Land and Appointment of Trustees Act 1996; the job was originally done by s 40 of the Law of Property Act 1925.

Overreaching

Now, we have seen that where title to land is registered, beneficial interests could not be entered on the register. And, for reasons to be explained, it was not supposed in 1925 that trust interests could be overriding interests. Where title to land was not registered, beneficial interests bound a purchaser by notice just as they always had done because they were not registrable on the Land Charges Register. But the doctrine of overreaching meant that, despite this, beneficial interests would never trouble a purchaser.

Overreaching is a form of magic. It is a doctrine that says that when land is purchased, if and only if certain conditions are met, certain equitable interests cease to affect the land. The rights that can be overreached are equitable ownership rights; thus not equitable leases, equitable mortgages, equitable interests, nor the contractually based interests such as options. Overreachable interests include life interests in land, or a fee simple which is subject to a current life interest so that the holder cannot access the land until the life interest ends (he does not have a fee simple *in possession*). They include the fees simple of brothers 5 to 10 of the group mentioned above. Overreaching means that when land is sold, the only claims the holders of those interests can have is against their trustees who sold the land and now hold the proceeds of sale; they have no claim on the purchaser.

Overreaching applies only on purchase. The protection given here is for buyers, not for anyone taking the land as a gift. The aim is to protect the market. But the main condition for the operation of overreaching, set out in section 2 of the Law of Property Act 1925 (the position of the provision, next to section 1, reminds us just how central it was to the reformers' thinking), concerns the identity of the seller of the land. In order for overreaching to happen, the purchase money must be paid to at least two trustees of the legal estate.[20] In other words, all the purchaser has to do is to be careful about who he pays his money to. Provided the conditions are met, the rules of notice (where

---

[20] Or to a trust corporation (a commercial organization set up to operate trust funds).

title was unregistered) do not apply, and overreaching takes place even though the purchaser knew of the existence of beneficial interests.

The upshot is that if a purchaser is buying from two or more legal owners then he knows, with absolute certainty, that even if the land is held on trust he will take it free of any equitable interests. If sale is offered by a sole owner, and the purchaser knows that the land is held on trust, he must insist that it is conveyed to him by two individuals, not one. Again, if he does so, the purchaser is safe. The process is quick and easy; the transfer document simply takes two steps: it consists, first, of an appointment by the sole owner of an additional trustee of the legal estate, and then proceeds to be a sale by those legal owners. The proceeds of sale of the land are then held on trust by the two trustees, and the existence of *two* trustees is supposed to afford some protection to beneficiaries. And the 1925 reformers' expectation was that trusts would in any event be properly managed so that they normally had two trustees.

Overreaching was not invented by the 1925 reformers; it was extended and given fresh importance as a major mechanism for the protection of purchasers. It was intended to be a fail-safe mechanism. The expectation was that where there was a trust of land, there would be more than one trustee, and that over-reaching would take place. Purchasers were safe.

Hidden beneficial interests: the problem and the solution

As it turned out, purchasers were not safe. Overreaching did not prove to be the fail-safe that the 1925 reformers had expected.

The problem was that the reformers assumed that in all cases where overreaching was actually needed, those involved would be aware of the need and would ensure that the two trustees requirement was met. A quick trawl through the different types of trust shows that this appeared to be a safe assumption in 1925.

First, there were formal, family settlements of land. These were almost always governed by the Settled Land Act 1925. That statute is now virtually obsolete because it has not been possible to create new settlements under it since 1996, but in

1925 conveyancers were familiar and comfortable with it. Conveyancing rules ensured that the existence of the trust (without any details of its provisions) was obvious from the deeds, and the purchaser was therefore alerted to the need to pay his money to two trustees. The trustees themselves could normally be relied upon to ensure that this would happen in any event. It was unlikely that title to land held on this sort of trust would be registered (registration is required when land is sold, and such land tended to remain in families), but if it was, overreaching was not even needed: the beneficiaries' interests could not be protected by registration, and the statute provided that beneficial interests in a Settled Land Act settlement could not be overriding interests by virtue of the beneficiaries' occupation of the land (now replicated in paragraph 2(a) of Schedule 3 to the 2002 Act). They could not therefore bind a purchaser.

Most other trusts were implied ones, arising by virtue of joint ownership, whether joint purchase or as a result of inheritance. These trusts, by contrast, were governed by provisions in the Law of Property Act 1925, not the Settled Land Act. The fact of joint ownership would be readily apparent to a purchaser from the deeds or the register; if all but one joint owner had died so that the legal estate was held by a sole survivor, the purchaser would know that he had to insist on the appointment of an additional trustee.[21] Moreover, if title was registered then, again, overreaching was unnecessary because of the safeguards built into the registration system. One was that beneficial interests could not be protected on the register. The other was that these trusts, governed not by the Settled Land Act but by the Law of Property Act, derived their structure and rules from nineteenth-century investment practice and the management of land bought only for its value and not as a home. They were therefore known as trusts for sale. If it sounds strange to label ordinary joint ownership as a 'trust for sale', recall that where land is inherited by, say, five brothers they will normally sell it, sooner

---

[21] The register was at that date a series of typed cards; former proprietors were struck out when they sold on or died, but the deleted entry remained visible. There is a further point to make about the survivor of joint owners, discussed in Chapter 5, p 132.

or later; and that joint ownership of the family home by husband and wife was extremely rare. And because of that derivation from investment practice, interests under such trusts were regarded not as interests in the land itself, but in the proceeds of sale of the land. That meant, according to the then current interpretation of the Land Registration Act 1925, that they could not be overriding interests in registered land. They could not therefore bind a purchaser.

Just a few trusts did not fall within either of these categories, in particular cases known as 'bare trusts' where a trustee held land for someone who was entitled to the legal estate, but chose to have it held for him by a nominee. Outside these narrow exceptions, beneficial interests virtually lost their proprietary status. By sleight of hand the reformers achieved what had been proposed and rejected earlier in the reform process.

Social changes made this tidy structure break down. One was the rise in owner-occupation. In 1925 more than 70 per cent of the population—the less wealthy end of the social scale—rented their homes. Nowadays, over 70 per cent of homes are owner-occupied; we are a 'property-owning democracy'. Another was the change in the economic status of women. In 1925 few were economically independent or had means of their own; during the following forty or fifty years that changed radically. Add to this the rule that is the foundation of another type of trust, the resulting trust: that if I finance the purchase of land by someone else, he will hold it on trust for me, to the extent of my contribution.[22] These factors came together to produce a case which badly frightened conveyancers. In *Williams and Glyn's Bank Ltd v Boland*[23] Mr Boland was sole legal owner of a house. He mortgaged it, post-acquisition, to the bank to secure a loan. The bank did not appreciate that Mrs Boland had paid a substantial part of the purchase price and therefore owned a proportionate share of the house on a resulting trust. Mr Boland defaulted on the loan and the bank sought to repossess, only to

[22] The central importance of the resulting trust in such cases has been displaced recently (see Chapter 4), but was crucial to the reasoning in *Williams and Glyn's Bank Ltd v Boland*, see p 120.

[23] [1981] AC 487.

be met by Mrs Boland's claim that she was a part-owner of the house. She was in actual occupation of it at the time the mortgage was granted and therefore at that point her interest bound the bank, and the mortgage did not affect her share. The bank argued that Mrs Boland's interest was held under a trust for sale, so that her interest was in money and not in land and she could not have an overriding interest. This was rejected by the House of Lords as an unrealistic way of regarding home owner-ship. The bank also argued, following earlier precedent, that she was not in actual occupation of the house because her presence was simply an extension of that of her husband. Being a wife, she simply did not count; and the older cases supported that argu-ment. It was robustly (and inevitably by that date) rejected. Mrs Boland won, and the bank could only take Mr Boland's share of the value of the house, and in any case could not, at this stage, get possession of the property in order to sell it and realize that interest because of Mrs Boland's right to live there.[24]

Thus it is clear that overreaching is not the guaranteed safe-guard that it was supposed to be. Trusts with a sole trustee could arise where there was no clue for the purchaser that overreach-ing was needed, and no professional trustees involved to ensure that it happened. And registration was not the safeguard it was intended to be in these cases because of the re-conceptualiza-tion, in *Boland*, of the trust for sale.

The danger for purchasers was intensified by two other de-velopments. One was the rise in unmarried cohabitation. The advice given to the writer as a student, 'never take a conveyance from a sole married vendor', does not cover the multitude of relationship possibilities. The other was the development, in equity, of additional means for those who are not legal owners to acquire, informally, a share in the property. Principal among these is the common intention constructive trust, to be discussed at length later.[25] Briefly, it enabled non-owners to acquire a

---

[24] The eventual solution for the bank would be to take insolvency proceed-ings against Mr Boland, since under the insolvency legislation the wife's right to occupy would be subordinated to the bank's right to possession. See Chapter 5, p 127.

[25] See Chapter 4.

share, on a much more generous basis than did the resulting trust, and without such stringent requirements for direct contribution. A spouse or cohabitant who had contributed just a few hundred pounds to the acquisition of the property might be discovered, later, to own a half share in equity.

Controlling the enforceability of informal trusts

So it is clear that overreaching is not the guaranteed safeguard that it was supposed to be.

What could be done to protect banks and buyers? One proposal, made by the Law Commission,[26] was that the Land Registry should compensate any purchaser who suffered loss because of an overriding interest. The proposal was not followed up. The register provides a guaranteed title to land, largely in the interests of purchasers, but the system is designed to ensure that the Registry rarely has to make any payment in support of that guarantee.[27] Instead, the answer devised to the problem of unexpected occupiers is simple, conceptually unsatisfying, and reasonably effective. Standard conveyancing practice introduced soon after *Boland* is for the purchaser (whether buyer or mortgagee) to ask the owner to disclose the names of all adult[28] occupiers of the property. Each of those occupiers is then asked to consent to the disposition and to give up, as against the purchaser, whatever rights, if any, they have in the land. This is unsatisfying because it does not protect the purchaser if the owner lies; the purchaser is left with a personal remedy only, ie the right to seek damages from the owner for misrepresentation. Yet it seems to have laid the *Boland* problem to rest. Either misrepresentation has not happened, or it has done so seldom enough for the institutional lenders to regard it as an acceptable risk. Equitable ownership rights in land do not generally pose a problem for purchasers—which is what the 1925 reformers

---

[26] The Law Commission is an independent statutory body charged, by the Law Commissions Act 1965, with keeping the law under review and recommending reform to the government.

[27] See pp 65 ff.

[28] It has been held that children cannot have an overriding interest under Sch 3, para 2.

intended, although it has not been done anywhere near so tidily as they planned.

The upshot, curiously, is that provided normal conveyancing safeguards are observed, the holder of an equitable ownership right in land is unprotected against a purchaser. The result is the same as if the equitable interest were not proprietary, provided that either overreaching takes place or the post-*Boland* safeguards are observed and no misrepresentation takes place. A complex route has been taken to achieve a very simple result.

Overriding versus overreaching

One final point about overreaching. Where a trust interest has overriding status because of occupation, but can also be overreached, does overreaching trump overriding, or vice versa? The statute does not say because the issue was not supposed to arise. Settled Land Act interests were excluded from being overriding interests; and interests under trusts for sale were conceived as financial interests which could not therefore be interests *in the land* as required for overriding status. But *Boland* of course opened that door. Mrs Boland's interest could not be overreached because the legal estate was held by a sole trustee. But what if the conditions for overreaching had been met? The issue went to the House of Lords in 1988.[29] The case concerned a couple, Mr and Mrs Flegg, who bought a large house which included a 'granny flat'. Into the granny flat moved the wife's parents, Mr and Mrs Maxwell-Brown; in a not-untypical arrangement, they sold their own home and put the proceeds into this one, amounting to approximately a quarter of the price. The four of them were therefore joint owners in equity; but the Maxwell-Browns did not wish to be legal owners, because they did not wish to take on responsibility for the Fleggs' mortgage repayments. So the Fleggs bought as joint legal owners, holding on trust (they were probably unaware of this) for the four of them. Later, they re-mortgaged the property. Later still, they defaulted on that loan. The bank sought to repossess the house. Up jumped the Maxwell-Browns, who lived there and owned a

---

[29] *City of London Building Society v Flegg* [1988] AC 54.

one-quarter share in the property. They were in actual occupation, and so their equitable ownership was an overriding interest which bound the bank. In answer, the bank claimed that it took its mortgage, as security for the loan, from two trustees of the legal estate. Any equitable interests should therefore have been overreached, and should not affect the bank. So which form of magic prevails: overriding or overreaching?

Perhaps surprisingly, the statute did not say. Arrangements like this, though normal now, were not thought of in 1925. Much was said in the judgments in *Flegg* about statutory interpretation and about the protection of the home. Nevertheless, in this writer's view the statute left the court a free choice as to which should prevail; there is simply no decisive provision. The case is an excellent illustration of the fact that a 'purchaser' can be either a buyer or a mortgagee, or indeed anyone acquiring, for value, an interest in land. And it is a good illustration of the courts' prevailing policy: to protect purchasers. The bank won.

INDEFEASIBILITY AND THE REGISTER'S POSITIVE WARRANTY

What is indefeasibility?

Most of what we have said so far about enforceability has tended towards dynamic rather than static security. Assuming an owner willing to sell, the purchaser is favoured by the system, in preference to those who hold interests in the land. A purchaser can be confident that he will not be bound by non-ownership rights unless they were protected (and were therefore visible to him) by registration or by actual occupation, and he can also be sure that in virtually all cases he cannot be caught out by unexpected equitable ownership rights. This, we said, is the negative warranty inherent in section 29 of the Land Registration Act 2002: there is nothing else to worry about.

Writers on the Torrens system also speak of the register's positive warranty: it guarantees the validity of the registered title. This too is part of dynamic security. A system that gives a strong positive warranty tells a purchaser that what he buys will be stable, and cannot be taken away from him because of a defect in the transaction by which he acquired it. That guarantee is also known as indefeasibility. Different levels of indefeasibility are possible, and the English system's version is significantly different from either of the two found in the Torrens systems.

To see why this matters, consider some examples. In the first, X's registered estate is transferred to Y. Y forged the transfer. We can call this the 'straight fraud' case. In the second example, Mr and Mrs X own a house. Mrs X mortgaged it to the Y bank, by forging her husband's signature, and the Y bank now has a registered charge. This is the 'innocent Y' case. In the third example, there is a void transfer from X to Y, whether because of fraud or because of 'double conveyancing', that is, the sale of the same piece of land twice usually by mistake (this is far less likely to happen where title is registered). In a few years' time, it might be void because of the fraudulent use of the electronic conveyancing system. The land is then bought by Z, who is unconnected with and uninvolved in the void transfer. This we shall call the 'acid-bath' case, after the series of transfers made by Haigh, who forged the signature of some of his victims, transferring their land to him, and then sold the land on.

In all the examples there is a void transfer from X to Y. In the straight fraud case, Y is the forger; in the innocent Y case, he is not. And in the acid-bath case, the chain of title has gone from X to Y to Z, but the first link is void. In all cases, if title were unregistered X's title would be unaffected and he would not lose his legal estate, because the transfer is simply void. If title is registered, section 58 of the 2002 Act states that the registered proprietor, Y or Z as the case may be, has the legal estate. What should happen now? In the straight fraud case the register clearly should be altered to restore X's legal estate. Where Y is innocent of the fraud—be he a buyer or a mortgagee—it is not entirely obvious which of two innocent parties, X or Y, should benefit from the register's guarantee of title, but in the second example above it seems very wrong for the mortgage to be valid and to prejudice Mr X (when the property is sold). If an innocent Y were a buyer who had moved into the property (perhaps the fraud was carried out while the Xs were away from home for a long period) then the answer would not be so obvious.

Moving on one step: if the land has passed to Z, should he be able to rely on the register, or is he in danger from the invalidity of a transaction once removed from his own? One of the ingredients of the problem—one of the values to be weighed—is the security of the register, and therefore the confidence of the market.

Indefeasibility in the 2002 act

The theory of indefeasibility has been worked out in great detail in the Torrens registration systems. They all give security of title to Z. Some also give security of title to Y, always provided he is innocent of the fraud. Where Y's title is guaranteed, the system is said to be one of immediate indefeasibility. Where X is able to recover the land from Y, but not from Z, there is said to be deferred indefeasibility. In very nearly all Torrens systems there is a system of indemnity, or insurance, funded by the Land Registry fees system, which will compensate X.

By contrast, English law operates a compromise. It does not guarantee Y's title, but it makes Y's title secure if he is in possession of the land. It does so by using the concept of mistake. Schedule 6 to the Land Registration Act 2002 states that the register can be altered in order to correct a mistake. This is obviously needed for typographical errors, for example. But the Schedule goes on to define a sub-set of cases where an alteration to correct a mistake prejudicially affects the title of a registered proprietor of the land. Such cases are called rectification. Rectification will not be ordered if a registered proprietor *in possession of the land* objects to it, unless he has caused or substantially contributed to the mistake by fraud or carelessness, or unless it would for any other reason be unjust not to order rectification. This gives a clear answer in our first two cases. In the straight fraud case, Y loses; but where Y is innocent, he keeps the land provided he is in possession of it. Moreover, possession is carefully defined, so that if land is in the possession of a tenant, the landlord is treated as being in possession; if it is in the possession of a licensee, it is deemed to be in the possession of the licensor; if it is in the possession of a beneficiary, it is deemed to be in the possession of the trustee. So Y is safe even if he is a buyer (unlike our example) and has let the land, or taken in a lodger, or declared a trust of the land. However, if land is in the possession of a mortgagee, it is deemed to be in the possession of the mortgagor. So in our example, the Y bank does not keep its registered charge.

Where Y *is* in possession, the Schedule gives the court a discretion to rectify nevertheless if it would be just to do so. A good example is where the land concerned is a tiny piece of land, of no benefit to Y, but important to X.[30] It would be unjust to allow Y to keep it and then demand a ransom price from X.

The English system has been described as qualified indefeasibility. It is kinder than immediate indefeasibility, because it tends to keep the land with those to whom it matters most: proprietors who are living on it or running a business on it. And the rules about rectification have to be read side by side with the provisions of Schedule 8 to the Act, on indemnity. Schedule 8 provides that in all cases where someone suffers loss because of the rectification of the register, or because of a mistake whose correction would involve rectification, he will be compensated. So in our second example, the innocent Y bank is compensated for losing the security of half the land (the loss will be whatever part of the debt Mrs X, or her share in the property, cannot pay). But if the innocent Y were a buyer from X under a void transfer, who kept the land because rectification could not be ordered against him, X would be compensated.

Under the Land Registration Act 1925, Z, too, was vulnerable and could lose his title unless he was in possession of the land. This was not a problem for the ordinary domestic purchasers in the acid-bath cases, but it left some purchasers, particularly mortgagees, insecure. The 2002 Act is not explicit on the point but the best view is that Z's title is secure, because there is no mistake in the transfer to him. He can rely on the title he sees on the register, provided the disposition to him is itself valid. There is thus qualified indefeasibility for Y, but true deferred indefeasibility for Z, as we would expect in a system so firmly orientated

---

[30] *James Hay Pension Trustees Ltd v Cooper Estates Ltd* [2005] EWHC 36 (Ch).

to dynamic security. And where Z gets to keep the land, despite the discovery of a mistake further back in the chain of title, again, X can look to the indemnity fund for compensation.

The 1925 provisions for rectification generated a number of awkward cases, some of them betraying serious misunderstanding of the operation both of registration and of indefeasibility. In some, the courts succumbed to the temptation to use a trusts analysis, on the basis that Y might hold the land on trust for Z following a void transfer. This is unhelpful. It cannot be correct in cases where Y is innocent. Where Y is guilty of fraud, the remedy should not depend on the existence of a trust interest which can be overreached. Much of the confusion arose from the poor drafting of the relevant provisions of the 1925 Act. The 2002 Act represents a great improvement; a consistent set of results can be achieved, for X, Y, and Z, from the mechanism in Schedules 4 and 8, without the need to rely on concepts not intended for the purpose of defining indefeasibility.

The final chapter of this book reverts to the tension between legitimate acquisition of land and the value placed on possession, in the context of the law of adverse possession. We shall see that in that context the tension is under acute strain at present and that one of the problems is the absence of any provision for compensation in order to restore a balance.

Bringing the register up to date

Schedule 4 to the Land Registration Act 2002 also provides that the register can be altered in order to bring it up to date. Again, this covers some very simple cases in the 'oh, of course' category, for example where a street name or number has changed or where a death certificate is sent in to record the death of one of joint proprietors. It covers the registration of transactions carried out by the registered proprietor and events subsequent to his acquisition such as the registration of an easement acquired by prescription (long use).[31] And it also covers two quite difficult instances.

---

[31] See Chapter 8.

One is what the Torrens writers call the *in personam* exception—where a registered title has been bought in circumstances which make the purchaser hold it on a constructive trust for another party. We discussed this in the case where a third party has an unregistered interest. Mere notice of this interest will not bind a purchaser. But if he has actively engaged in a deal whose object is the defeat of that interest, or otherwise behaved with serious dishonesty—the issue has not been explored in English case law—a trust may be imposed. In such a case the register can be altered, for example to give effect to the unregistered interest. This is not rectification, because there has been no mistake on the registrar's part.

Second is the voidable transfer. This is a transfer tainted by a problem such as misrepresentation or undue influence, but not actually void. The party who is the victim of the wrongdoing can choose to *avoid*, that is cancel, the transaction, subject to rules about taking action within a reasonable time. Until he does so, he has an 'equity', that is, a right falling short of an equitable interest but which may nevertheless bind a purchaser if protected on the register or by actual occupation. So a purchaser of a registered estate may be bound by an earlier owner's right to avoid a transaction, one or more steps back in the chain of title. This leans rather more in the direction of static security than do the indefeasibility rules and the principles of rectification; it may arise from a particularly unfortunate decision under the 1925 Act.[32]

CONCLUSION

This chapter has explored the heart of modern English land law. We have seen why the law has to organize complexity because it is a source of uncertainty to purchasers of land, and to those who hold rights in land. In organizing complexity, the law has to make a choice: will it protect the holder of, say, an equitable easement or a trust interest in the land, or will it protect the purchaser who wants to be free of them? The draftsmen of the

---

[32] *Norwich and Peterborough Building Society Ltd v Steed* [1993] Ch 116.

1925 legislation were quite clear that they wanted to protect the purchaser. The legislation they drafted was not entirely watertight, but the decisions of the courts and the practice of conveyancers have filled in the gaps and the 2002 statute has largely followed the 1925 pattern. In cases of conflict the odds are stacked in favour of a purchaser of land. This is closely linked with our perception of what land is for; there is no getting away from the fact that we value it as capital. The buyer of land may or may not want to live there, but he certainly wants to have a marketable asset. It is in the interests of both purchasers and landowners to have a land law system that protects purchasers and maintains a brisk market in land, even at the expense of those who have rights in land but are not owners.

There is a contradiction inherent in this preference for dynamic security, in the effect upon long-term stability for purchasers. We have seen that section 29 of the 2002 Act gives a negative warranty that is, in practice, robust. The three items that it lists are all of the pre-existing interests that a purchaser need be concerned with. The provisions on alteration of the register control the register's positive warranty—the promise that the registered title is secure. We have seen that, again, the odds are stacked in favour of a purchaser insofar as his own acquisition is in question: provided that he is in possession of the land, he will be able to keep it despite any defect in the transfer to him, and provided the defect was not his fault. This is splendid for a purchaser contemplating his own acquisition of the land. But once he steps past that acquisition, it makes him vulnerable to fraud in the future. The purchaser interested in dynamic security has become the owner interested in static security, and in that capacity he may find the registration system disappointing. But he will not find it disastrous, because of the existence of the indemnity fund.

The chapters that follow explore further the acquisition of land and of interests in it, and the nature of those interests. All are affected by registration and by this tension between dynamic and static security. The challenge for the system is to find a balance between the two and, increasingly, to do so in a way that does not conflict with human rights. For dynamic security may well involve people being deprived of their possessions.

In the context of indefeasibility, compensation provisions provide that balance. In the context of adverse possession, as we shall see in Chapter 9, the absence of compensation provisions have led to a serious conflict between land law principle and human rights. For most holders of non-ownership rights in land, registration provides a safeguard, and is consistent with dynamic security. For some, in particular the beneficiaries of informally constituted trusts (to be explored in Chapter 4), there is little safeguard because their interests have little proprietary effect. They might be said to be the main victims of our purchaser-focused registration system.

BIBLIOGRAPHY

E. Cooke, *The New Law of Land Registration* (Oxford, Hart Publishing Ltd, 2003).

E. Cooke and P. O'Connor, 'Purchaser liability to third parties in the English Land Registration System: a Comparative Perspective' (2004) 120 *Law Quarterly Review* 640.

A. Pottage, 'The Originality of Registration' (1995) 15 *Oxford Journal of Legal Studies* 370.

R. B. Roper et al., *Ruoff and Roper: Registered Conveyancing* (London, Sweet and Maxwell Limited, 2005) Ch 46.

P. Sparkes, *A New Land Law* (Oxford, Hart Publishing Ltd, 2003) Ch 1.

4

CREATING AND ACQUIRING INTERESTS IN LAND: WORDS AND INTENTIONS

This chapter is about the way the law controls the creation and transfer of interests in land, when we buy houses, grant a lease, acquire an easement, grant a mortgage in exchange for a loan, and so on. To grasp this topic, we have to embrace a contrast. On the one hand, the law likes these things to be done unambiguously, deliberately, and publicly. On the other hand, the law recognizes that in some cases it would be oppressive, perhaps even discriminatory, to require this. Besides, some transactions are too trivial, in the sense of being short term, for it to be worth insisting on formal procedures.

So how does the law deal with this contrast? We need to examine the formal requirements for the acquisition of interests in land. *Formal* requirements are rules about the practical, physical way in which such transactions are carried out, for example that they be done in writing or by deed. Then we need to look at short leases, where informality is not a problem, and at implied trusts and estoppel, which enable informal acquisition. These latter two ideas are closely linked, and in some cases are alternative responses to the same set of facts. A very different method of informal acquisition is adverse possession, to be considered in Chapter 9; its diminishing importance means that it is not discussed here alongside other methods of informal acquisition.

The impression that this chapter aims to give is one of a battery of rules about formality, a carefully built wall of requirements, behind which we find a limited area where there is scope for informally created interests. Here, again, is the land law dilemma of clean titles versus grace for the vulnerable, or of dynamic versus static security.

FORMALITIES

The law requires that certain land transactions be done in writing; that some be done by deed; and that some be done by deed and then registered. The penalty for failing to comply with the rules is that the transaction does not work; in some cases it is wholly ineffective, in others partially so.

Why? The earliest statute imposing formality requirements for land transactions was the Statute of Frauds 1677. Its title explains its purpose and a principal motivation for all formality rules: the avoidance of fraud, because informal transactions are so easily concealed. More generally, we can say that the rules are imposed to protect people. One aim is to make sure that they know what they are doing; there is no 'cooling-off' period for land transactions as there is for some consumer contracts, but making people write things down (as we used to: nowadays we type things up) serves a similar function, bringing the transaction itself and many of its details to the parties' attention. Another aim is to make sure that people can check what they have done, and that other people can see what they have done. Where formalities include registration, the evidence is made public so that it is hard to conceal. For the same reasons, publicity and registration requirements were introduced for marriages in 1753, although land transactions in this jurisdiction, unlike weddings, do not now have to be actually performed in public. Other purposes for formalities include the government's interest in seeing what has been done and, in some instances, in taxing it.

Contracts

Contracts are not a necessary preliminary to the creation or transfer of property rights. If I am going to give, not sell, a plot of land to you, there would be no contract between us beforehand, and the formalities we would need to think about would be those necessary for the transfer of a legal estate. But most sales of land (leasehold or freehold) and grants of leases will be preceded by a contract. The context in which most people meet land contracts is domestic conveyancing, where the contract has a vital role in practical and financial planning: it locks both seller and buyer into the deal and fixes the date of completion, enabling removal vans to be booked and mortgage arrangements to be finalized. It is of course possible to sell and buy land without a prior contract, but it is rarely convenient to do so.

Contracts are therefore a frequent preliminary to the creation or transfer of legal rights (usually ownership rights) in land, and the layman regards them as just that. But they play another role; they are fundamental to the creation of equitable rights in land.

We noted in Chapter 2[1] that a contractual right to buy land is an equitable interest in it. It was explained that this is because of the availability of specific performance of the contract. It means that the purchaser's pre-completion rights can be inherited and, like any other equitable interest in land, they can be enforced against at least some purchasers of the land.

Other equitable rights can all be seen to have their roots in contract: a contract to grant a lease generates an equitable lease; a contract to grant a mortgage generates an equitable mortgage. Moreover, it has been explained that equity will rescue deals which are insufficiently formal to generate legal rights, so that equitable rights can be seen as a sort of consolation prize, or a rescue effort for those who have missed the boat by failing to complete the formalities required for an effective transaction at law. The reason for this is the readiness of equity to recognize the proprietary nature of rights arising from contracts. But it follows from this that if a deal fails to be a valid contract, it will not generate rights at law *nor in equity*.

With that in mind we turn to the formality requirements for contracts. With a few exceptions, contracts for the creation or transfer of any interest in land must be in writing; the document must be signed by both (or all) parties; and all the terms they have agreed must be written in the one document. The law implies some terms in some contracts, and these implied terms do not need to be written. For example, if the parties to an agreement to sell land do not state when they will complete the sale, the law implies that it will be done in a reasonable time (for what that is worth). The rules allow for transactions where

---

[1] At p 34.

contracts are 'exchanged', a practice familiar to anyone who has bought a house. In that case, two identical contracts are prepared, each party signs one, and the contract comes into effect when contracts are exchanged—once a physical ritual, nowadays a moment declared by lawyers in accordance with rules of professional practice.

These requirements are set out in the Law of Property (Miscellaneous Provisions) Act 1989—a relatively recent enactment. Until 1989, the requirements for land contracts were more subtle; they did not have to *be* in writing, but if there was no written *evidence* of a land contract, they were 'unenforceable by action'. For example, suppose you and I agreed, over a pint and a handshake, that you would buy my house, and you paid a five per cent deposit. Nothing was written down. Come the agreed day for completion, you refused to complete; it would have been perfectly proper for me to keep your deposit, because that is what a deposit is for—agreed compensation for a failure to complete. But if you were ready to buy and I refused to complete, you would not be able to retrieve your deposit; the contract was unwritten and so you would not have been able to get a court to order me to pay the money back. That is the consequence of the contract's being unenforceable by [court] action.

This rule was difficult to understand, and could lead to inconsistent results. The current law was constructed by the Law Commission with the aim of better serving the protective purpose of formalities. And so it does; it makes it unlikely, for example, that anyone will get trapped into a land contract inadvertently, and therefore renders superfluous the 'Subject to Contract' slogan still used in conveyancing correspondence. It makes the deal described above completely void: I would have to give your deposit back because there would be no reason to keep it. Note that the 1989 rules apply both at law and in equity; a deal that fails to meet their requirements will create neither a legal nor an equitable interest.

What the new rule also did was to complicate some well-established ways of dealing with land. It made the traditional analysis of options untenable, for example. An option is a deal whereby I give you the right to buy my land from me at any time you choose within a defined period, say five years, at a price we have agreed or to be determined in an agreed way; you exercise that right by sending me notification. Options are useful for structuring transactions and their finance, and they are robust devices because equity has turned these contractual rights into property rights. The difficulty is that the option structure had always been analysed so that the initial agreement was seen as an offer, to be held open for the option period; the notification that the option is to be exercised was the acceptance. Together, they made a complete contract. Clearly, this would not work in the new dispensation, as it was a contract that was not comprised in one document. So were options now impossible? No, said the court; they are to be re-conceptualized as conditional contracts, complete at the point of agreement, but activated by the notification. What the courts could not save was the mortgage by deposit of title deeds; the ancient and handy arrangement whereby A lends money to B on the security of his land, and, instead of drafting documentation and then registering a legal mortgage, A simply takes the title deeds. Such a transaction took effect before 1989 as an equitable mortgage, but cannot now do so because the contractual basis that underpins all equitable property rights has gone; for an equitable mortgage to take effect now the deal must be written down in a single document complying with the terms of the 1989 Act. The same goes, of course, for equitable leases and equitable easements; these are still subject to less onerous requirements than are their legal counterparts, but the 1989 rules stand as a minimum for equity as well as for law. Despite its ancient role in rescuing deals that have not complied with the rules, equity has never been entirely insouciant about formalities; but the 1989 Act is rather disturbing in its restriction of equity's scope. It brings a loss in freedom and in time; a gain in lawyers' fees; a gain in certainty; and a gain in evidence.

More generally, we can say that the 1989 rules make it easier for people to get things wrong. It is more likely now that people who seriously intended a transaction will fail to effect one. Should they be given any help in enforcing it? In order to answer that, we might ask whether or not we would have expected either party to take legal advice and therefore to get it right; we might also ask what are the effects, on either party, of their transaction being void. We shall have more to say about this later.

Transactions: creating or conveying

As we might expect, transactions which actually create or transfer an interest in land are subject to more onerous formality requirements than are contracts to do so. We use the word 'transfer' now, to conform to the terms used in the land registration legislation, whereas the older statutes use the word 'convey', which was appropriate to unregistered land. But in this context, the terms mean the same thing. With some exceptions, section 53 of the Law of Property Act 1925 requires that interests in land, whether legal or equitable, can only be created in writing, and that a declaration of a trust of land (which creates equitable interests) must be evidenced in writing. Thus a declaration of trust is effective if done orally, provided there is written evidence of the declaration—a tricky distinction which has generated some tortuous case law. Section 52 of the same Act goes a step further and states that to be effective at law—to create a legal interest with the extra strength that such interests have in the face of buyers or mortgagees—a transaction has to be done by deed. This takes us a step beyond mere formality and into the realm of ritual.

In medieval times, in practice until the mid-sixteenth century, land had to be transferred by livery of seisin. The transaction was carried out publicly, in the presence of witnesses (in an era before folk were willing to rely on mere documentation), and very physically: the parties stood on the land, and the transferor would hand a bit of it—a twig or a turf—to the tranferee. By the mid-nineteenth century the ritual was formally abolished, so that all legal estates in land could be transferred by deed. A deed was sealed writing; literally sealed, with hot wax (as much correspondence still was at that date).[2] As the use of

---

[2] 'He wrote with his own hand his love to his cousin William, and sent him half a guinea under the seal', Jane Austen, *Mansfield Park* (London, Penguin Books, 1966) 52.

wax and seals became obsolete, the seal was represented by a little circle of red, self-adhesive paper. The seal is a rite—a visible sign of something invisible yet deeply significant. A seal by itself did not do the job; the document had to be signed by the parties, witnessed, and then delivered, ie put into effect by the delivery of the deed to the party whose title it completed.

Another modernization effected by the Law of Property (Miscellaneous Provisions) Act 1989 was a change in the requirements for a deed. A document is a deed if it 'makes clear on its face that it is a deed', ie if it claims to be a deed. A heading will do; and the requirements for witnessing remain.

Originally, a deed was a sufficient condition for the transmission or creation of a legal estate; now it is only a necessary condition; in most cases (though not all) even the delivered deed will not do the job by itself. As we have seen,[3] it is not possible to transfer a registered estate in land, or to grant a legal lease of more than seven years out of it, or to create a legal interest in it (such as a mortgage), without registering the transaction. And the creation of a legal lease of more than seven years out of an unregistered estate (a fee simple or a lease) triggers a requirement that that new lease be registered as an independent title, on pain of its losing legal status.

Three rather mechanical, but crucially important, conclusions follow from what has been said above. First, transactions that should be in writing but are not will be wholly ineffective.

Second, those that should be done by deed but are merely in writing will be effective in equity but not at law. A mortgage effected in writing (complying with section 2 of the 1989 Act) but not by a deed will be an equitable mortgage; an attempt to register it, so that it has the benefit of guaranteed status,[4] will be unsuccessful (although the registrar will record it against the title of the mortgaged land so that its priority is protected). It is more likely, of course, that parties who do not get round to using a deed will also fail to get round to registering the deal, so that the mortgage remains unprotected and will not be of any effect against a subsequent purchaser of the land.

---

[3] Chapter 3, p 48.   [4] Chapter 3, p 65.

Third, a transaction that is done by deed but not registered works only in equity, consistent with the tradition of equity's rescuing transactions that miss the legal boat. A mortgage done by deed but not registered is an equitable one; a purchase of a house, done by deed but not registered, gives the buyer an equitable title only. This happens every time a purchase is 'completed', and continues until it is registered.

We can now build on what was said in Chapter 2 about the distinction between legal and equitable ownership, and non-ownership rights, using formalities to distinguish between the two kinds. Given a property right, for example a right of way, how can we tell whether it is legal or equitable? We have to look first at what it is: it may be something that can only be equitable. But a right of way is an easement, and easements can be either. Second, if it was created using words, whether unwritten or documented, it may be clear from what was said that the people involved deliberately created an equitable right when they could have created a legal one. There are reasons why someone might want to grant an equitable mortgage, for example. Third, if the right is one that could be either legal or equitable and no deliberate choice is evident, then we have to look again, and more precisely, at the way in which it was created or transferred. If the legal requirements for its creation are met, then the right is legal; otherwise, if it has missed the boat by falling short of the formal requirements, it is equitable.

A few examples may help.

First, the creation of a property right. Adam has been granted a ten-year lease of a shop. The requirements for a legal ten year lease are that it be written down in the form of a deed, properly executed (ie signed and witnessed), and registered at the Land Registry. If and only if this has all been done, the lease is legal. Contrast a weekly tenancy granted to Zoe, orally. Nothing is even written down, let alone turned into a deed or registered. Nevertheless Zoe has a legal lease, because for leases for a term of three years or less (provided that a full rent is charged), no formalities are required, so there is no boat to miss.[5]

---

[5] See p 82.

Second, a transfer. Bertha has bought a house from Colin, who was the registered proprietor, holding a legal fee simple. The transfer of the land to Bertha was in the form of a deed, and has been registered at the Land Registry. Bertha now holds the legal fee simple.

Third, a transfer that has failed to meet the requirements for legal validity. Adam sells his lease to Dennis, so that Dennis will stand in the original tenant's shoes and take over Adam's relationship with the landlord (just as Bertha took over Colin's relationship with the Crown, though that is far less important). The transfer of the lease to Dennis is done by deed, but Dennis (or his solicitor) forgets to send the transfer to the Land Registry. Unless and until he does so, he holds only an equitable lease. The legal lease is still held by Adam, on trust for Dennis, even though neither Adam nor Dennis knows of the trust.

Electronic land transactions

Notice how much less physical the formalities for land transactions have become. We have moved away from the era where we had to get earth on our hands in order to own it. Gone, too, is the ritual with hot drippy wax, and even the little red-gummed paper circles that pretended to be seals. All that is needed now is paper and ink . . . but this book is being written without either. No sooner has the law become accustomed to a business world of printing on paper, than paper is *passé* and the law needs to work out how to manage electronic dealings without sacrificing the protection that formalities give.

The Land Registration Act 2002 lays the legislative foundation for electronic conveyancing. The idea was that within the next few years the Land Register, which by the beginning of the twenty-first century was already held in electronic form, and was already available for inspection online (for a fee), would become accessible *and changeable* from the conveyancer's computer. Completion of a land transaction would take place, not by signing and delivering a piece of paper, but by clicking a mouse and thereby, in one instant, creating or transferring a registered estate. The intention was that transactions—including contracts—not made electronically would be of no effect either at law or in equity; equity's rescuing role would be further diminished.

That was the vision. Reality has involved a more gradual change. Mortgages can now be discharged electronically by the lender's computer and without intervention by Land Registry staff. Mortgages can be created electronically; but transfers cannot, and therefore in effect only re-mortgages will be created in this way. Consultation by the Land Registry about the possible introduction of 'e-transfers' in 2011 revealed insufficient support for that step to be taken, and the plan has been shelved. Moreover, what was envisaged was not electronic completion (as described above), but electronic notification of the transfer to the register. Thus there is no conceptual change, and there is still a 'registration gap' albeit greatly reduced. One of the reasons for this is the depressing fact that the development of an integrated system for the electronic transfer of funds has not been possible. Another reason is heightened concern about fraud, which has been on the increase in recent years. There is more amiss than unfamiliarity; the world of electronic communication and transaction is not regarded as sufficiently safe for the sale and purchase of land.

INFORMAL TRANSACTING

So far, then, we have a relatively tidy picture. One statute regulates the formality requirements for land contracts; another sets out the requirement of writing for creating all interests in land, and the additional requirement of a deed for creating or transferring a legal interest; and in most but not all cases registration is a further requirement for legal validity. The rest of this chapter is about the exceptions to the formality rules, exceptions made because formality would be inconvenient or oppressive.

Exceptions for short leases

All the statutory formality requirements make an exception for short leases. Leases are both contracts and estates in land. Yet most leases of three years or less, for which a market rent is charged, do not have to be created in writing, and are valid at law even though they are not made by deed. The 1925 and 1989 Acts provide this explicitly. This makes it unlikely, by the way, that a short lease will ever be equitable, unless the rent condition is not met or unless the grantor has only an equitable estate so that he cannot create a legal one. In the short leases category come all periodic tenancies, of course, where informal arrangements made on the doorstep or by telephone have always been commonplace and whose validity the law simply has to recognize. Trivial though it sounds, this deserves a paragraph to itself: it shows the law accommodating itself to the convenience of its users. For the same reason, auction contracts—complete when the hammer falls—are exempt from the formality requirements. The concession for short leases is thought to be a safe one so far as purchasers are concerned, because a tenant paying a weekly or monthly rent is likely to be in occupation of the property, and the law continues to make the assumption that a purchaser will actually inspect the property he is buying (as he probably will) or of which he is accepting a mortgage (yet in that case inspection is very unlikely). Short leases are also kept off the Land Register, partly at least to keep the register uncluttered, and to avoid an excessive workload for the registries. Notice that this paragraph had to start by saying '*most* leases of three years or less'; there are exceptions to the exception, where special factors make publicity desirable. One example is reversionary leases where possession is given at a date later than the grant of the lease and where therefore the tenant might not be readily discoverable by the purchaser.

It is odd, however, that the assignment of a periodic tenancy, whether as a gift or as a sale, is subject to the full rigour of the formality requirements; the periodic tenancy is a legal estate and so a transfer must be done by deed in accordance with section 52 of the Law of Property Act1925. Lawyers had not noticed this until it was exposed in a 1990s case;[6] the exception in the Act is only for creation.

The exception to the registration requirement is for leases of seven years or less; these can be created and transferred off-register.

---

[6] *Crago v Julian* [1992] 1 WLR 372, CA.

There is therefore a group of leases—for seven years or less, but for more than three years—where writing and a deed are required for creation and transfer, but registration is not, so that the deed remains a sufficient condition for the manipulation of the legal estate. It may be that this will be tidied up by moving the threshold for registration down to three years, to match the requirements for contracts in the 1989 Act and the requirements for creation and transfer in the 1925 Act. Whatever the eventual threshold for registration of leases will be will also be the threshold for the requirement of electronic dealing.

Implied trusts and estoppel; introductory points

The exception for short leases generates legal estates. So does the doctrine of adverse possession, the other exception to informality which we have already mentioned. A further provision found in the 1925 and 1989 Acts is for 'implied, resulting and constructive trusts' to be exempt from the requirements of writing. Here we move into equity and the creation of equitable interests in land. Note that it is generally accepted that resulting and constructive trusts are a subset of implied trusts, and this narrative proceeds on that basis.

When the exception for implied trusts was written into section 53 of the Law of Property Act 1925, it was expected to cover quite a narrow range of circumstances. Its importance has grown considerably, however, thanks to developments in the second half of the twentieth century. As we have already observed, the courts became very creative during that period in adapting ancient doctrines to modern contexts. Much of what we are about to discuss has been developed as a way of bringing ownership into line with the reality of a relationship. How does that happen? Equity is a community of judges and a body of legal thinking; the development of the law of implied trusts and estoppel has proceeded gradually and has reflected the instincts of succeeding generations of judges about what is fair between the litigants before them, about what is legitimate within the doctrine of precedent, and about what is the appropriate balance between the courts and Parliament. We have legislation for the redistribution, on a very wide discretionary basis, of the property of divorcing couples; we have no statutory provision for cohabitants. How much discretion can the courts exercise in the absence of Parliamentary intervention? Couples who are, or have been, cohabiting have formed a large proportion of claimants under the doctrines to be discussed. The common intention constructive trust was actually developed in response to their needs; resulting trusts and estoppel were not, although estoppel in particular has proved very adaptable for use in this context.

It follows from what has just been said that divorcing couples will not normally need to use any of the following doctrines; but some of the cases involve married couples because the trigger for litigation was not divorce but bankruptcy, and sometimes succession, when it is vital to know precisely who owns what. Even if the law is reformed so as to introduce for cohabitants a statutory basis for financial remedies on the breakdown of the relationship, it seems inevitable that property law doctrines will continue to be needed for married couples, civil partners, and cohabitants in cases arising on bankruptcy or death.

And what if the law is not reformed so as to introduce financial remedies for separating cohabitants? Then the law of implied trusts and of estoppel will continue to be the only route for financial redress in those circumstances, aside from the law relating to child support. It will be seen that this body of law is wholly inadequate for that purpose. It is not sufficiently clear to enable couples to negotiate in the shadow of the law; nor is it sufficiently comprehensive, because insofar as it provides answers it does so in general only for the family home. It is makeshift law, at best. Developments since the first edition of this book have not improved that position.

We turn now to the individual doctrines: the resulting trust, the common intention constructive trust, and proprietary estoppel.

RESULTING TRUSTS

Resulting trusts are ancient. The idea is that where one person supplies the money to buy a property which is purchased in another's name, then, unless it is clear that the one who

provided the funds was making the other a gift, the buyer holds
it on trust for the one who supplied the money. I send you a
large sum of money and ask you to buy a house with it, and you
do so; unless it is clear that this was a gift, equity regards you as
trustee for me. The house is really mine. (The word 'resulting' is
supposed to be a Latin derivation, because the equitable interest
jumps back to the one who gave the money: *re-salire*). If
I provide part of the money for the house purchase, we become
co-owners in equity.

In a family context, the concept is skewed by the 'presumption of advancement'. In certain circumstances the law starts
from the assumption that a gift is being made. A father buys a
house in the name of his daughter for her to live in while she is at
university; the house is presumed to be a gift to her unless (in the
event of dispute) he can show that both parties regarded the
daughter as holding the legal title on trust for him. The presumption also applies when a husband provides money for a
purchase in his wife's name, but not vice versa—fortunately for
women, because the resulting trust has been very useful in an era
when the purchase of the family home was often done in the
husband's name. When part of the funds for the purchase were
provided by the wife, the husband was regarded as holding the
house on trust for her to the extent of her contribution (she puts
in 25 per cent, she has a 25 per cent share, etc). The courts are
now very reluctant to apply the presumption of advancement,
because of its gendered nature. Section 199 of the Equality Act
2010 abolishes the presumption of advancement, but has not yet
been brought into force.

The downside of the resulting trust is that the beneficiary gets
exactly what he contributes to the property, in terms of proportion of value. A five per cent contribution to the purchase of the
family home, followed by years of hard labour, self-sacrifice, and
devotion of income to the household bills, will only ever
generate a five per cent share in the value of the property.
Contribution is closely defined: making mortgage repayments
does not seem to be recognized for this purpose. The existence
and extent of a resulting trust is fixed at the moment of acquisition of the property. The Supreme Court has now said that the
resulting trust is unlikely to be relevant in the domestic context,

as between couples (and has made it clear that it is not to be used where the couple were joint legal owners).[7] Accordingly the common intention constructive trust will almost invariably be the appropriate doctrine for the resolution of disputes about equitable ownership.

COMMON INTENTION CONSTRUCTIVE TRUST

Origins

The common intention constructive trust was invented in response to a failed attempt to create a discretionary jurisdiction for the assistance of married claimants, in the days before the divorce reforms of 1969. The story goes like this.

Lord Denning has become an almost mythical figure to law students in the last thirty years or so—starting from those of us who began learning the law just after he left the Bench. The 1960s and 1970s must have been exciting times. What would he come up with next? And would the House of Lords let him get away with it? There was something of a cat-and-mouse game going on. In 1967 Lord Denning, then a member of the Court of Appeal, invented 'deserted wife's equity', the doctrine that where the family home belongs to the husband, the wife automatically has a proprietary interest in it. The purpose of the invention was to give the wife a stake in the home when the husband defaulted on the mortgage, to save her from homelessness; had Denning's invention been allowed to stand, it would have had a most revolutionary effect on family property in this jurisdiction. It would have brought us into line with the European doctrine of community of property, whereby marriage automatically generates a form of joint ownership of the family home and some or all of the couple's other assets (the extent of co-ownership varies from one jurisdiction to another). But the House of Lords overruled Denning's efforts in this instance, being more anxious to ensure that the mortgage industry would function smoothly than to make a significant move towards European legal integration (this was 1967!).

---

[7] *Jones v Kernott* [2011] UKSC 53 at [25].

As it turned out, the overruling was softened a little by a statute enacted shortly afterwards and in response to the House of Lords decision: the Matrimonial Homes Act 1967. Its key provision is now found in section 30 of the Family Law Act 1996. It asserts the right of spouses to occupy the couple's home, even where they do not own it; and it enables that personal occupation right to be registered so that it can bind a purchaser. It thus takes on, through registration, a partially proprietary status. Only partially: the right can be made enforceable, as if it were a property right, but it is not alienable. It means that a wife who is aware that her husband is planning to sell or mortgage the house, against her wishes, can register her occupation right on the Land Register, just as if it were the burden of an easement or a lease. If title is unregistered the registration can be done through the Land Charges Registry. A potential purchaser, whether a buyer or a mortgagee, will not deal with the husband or make any commitment to the property in the presence of that registration. The Act has given the non-owning spouse a right to veto transactions. Its weakness is that very few individuals are aware of it and by the time the need for protection is known, it will probably be too late. The occupation right cannot be an overriding interest, and so in the absence of actual registration it gives no protection at all against third parties.

The swift suppression of the 'deserted wife's equity' left us with the system of separation of property, whereby marriage has no effect upon the property rights of the couples as individuals (until they divorce, that is). Separation was a considerable improvement upon the law before 1882, whereby a married woman was unable to own a legal estate in land at all. That disability was removed by the Married Women's Property Act 1882. And that statute provided the tool for Denning's next attempt to reform the law of family property. He took section 17 of the Act, which was intended to enable the court to declare the respective interests of the parties, and read it as if it enabled the court to determine, and therefore to redistribute. The statute enabled the court, said Denning, to declare that a contribution to the home, in labour and materials, entitled a wife or husband to a beneficial interest. His views prevailed in the Court of Appeal for a short period. But the House of Lords decisively overruled this use of the 1882 statute, in a case where a Mr Pettitt was claiming an interest in his wife's property by virtue of his contribution in work and materials.[8] Mr Pettitt was found to have no property rights. His contribution was not in fact substantial and he was perhaps not a claimant who prompted a great deal of sympathy. But the House of Lords made the principle very clear, that property rights are not granted merely because the claimant needs or deserves them.

That sequence of decisions triggered two responses. First, a small and little-used statutory provision,[9] to the effect that where someone carried out substantial improvements to his or her spouse's property, that person would acquire a share (or an enhanced share, if already a co-owner) in the property in equity. The provision is useful only to spouses (who do not normally need it); and it would not have helped Mr Pettitt, whose work was hardly substantial. A much more exciting response to the *Pettitt* saga was the case of *Gissing v Gissing*,[10] where the House of Lords, having closed the door rather firmly on Lord Denning, opened a door of its own—the common intention constructive trust.

Constructing a trust

Constructive trusts are nearly as ancient and respectable as resulting trusts. They arise in a number of contexts where the courts have concluded that there ought to be a trust even though one has not been formally set up. They may arise as a response to wrongdoing, for example when someone has received trust property and is then obliged to hold it as a trustee rather than for his own benefit because he knew about the trust. In the context of land registration, for example, a constructive trust may in exceptional circumstances be imposed on a purchaser whose conduct is so dishonest that he cannot be allowed

---

[8] *Pettitt v Pettitt* [1970] AC 777, HL.
[9] Section 37 of the Matrimonial Proceedings and Property Act 1970.
[10] [1971] AC 886, HL.

the protection that registration normally gives a purchaser, but is obliged instead to hold the land for the benefit of someone else.[11] The common intention constructive trust harnesses the idea of a response to wrongdoing, and of the imposition of trustee status on someone who did not want or expect it. But it extends the conditions under which a trust may arise. The House of Lords held that where there has been an agreement (also called a 'common intention') between the landowner and the claimant that the claimant is to have an interest in the property, and she has acted to her detriment in reliance on that agreement, then the landowner holds the property as trustee for her—or, more usually, for the two of them together.

From this formulation we can construct a claim for a disappointed cohabitant. She can say: he promised that the house was as much mine as his; that was our shared intention; I relied on that and helped with the finances, or gave up my protected tenancy, or worked hard at renovating the property. The house should therefore belong, in part, to me. The House of Lords is doing something apparently quite close to what Lord Denning wanted to do, albeit with better roots in precedent. The result is a doctrine that will not help every claimant, but is nevertheless very flexible and is something that the courts have worked with creatively, if not entirely consistently.

The introduction of this recipe (agreement plus detrimental reliance generates an equitable interest) has given the courts scope to explore the ingredients. What sort of agreement will give rise to a trust? What counts as detrimental reliance upon that agreement so as to generate a beneficial interest? And what is the quantum of that beneficial interest—in what proportions do the equitable joint owners hold the property?

That last ingredient is important also in cases where the existence of a beneficial interest is not in dispute—where the parties bought the property jointly but the extent of their shares is now in dispute. It has attracted a great deal of attention recently because two highly authoritative decisions, of the House of Lords (*Stack v Dowden*[12]) and then of the Supreme

Court (*Jones v Kernott*[13]) concerned cases of joint purchase where the fact of joint beneficial ownership was not in dispute but the extent of the shares was. This is therefore relevant to our discussion of joint ownership, and the disputes to which it can give rise, in Chapter 5. In this chapter we are concerned with the issue of acquisition; how do I acquire a beneficial interest in the house of which you are the sole legal owner? The recent leading cases have things to say about this situation too.

First, the agreement or common intention. If the parties made a verbal agreement, then there is no difficulty; but who does? The business of falling in love and setting up home together does not generally involve cosy discussions about the beneficial ownership of the property, even if the parties know what that means. The cases are marred by squabblings over who said what and what it meant, when in fact, at the time, the words were not about property rights and may have been no more than pillow talk. The courts have even found express agreement in words which were actually lies and excuses, when he said to her that the house could not be put in their joint names because she was under 21 (at a time when the age of majority was 18), or because it would complicate her divorce proceedings. In these cases, the courts have found an express agreement, forcing the speaker to stand by what he said (compare the ideas behind proprietary estoppel, discussed below). So he should; but to label the conversation an agreement, or to say that the two shared the same intention, is ridiculous.

Then there are the cases where nothing was said. The courts are willing to discern an agreement from the parties' conduct; the idea is that if the parties have behaved in a particular way then they *must* have both intended that the claimant should have a share in the property. And from that idea have arisen two difficult controversies. First, what are the courts doing here? Are they discovering an unspoken but real agreement? Or are they constructing a bargain where in fact there was none? To be blunt, are they pretending that there was an agreement? The Supreme Court has said that wherever possible the courts must

---

[13] [2011] UKSC 53.

seek out what the parties in fact agreed, even where nothing was said. They must infer, not impute. It may be that an agreement—where in fact there was none—will be imputed as a last resort.[14] And that would appear to involve assuming that the parties intended what would in fact be fair in the light of all the circumstances. It is a far cry from giving effect to the actual intentions of real people.

Second, on what basis will the courts infer or, perhaps, impute an agreement? What evidence can the court take into account in a particular case? There has been clear authority to the effect that only a direct financial contribution to the acquisition of the house will suffice.[15] But what the courts have regarded as a direct financial contribution is considerably wider than the type of payment that would be regarded as a contribution sufficient to give rise to a resulting trust. The contribution may be in the form of a capital payment, or of contributions to the mortgage payments. It may be made at the time of purchase, or it may be made later; it may be the financing of an extension, rather than the purchase of the house itself; but repair and maintenance will not suffice. The 'contribution' may actually be the right-to-buy discount, that is, the reduction in the purchase price earned by a public sector tenant; this is important, as so often council houses are bought by the tenant who has earned a discount, and a family member who pays the rest or raises it as a loan.

More recently, doubt has been cast upon the authority of Lord Bridge's famous structure in *Rossett*.[16] The House of Lords[17] and the Supreme Court have expressed the view that his criterion was too narrow. So we may have to examine again the situation where it is claimed that the contribution from

---

[14] *Jones v Kernott* [2011] UKSC 53. This was a case where the existence of joint beneficial interests was not in dispute, only their quantum; so what is said about inference and imputation is binding, strictly, only in the context of the ascertainment of quantum. But it is unlikely and unrealistic to suppose that the courts' approach would be different in the context of the ascertainment of the existence of the trust.

[15] *Lloyds Bank plc v Rossett* [1991] 1 AC 107 at 132H–133B, per Lord Bridge.

[16] Ibid.

[17] *Stack v Dowden* [2007] UKHL 17 at [26], per Lord Walker and at [63], per Lady Hale.

which a shared intention can be inferred is payment of household expenses alone. The most authoritative cases in this area have been clear that paying the bills (as in the common arrangement: you pay the mortgage and I'll pay the bills) is too ambiguous, insufficiently closely linked to the acquisition of the house. Yet the claimant's paying the bills may have freed up the other party's resources and enabled him to pay the mortgage; there are contradictory statements in the cases, and the steer given by the Supreme Court may mean that the courts now take a more generous view of this situation.

But what of poor Mrs Burns?[18] She lived with Mr Burns for 19 years (the fact that she took his name, although they were not married, dates the case); she earned very little, and put most of her time and energy into raising the couple's children. Without her, Mr Burns would have had to pay for childcare; had she not spent her life in this way, Mrs Burns could have made money elsewhere. Would the courts be prepared to infer or impute from those facts an agreement relating to the family home and sufficient to found a trust of it?

Of those claimants that get past the 'common intention' hurdle, many do so because they have put money into the property rather than because anything was said. As we shall see, what they get out is rather different from what is available to them on a resulting trust analysis. But before the claimant can succeed, she must prove detrimental reliance upon that common intention.

There are two issues here. Detriment is supposed to be something costly, or difficult; and reliance is about causation. The detriment suffered by the claimant is supposed to be something she would not have done but for the prospect of an interest in the property.

Financial contribution is itself an easy example. The courts have no difficulty accepting that anyone who puts money into the acquisition or improvement of someone else's property must be expecting an interest in it. This is legally uncontroversial, although it may not match how non-lawyers think. And in cases

---

[18] *Burns v Burns* [1984] Ch 317.

where there is no express agreement in the first place, but an agreement is implied from conduct, we may find that the same behaviour pattern does two jobs: the claimant's making mortgage payments may be the evidence for the claimed common intention, and it may also constitute the claimant's detrimental reliance on that intention.

Where the action or course of conduct alleged to be the detrimental reliance is not a money contribution, the courts have had more difficulty assessing the validity of the claim of detrimental reliance. Successful examples include giving something up, such as a protected tenancy elsewhere, or looking after the landowner or assisting his business endeavours. The courts have had difficulty with manual labour and homemaking; they have looked for something more than a wife or partner would normally be expected to contribute to her home. So claimants are vulnerable to the personal ideologies of the (mostly male) judges, however innocent or unconscious, which may mean that the odds are stacked against female claimants.

Outcomes

This section is labelled 'outcomes' rather than remedies because the court does not see itself as awarding a remedy. The theory is that the parties' own actions have generated a beneficial interest in the property. What the court is doing is declaring the existence of that beneficial interest and declaring the proportion of the property's value that it represents. This means that the outcome of a claim of an interest under a common intention constructive trust is the discovery of something that has already happened.

So how much does the claimant get? Again, the courts give primacy to an express agreement; if the parties actually put into words how much the claimant's share would be ('as much yours as mine'), that is what she gets. If there was no express agreement,[19] the latest authorities[20] state that the court will look at the whole course of the relationship and of the parties'

---

[19] As there was, eg, in *Crossley v Crossley* [2005] EWCA Civ 1581.

[20] In particular, *Midland Bank plc v Cooke* [1995] 4 All ER 562, CA; *Stack v Dowden* [2007] UKHL 17; *Jones v Kernott* [2011] UKSC 53.

behaviour. A wide variety of factors may be regarded as relevant—including such personal factors as the nature of the relationship, whether or not the parties had children, and how the parties organized their money. Moreover, the parties' intentions may have changed over the years; the shared life that would have given rise to an inference that they intended to share equally may give place to something quite different if the parties later separate, one of them leaves, and they reorganize and disentangle their financial relationship. The constructive trust does not mirror the resulting trust, and the outcome may not yield proportions that match what was put in, although in the recent leading cases it has done so.

The courts have come a long way with the common intention constructive trust. Something like a concept of family property has been created, although only for the family home. And whereas in the past it has been the law that what the courts respond to is either words or money (there had to be an express agreement, or a direct contribution to the purchase of the house), the leading decisions now seem to be moving away from that restrictive formulation. At the same time, the courts continue to express dissatisfaction with the absence of a statutory structure for financial remedies between separating cohabitants, such as the one recommended by the Law Commission.

Whether or not reform along those lines ever takes place, there will remain an important role for the law of implied trusts when the dispute arises not between the couple, but with third parties. In that context, the courts' generosity is constrained by the conveyancing safeguards; although the common intention constructive trust gives rise to a property right for the claimant, which in theory will bind a purchaser, in fact it will very rarely do so. As we saw in Chapter 3, equitable ownership in fact has very little proprietary effect. What looks like a protection of static security in fact has had very little impact on dynamic security.

So if the claim is made in a context where someone else—a mortgagee or a buyer—is claiming ownership of the property, the claimant needs to show that she has had an interest in it for some time and that it is enforceable against that purchaser. Where the legal owner's title is registered, the story she needs to construct is something like: he bought the house, I moved in with him, I paid off a substantial part of the mortgage. So I have made contributions to the acquisition of the property which demonstrate our common intention that I should be a joint owner of it. The partnership in which we lived and the extent to which we shared our lives indicates that I have had, in equity, a half-share in the property for some time now, and certainly since before my partner mortgaged the property to the bank. I was in actual occupation of the property so I have an overriding interest in it under the Land Registration Act 2002;[21] and as my partner is the sole legal owner my interest was not overreached when the mortgage was created;[22] so my interest binds the bank. The bank can take possession of the property and sell it, but it will have to give me a half-share in the value of the property as if there were no mortgage.

If the bank is lucky, and if the legal owner has been honest, the normal conveyancing safeguards of making enquiries of occupiers[23] will prevent this disaster. We have to contemplate it to understand the mechanics of the claim, and to appreciate the disaster that the conveyancing safeguards will normally prevent.

PROPRIETARY ESTOPPEL

Origins

Resulting and implied trusts are expressly contemplated in the statutory provisions that require formalities for land transactions, and are accepted explicitly as exceptions. Rather more on the edge of land law lies proprietary estoppel, which has the effect of enforcing informal transactions involving land but is rather different. Its origins are older than those of the common intention constructive trust. It is an amalgam of ideas rather than a deliberately constructed doctrine. It works in a wide variety of contexts meeting a number of very different needs, and its effect is not to generate a property right automatically. It is a more

---

[21] Chapter 3, p 52. [22] Chapter 3, p 58.
[23] Chapter 3, p 64.

unwieldy instrument than the common intention constructive trust, and rather more of a loose cannon.

Estoppel in its most basic form is a rule of evidence. It prevents someone from contradicting himself, in certain circumstances.[24] It has been extended to form part of the law of contract, as a result of the requirement for consideration. English law does not enforce promises, however serious, unless they form part of a bargain. Something must be given in return, whether a promise or an action, and that something is known as 'consideration'. The fact that a promise has been relied upon will not make it enforceable. It is still the law that if I promise to give you £10,000 next Monday and you, relying on my promise, spend £5,000 on a new piano, I am free to pay you nothing. (Whether or not that would actually be the law's answer would depend upon whether or not, after years of academic badgering, the courts were prepared to adopt American precedent; but that is another story.) But occasionally one may be estopped, that is, prevented, from going back on a promise to let someone off a contractual obligation. The leading case on this concept, known as 'promissory estoppel', concerned a letting arrangement in the 1940s, when the landlord agreed to accept a lower rent for the duration of the war. After the war he was able, of course, to charge the full rent; but he was not allowed to recover for the arrears of rent that had built up during the war, even though the tenants had given no consideration for the promise to charge less.

Proprietary estoppel is older than this and it grew from the rather stronger requirements for contracts concerning land, already discussed in this chapter, and from the fact that where there are strict rules for formalities in contracts, there is bound to be demand for the law to enforce promises made less formally.

Although there are a number of more ancient precedents, the major inspiration for proprietary estoppel was a case in the 1860s.[25] The context is urban expansion following the industrial

---

[24] The word comes from Norman French, and is derived from the word for a bung or stopper: cf those handy little things for stopping up open bottles of wine.

[25] *Ramsden v Dyson* (1866) LR 1 HL 129.

revolution. A landowner offered short-term tenancies to a large
number of tenants, and encouraged them to build on the land,
promising that they could have a long lease for the asking at any
stage. Later, he tried to evict them on the basis that they had
only short-term tenancies (this was long before the security of
tenure legislation). The tenants pleaded the landlord's promise,
upon which they had relied. They failed; the majority of the
judges in the House of Lords held that they could have succeeded only if they had been under an actual mistake about their
title to the land. They knew they had only short-term lettings;
the promise to give a long lease was simply unenforceable. Lord
Cranworth said:

> If a stranger begins to build on my land supposing it to be his own, and
> I, perceiving his mistake, abstain from setting him right, and leave him
> to persevere in his error, a Court of equity will not allow me after-
> wards to assert my title to the land on which he had expended money
> on the supposition that it was his own.

That in itself was a powerful authority, even though it did not
help the tenants in this case. A modern application of it is where
I build my garage 20 cm beyond my boundary and on your
land, supposing that 20 cm strip to be my own, and you stand
watching without correcting my mistake; you may be prevented from asserting your ownership of the strip, and indeed
be ordered to transfer it to me.[26] The doctrine which developed
from Lord Cranworth's judgment depended upon the idea of a
statement, known as a 'representation', being made and relied
upon (echoes of the common intention constructive trust spring
to mind; but proprietary estoppel was the earlier doctrine).
Debate has focussed on how much the defendant (the 'representor', the one who made the statement) must know about the
claimant's state of mind: must he know that the claimant has
made a mistake about the boundary; must he have intended the
claimant to rely on his statement, etc? A body of law also built

---

[26] A different way of solving boundary problems in this form is adverse
possession; see Chapter 9. The use of adverse possession in this context has
been severely curtailed by the provisions of the Land Registration Act 2002, but
the use of estoppel appears to survive: Chapter 9, p 260.

up about the way the statement could be made: as well as words, there might be actions, or even silence, provided there was communication. As Lord Cranworth envisaged, silence can communicate, in circumstances where the landowner might be expected to speak up (eg 'but he watched me building the garage; if I was on his land he should have said'), so that his failing to do so when he is obviously aware of the situation may speak volumes.

But there was more in *Ramsden v Dyson*. This being a House of Lords case, even a dissenting judgment is authoritative. Here is what Lord Kingsdown said:

> If a man, under a verbal agreement with a landlord for a certain interest in land, or, what amounts to the same thing, under an expectation, created or encouraged by the landlord, that he shall have a certain interest, takes possession of such land, with the consent of the landlord, and upon the faith of such promise or expectation, with the knowledge of the landlord, and without objection by him, lays out money upon the land, a Court of equity will compel the landlord *to give effect to such promise or expectation*. (emphasis added)

This is much stronger; and although the majority of their lordships did not recognize it as the law in *Ramsden v Dyson*, a number of authoritative decisions later adopted this statement, placed it alongside Lord Cranworth's, and combined both as the foundation of the doctrine we now call 'proprietary estoppel'. It is estoppel because it prevents someone from going back on a promise, but it does much more than an estoppel because it has a positive effect. It results in the award of a remedy, which may (not must) be an interest in land.

Constructing a flexible doctrine

The term 'proprietary estoppel' was not coined until the twentieth century. The controversial element was the idea of enforcing promises about future ownership, rather than just statements about current ownership. Expanded in this way, its scope is huge. The farmer who was promised an easement by the neighbouring landowner, and therefore goes ahead with a deal that leaves his field land-locked if the easement is not granted, will be able to claim the right to an easement;[27] the holder of an option to extend a lease, which seemed to be unenforceable because it was not registered against the landlord's title, could claim that the option was enforceable anyway because the landlord assured him it would be.[28] A father with lots of land encouraged his son to build a house on it, promising that he could have the land; the father's executors were not allowed to build on the land.[29] And the cohabitant who was promised 'this house is as much yours as mine' was able to make a claim on the basis that so it should be, if she has relied on the promise to her detriment. She may be allowed to stay there for life; or she may be awarded a beneficial interest in the property so that it really is half hers. Common to these situations is an element of faith; something was said, or promised, and the claimant believed that it would be so. It follows that where the claimant knew perfectly well that things were not as the other party said they were—particularly in a commercial context—then there can be no estoppel.

So proprietary estoppel has been used in a wide range of contexts, just one of which overlaps with that of the common intention constructive trust, namely the provision of an interest in property following cohabitation.

The 'recipe' for proprietary estoppel is remarkably similar to that for the common intention constructive trust: there must be a representation (a broad term covering express statements but also other forms of communication) that the claimant has or will have an interest in land; and the claimant must have relied on that, reasonably, and to his detriment, so that it is unconscionable for the representor to go back on his promise or statement. It does not take much imagination to see that a 'representation' may be made in a conversation which could equally found the inference of a common intention. Exactly what is meant by 'unconscionability' is simply not known—there is no consistent policy in the judges' use of the word—and so it is easy to build up theories about what it does mean. Sometimes it is used as a

---

[27] *Crabb v Arun DC* [1976] Ch 179, CA.
[28] *Taylors Fashions Ltd v Liverpool Victoria Trustees Co Ltd* [1984] 1 QB 133.
[29] *Inwards v Baker* [1965] 2 QB 29, CA.

way of describing the rest of the recipe (representation + detrimental reliance); sometimes it is an extra ingredient, for example where the recipe ingredients are present but for some other reason the claimant should not be given anything (for example because she does not need the property and the defendant does).[30]

Outcomes: the equity and the response

How much does the claimant get? Here there is a significant theoretical distinction between estoppel and the constructive trust. The presence of the ingredients that make up estoppel does not of itself give rise to an interest in land. It gives the claimant an 'equity': that is, a claim, to which the court must respond in some way.

The 'equity' idea is a very unsatisfactory one. It is used in other contexts to indicate a very weak interest in land, rather less robust than an equitable interest. Here it seems to indicate even less than that, because the court's response to an equity by estoppel may be to do nothing. But it is more than just a right to seek relief, because anyone can go to court to seek relief. We might say that it is a prima facie case for relief, or perhaps a presumption that some relief will be given.

And there is in principle complete freedom for the court to grant whatever relief it thinks best; in doing so, the court is said to be 'satisfying the equity'. It might give the claimant precisely what was promised, whether that is an easement, or an interest in land, or simply permission to occupy a home (ie a licence). Or it might give the value of that in money. An award of what was promised, or its value, is known as 'expectation-based relief'. Equally, relief may be reliance-based, aiming to compensate the claimant, by a money award, for the detrimental reliance suffered. But any other basis of calculation is acceptable in principle. In fact, in the vast majority of cases up until the end of the twentieth century the award was expectation-based. This reflects the doctrine's basis in contract, where relief is almost

---

[30] *Sledmore v Dalby* (1996) 72 P & CR 196, CA.

always expectation-based; and it reflects the difficulty, in many cases, of truly putting right the claimant's detriment by anything less than the meeting of his expectations. There is a very human factor at work here. In almost all the cases, what the claimant wants is expectation-based relief. And once the court has been swayed by an argument to the effect that the claimant has an equity, and that it would be unconscionable not to give relief, the court is then predisposed to give the claimant what he wants.

The problem with this is that it may turn out to be a very severe penalty for admittedly unconscionable behaviour. In the early years of this century we have seen a swing in the courts' response to the estoppel equity; and one suspects that this has been caused by a particular trend in the type of cases reaching the higher courts. We have seen a number of cases concerned neither with boundaries nor with cohabitants, but with carers to whom a promise of an inheritance has been made, and where the promise has failed to meet the formality requirements for wills rather than for contracts. Typical is the elderly person who is looked after by someone who is not a family member, who spends a good deal of time looking after her, perhaps undertaking personal care; and the elderly person promises to 'see them right'. Sometimes there is an explicit promise of a gift of a property in a will. Sometimes a more general promise of a gift of everything—the 'all this will be yours'-type of reassurance. Then the person dies without making such a gift in her will, and the claimant challenges the executors and the beneficiaries of the estate. And it may well be that the court can find a promise (whether expressed in clear words or inferred from conduct), relied on by the claimant to his detriment in time and money over a considerable period. To respond to this equity by the gift of a house, or perhaps of more extensive property, can seem out of proportion to the detriment suffered. So the courts in recent years have stressed the need for proportionality; and inevitably that means a move towards a more reliance-based response, at least in this context. In the context of cohabitants, we may expect this approach to be used with care, and that the relief given will be proportionate to need rather than just to the cost of reliance; this would be consistent with the courts' traditional approach to such claims, as well as ensuring a response that is consistent with what a claimant would get out of a common intention constructive trust. In the wider context, the courts' freedom to tailor the remedy to the facts must be a factor that has led the courts not to insist that the promise or representation that founds the estoppel need be as clear as it would have to be in a contractual context.

IMPLIED TRUSTS, ESTOPPEL, AND FAMILY PROPERTY

Implied trusts and proprietary estoppel have been very fluid concepts. Until a few years ago there was some difficulty in distinguishing resulting and constructive trusts, until the courts made it clear that in the latter case, what the claimant gets out is not necessarily the same as what he put in. The generosity of approach seen in *Midland Bank plc v Cooke*[31] opened up the scope of the common intention constructive trust, so that it can be an answer, not really to a type of transaction, but to a relationship.[32]

The same could readily be said of proprietary estoppel, and indeed in the context of the cohabitant claimant it is very difficult to distinguish the two. If he said to her 'the house is yours, darling', or 'you can live here for as long as you like' there is no point trying to decide whether that was a common intention or a representation.

The common intention constructive trust and proprietary estoppel are truly distinct in their consequences. The constructive trust is supposed to arise when detrimental reliance takes place, and so may have given rise—supposedly—to a beneficial interest long before any court order given in recognition of that interest. But only the court can determine the response to estoppel, which therefore crystallizes, as it were, only at the point of the court order. This made the common intention constructive trust the obvious better choice for a cohabitant claiming *now* to have priority over a lender who took a mortgage a while ago. The effect of estoppel on a purchaser, by

---

[31] Note 20.
[32] The other leading case is *Oxley v Hiscock* [2004] EWCA Civ 546.

contrast, was unclear. If the representor—a cohabitant, say—sold the property while the claimant's equity by estoppel was still unsatisfied (she might not at this stage know that she had one), would the purchaser be bound by it? Various cases gave inconsistent and ambiguous answers to this; but section 116 of the Land Registration Act 2002 states that an equity by estoppel 'has effect from the time the equity arises as an interest capable of binding successors in title (subject to the rules about the effect of dispositions on priority)'.

The full implications of section 116 have yet to be explored. The principle remains that until the court makes a decision, we do not know what will be the response to the estoppel equity. If A has an estoppel claim against B, which is litigated after B sells to C, then if the response to the equity raised against B is a beneficial interest in the land that interest must be enforceable against C. If B is in fact two people, is it also overreachable? If the response is a licence to occupy the property, will that licence take on proprietary effect and bind C? What happens if the response is a monetary award—does section 116 transform an award of damages into a charge upon the property? These and other questions are still matters for speculation.

Section 116 is both generous and strict. It is generous because it makes clear that a purchaser can be bound by an estoppel equity before any determination has been made as to the appropriate response to the equity, and without any need for the purchaser to have actually done anything unconscionable. It is strict because it makes clear that this will only happen if the claimant has recorded her equity on the Land Register—which is highly unlikely—or if she has an overriding interest by virtue of her actual occupation of the land, as she probably will in the cohabitant cases only. That brings the estoppel claimant into line with the constructive trust claimant. And again, if a mortgagee took the normal conveyancing precautions, inquiring about the occupiers of property and obtaining their consent to the transaction, then, again, the cohabitant's right has no proprietary effect.

That does not make it valueless. In both cases, the claim remains good against the owning cohabitant. So the strength of these claims is their use when a relationship breaks down.

They form a substitute for the discretionary jurisdiction of the Matrimonial Causes Act 1973—only, of course, for cohabitants who can meet the requirements of the trust or the estoppel. That makes them unhelpful as a tool for family law. They are not designed to meet need, nor to give compensation for economic disadvantage suffered because of a relationship, for example as a result of being the principal childcarer and home-maker. They are blunt instruments in this context.

ESTOPPEL AND THE RESCUING OF INFORMAL TRANSACTIONS

Back to land contracts

We began this chapter with an examination of the requirements for contracts to create or transfer interests in land; and we noted that estoppel grew out of the courts' need to find a way to rescue deals that did not meet the formal requirements for land transactions. The deals or arrangements where it has operated have been rather complex ones, often involving an ongoing relationship which adds an extra dimension beyond the failure to do the paperwork. Now we have to look at something which ought to be rather simpler and to look at the potential use of estoppel in the simple case of a contract for the sale and purchase of land; and it brings us back full circle to the beginning of this chapter.

The issue is this: if you promise to sell your land to me, and I rely on that promise to my detriment (perhaps by doing some building work), are you estopped from going back on it? There are a number of ways of analysing this. We can say that you are estopped from denying a representation that there was a contract; or that you are estopped from going back on a promise to enter a contract; or estopped from going back on a promise to transfer the fee simple (ie the promise that would have been contained in the contract if formalized). However we choose to put it, the issue is the same: are you estopped, or prevented, from refusing to sell me your land even though you have not entered into a contract to do so? If so, what would be the courts' response to this estoppel equity?

When the Law Commission advocated the reform which is now section 2 of the Law of Property (Miscellaneous Provisions) Act 1989, discussed above, it assumed that estoppel could be used in that way, the courts' response being normally to enforce a sale. Clearly estoppel was a way of rescuing informal deals, and so surely the most basic form of such a deal—a straight sale and purchase contract—could be rescued in this way. There was no direct English case like this, but there was a powerful Australian precedent. Indeed, when the 1989 Act was debated in Parliament, reassurance was given to MPs that informal deals that had 'missed the boat' could be rescued in this way.

Two things were not noticed. One was that estoppel, as used to date, could not possibly be used to help a seller in such a situation, because it has only been used when there is an assurance that someone has or will have an interest in land—never where there has been assurance that someone will buy, or accept, an interest. That problem remains outstanding.

The other was that the courts have always felt something of a reluctance to use estoppel to contradict a statutory provision. It is not forbidden; there is no difficulty in using estoppel to avoid the formalities required in the Wills Act 1837, so as to validate a promise of a gift to take effect after death, even though the giver has not made the gift in a will. But it is not possible, for example, for a tenant protected by the Rent Acts (and so having security of tenure) to be estopped from asserting that status; nor is it possible for a borrower to be estopped from claiming the protection given him under the money-lending legislation (which regulates who may lend, rates, etc). The possibility for undue pressure in such cases is obvious; there is a tendency for them to be one-sided deals. So estoppel is not used 'in the face of a statute', as the courts have put it, if the statute is there to protect a vulnerable party. Given this policy on the part of the courts, can estoppel be used to rescue deals that have fallen foul of the 1989 requirements for land contracts? It is hard to say whether or not the requirements are there to protect the vulnerable; it is suggested that they are not, since sellers are no more vulnerable than buyers. But the courts have nevertheless been extremely reluctant to use estoppel in this way without direct statutory authority.

Initially, therefore, the courts avoided using estoppel to assist claimants whose agreements failed for informality. Instead they looked at the explicit provision in the 1989 Act to the effect that the operation of implied trusts was unaffected, and used a constructive trust instead of estoppel. The idea is that the defendant has behaved unconscionably in going back on the informal agreement; therefore he must hold his land on trust for the claimant, ready to transfer it as agreed.

There were a lot of problems with this. For one thing, it limits the court's choice as to remedy; it is not obvious that in all these cases there has to be a full expectation-based remedy given. For another, if a constructive trust is awarded in cases where estoppel has been pleaded, there is a tendency to confusion between the two doctrines which are, as has been shown here, distinct.

It has been suggested that estoppel can be used in these cases because in using estoppel the courts are simply responding to unconscionable conduct, they are not enforcing the failed deal. That seems a little disingenuous—it is obvious what the end result is—but it meets the problem of principle, and it gives effect to Parliament's intentions.

That debate may now be at an end. The House of Lords in *Cobbe v Yeoman's Row Management Ltd*[33] made it clear that in a case where there was no contract, the parties knew perfectly well that there was no contract, and the parties had deliberately not entered into a contract, the doctrine of proprietary estoppel will not be available to rescue the deal that fell through. Arguably this is a welcome move; the case caused alarm when it was decided, because it appeared to curtail the operation of proprietary estoppel dramatically by forbidding its use in response to promises, and to limit its use to representations of fact (thus taking the law back towards the way that Lord Cranworth saw things). The Supreme Court in *Thorner v Major*[34]—another case arising from a promise (expressed with remarkable lack of clarity) of an inheritance (of uncertain extent)—made it clear that that is not so, and that promises can indeed found estoppels. But not, it seems, in a commercial context where both parties are

---

[33] [2008] UKHL 55.   [34] [2009] UKHL 18.

well aware of their legal position. We are not yet in a position to say what will be the eventual effect of the decision in *Cobbe v Yeoman's Row*; it seems, at any rate, that for the future proprietary estoppel may belong with the common intention constructive trust, as a concept that straddles property law and family law, rather than with the law of contract and the world of business.

BIBLIOGRAPHY

E. Cooke, *The Modern Law of Estoppel* (Oxford, Oxford University Press, 2000).

P. Critchley, 'Taking formalities seriously' in S. Bright and J. Dewar (eds), *Land Law: Themes and Perspectives* (Oxford, Oxford University Press, 1998) 507.

M. Dixon, 'The Never-Ending Story—Co-Ownership After *Stack v Dowden*' (2007) 71 *The Conveyancer* 456).

S. Gardner, 'The Remedial Discretion in Proprietary Estoppel' (1999) 115 *Law Quarterly Review* 438.

D. Neuberger, 'The stuffing of Minerva's owl; Taxonomy and taxidermy in equity' [2009] 68 *Cambridge Law Journal* 537.

N. Piska, 'Intention, Fairness and the Presumption of Resulting Trust after *Stack v Dowden*' (2008) 71 MLR 120.

R. Probert, 'Trusts and the modern woman—establishing an interest in the family home' (2001) 13 *Child and Family Law Quarterly* 275.

A. Robertson, 'The reliance basis of proprietary estoppel remedies' (2008) 72 *The Conveyancer* 295

5

JOINT OWNERSHIP OF LAND

Chapter 4 explored how sole ownership can become joint ownership, in ways which may be unexpected and unwelcome to one of those involved. This chapter looks at the wider issues involved in the joint ownership of land; and we begin by recalling that, for the most part, it is set up deliberately and is welcome to all concerned for a range of practical and emotional reasons. It is commonplace for a couple, married or not, to buy their home in joint names; business partners may hold the lease of their premises jointly; and the trustees of a charity are the joint owners of the charity's property.

We have already seen that whenever there is joint ownership of land, there is a trust, and that this is largely a way of keeping the title to property tidy for the sake of purchasers. In the cases we looked at in Chapter 4 there is one legal owner, and more than one owner in equity because shared ownership has been achieved informally. But in most deliberate joint purchases, trustees and beneficiaries are identical. When a married couple buys a house together there is simply no distinction between legal and equitable ownership; the same goes for, say, three business partners buying an office. When there are more than four owners, a maximum of four of them can hold the legal estate; but all are owners in equity ('beneficial owners' is another term).

Less common cases of joint ownership are the deliberately created trusts, set up as a way of sharing wealth across generations, or of looking after land for children. Such trusts are often created by will; but sometimes they are the result of a transaction *inter vivos*, as the jargon has it—'among the living'. The person who sets up a trust is called a 'settlor', because when property is placed in a trust it is said to be 'settled'.[1] A deliberate settlement

---

[1] Even when, as in most cases nowadays, the Settled Land Act 1925 is not involved.

may involve successive or concurrent joint ownership, or both; successive joint ownership is where more than one person holds an ownership right, but ownership is planned over time and not all have interests in possession. The typical case is when land is left to A for life, with remainder to B in fee simple. This type of settlement, with its many variants, used to account for the ownership of most of the land in this country, whereas today it is very unusual. A deliberately created trust might equally involve concurrent co-ownership; imagine parents buying an extra house and holding it on trust for their children for their use while at university.

A will may set up joint ownership on a temporary basis. Property may be left to a group of people—perhaps siblings—with no expectation that they will keep it. It is held on trust for them by the executors of the will—whether or not the will actually says so—until it is sold, and the proceeds divided. The same may happen under the rules of intestacy, where no will has been made but property passes automatically to, say, the parents of the deceased, or his brothers. Again, there is a trust, set up automatically; the trustees are the administrators of the estate, a task which falls to the nearest relatives of the deceased.[2]

So this chapter looks at four broad categories of joint ownership. Case one is the joint purchase, where ownership rights are concurrent and all or some of the beneficiaries are also the trustees. Such are the couple, or the business partners; in the former case, and sometimes in the latter, the parties may be unaware of their trusteeship. Case two is the Chapter 4-type co-ownership claimed or discovered, or perhaps agreed (at varying distances from the door of the court) when the relationship between the joint owners has broken down. Here it may be that just one of the beneficiaries is also a trustee; and probably an unwilling one. Case three is the deliberate settlement or 'express trust'—express because it must be set up expressly, deliberately, by a written declaration of trust. Case four is joint ownership set up by will, or by the rules of intestacy, just on a temporary basis for the sake of passing property along. Case four may become

---

[2] These provisions are the subject matter of the Administration of Estates Act 1925.

case one or case three. For example, the siblings of the deceased (say) decide not to sell his house but to keep it and let it out; the deceased's personal representatives[3] may transmit it to the three of them (or indeed the three of them may be the personal representatives), so that what looked like a temporary joint ownership becomes a deliberate joint venture as in case one. Or a will might leave land to the testator's children, who are under 18 when he dies. Minors cannot hold a legal estate in land, and so the trust set up by the will must continue at least until the youngest child is 18, perhaps longer, depending on its terms. The trustees would often be the executors of the will, who might be close friends or family members; one might be the testator's solicitor. The will has set up for them a years' long relationship with the land and its beneficial owners, and so case four has become case one.

In all these instances it does not matter at all, for the purposes of this chapter, whether the estate held on trust is freehold or leasehold—although it may matter a lot in the daily lives of the owners.

English law does not recognize the rather closer form of joint ownership used in some jurisdictions known as 'community of property', where the property of a married couple (and in some cases of registered partners) is automatically owned jointly (subject to contracting out) in such a way that the property can be taken by creditors in satisfaction of the personal debts of either, so that the way one of the couple conducts her business has a potential effect on her partner's share in the family home. In English law, and common law jurisdictions generally, this idea is unknown because our law of family property evolved in a different way from those of the civil law jurisdictions.

The issue for this chapter is the way the law manages joint ownership using the structure known as the 'trust of land'. Of its various sections, it will be noticed that not all are relevant to each of our four cases in equal measure. We begin by looking at an issue which concerns only concurrent joint ownership, which can occur in two forms.

---

[3] This means the executors of the will; or the administrators of the estate, where the will did not appoint executors or where there was no will.

LEGAL STRUCTURE OF CONCURRENT BENEFICIAL JOINT OWNERSHIP: JOINT TENANCY OR TENANCY IN COMMON

Take a Kit-Kat bar and give it to two people, X and Y, to own jointly; there are two bars, joined up and hidden in one wrapper; ask them to hold it in their hands (if not too warm). If they own it as joint tenants, then when X dies, both bars stay in Y's hand, still conjoined, still in their wrapper. There is nothing X can do about this, even if she has made a will leaving her share of the Kit-Kat bar to her son. But if they own it as tenants in common, then when X dies the two bars may separate. One will certainly stay in Y's hand; the other must go to whoever is entitled to it under X's will, or under the rules of intestacy if she has not made a will. It may actually be Y, in which case the two bars stay together; or it may be someone else, in which case they are split up.

There are two forms of beneficial joint ownership of land. Where two or more people are joint owners in equity, they may be either joint tenants or tenants in common (for reasons to be explained, at law they can only ever be joint tenants). If they are joint tenants when one of them dies, then the other automatically becomes sole owner of the land. If they are tenants in common at that point then the share of the land belonging to the deceased goes to whoever is entitled to inherit it. It is possible for a joint tenant to change the form of ownership, and make it into a tenancy in common—this is known as severing the joint tenancy; but it cannot be done by making a will. So if a joint tenant makes a will leaving her share to someone else, this is of no effect; she remains a joint tenant and her co-owner takes the whole property when she dies.

The words 'tenant' and 'tenancy' in this context have their ancient meaning derived from the Latin *tenere*, to hold. They indicate landholding, in line with the feudal tradition whereby land is held but not owned, and have nothing to do with leaseholds and the law of landlord and tenant. Joint tenants may be co-owners in fee simple or of a lease, or, less likely but possible, of a life estate or an entail.

The theoretical distinction between joint tenancy and tenancy in common during the currency of the co-ownership is that tenants in common are said to have shares in the property while joint tenants own the whole without division. Tenants in common are said to have *undivided* shares, since the property is not physically divided and each is still entitled to possession of the whole. This is not a helpful distinction while the joint ownership continues although it may entertain the theorists. Its practical consequence arises when joint ownership ends on sale. In that event, joint tenants take half the proceeds each, whether or not they contributed equally to the purchase. Tenants in common will take the proceeds in whatever proportions they have decided, if they have actually made a declaration of trust and defined their shares; if they have not, they will take the proceeds in proportion to their contributions. Thus only tenants in common can take an unequal share of the sale proceeds.

That, in a nutshell, is the structure of beneficial joint ownership of land. The detail we need to look at includes: how do you tell what form of joint ownership is in operation in a given case? How can a joint tenancy be severed? Why do we have the two forms?

Identification

Equity is supposed to prefer tenancy in common. The point is that joint tenancy limits the parties' freedom (to dispose of their property effectively by will) and so the courts will discover a tenancy in common where possible. But it is not a default option; the default option is actually the beneficial joint tenancy in cases where the parties have not said which form of co-ownership they want, and where they have the same interest in the property, acquired at the same time, and in the same way. The principle was reiterated by the House of Lords in *Stack v Dowden*;[4] their Lordships expressed this by saying that there is a presumption of beneficial joint tenancy in such cases. There is nothing revolutionary about that; it is simply that

---

[4] [2007] UKHL 17.

beneficial joint tenancy is the default option and it is for the party who says that that is not the true position to prove it. The House of Lords also said that in cases where the property was bought by a couple as a shared home it will be very difficult to displace that presumption and to establish that, instead, the parties held the property on a common intention constructive trust for themselves as tenants in common in unequal shares.[5]

A purchase by joint legal owners will involve both, or all, taking the fee simple or the lease on the same day under the same transfer. These conditions are known as the unities; joint tenancy is said to have four unities, known as time, title, interest, and possession (but possession, being the right to possess the whole property, is a feature of tenancy in common too, so does not help with identification). The couples who became joint owners in Chapter 4 by virtue of a common intention constructive trust or, if the court so decides, thanks to the operation of proprietary estoppel, will always be tenants in common because they came by their interests in different ways (one by formal transfer and one not) and, often, at different times.

Ideally, joint owners should address this question explicitly when they buy the land. A transfer to joint owners should transfer the land 'to X and Y as beneficial joint tenants' or 'as beneficial tenants in common'. The courts have held that if the joint owners have done this, there is no scope for either of them to argue about the form of the acquisition subsequently— although of course either may claim that a joint tenancy has been severed subsequently, as we shall see; and we have to add that the flexibility of the regime now envisaged by the Supreme Court in its judgment in *Jones v Kernott*[6] means that it is no longer clear that an express declaration of trust can never be challenged as a result of later events. But certainly for a couple to make their intentions explicit in this way is the best protection against future litigation even if it can no longer be said that that protection is watertight; conversely, failure to set out the beneficial interests explicitly at the start is asking for trouble. Where

[5] *Stack v Dowden* [2007] UKHL 17; see Chapter 4, p 90.
[6] [2011] UKSC 53; see Chapter 4, p 94.

title is registered, or where the purchase triggers first registration, the Land Registry gives joint owners the opportunity, in their application for registration, to state which sort they are and to set out a declaration of their beneficial interests. But the Land Registry does not make completion of that declaration compulsory, and so failure to make this explicit statement remains a problem.

In our third type of co-ownership, the express trust, there will be a written settlement, whether a will or an *inter vivos* trust document, which should state how beneficiaries with concurrent interests will hold them.

However, if the parties have not stated which way they hold the land, and if the four unities are present, it may be possible for the courts to find that there is nevertheless a tenancy in common either from the words of the transfer (or will, etc) or from the surrounding circumstances. The words of the transfer will indicate that a tenancy in common is intended if its wording refers to shares or to any form of division, by transferring the land 'to X and Y in equal shares' or 'equally' or 'to be divided between them'. The use of such wording is now highly unlikely, and survives in the textbooks as examples of how not to draft wills. Circumstances that indicate a tenancy in common are: a business purchase (professional partners will not want the right of survivorship to operate); where the purchasers are in fact mortgagees (because their interest is financial and it is probable that neither would want the other to recover the whole debt secured by the mortgage); and where contributions to the purchase price are unequal, provided that the property is not a shared home. We have to add that proviso to that last point because the Supreme Court has now said that a resulting trust analysis based upon contributions is not appropriate for shared homes.[7] That must mean that unequal contributions to the joint purchase of a home should not (in the absence of other circumstances) displace the presumption of beneficial joint tenancy.

---

[7] See Chapter 4, pp 86–7.

Severance

A joint tenant who no longer wishes to be one can take one of
the actions specified in one case, *Williams v Hensman*[8] or in one
statutory provision, section 36(2) of the Law of Property Act
1925. The statutory provision is that a joint tenant can sever by
giving a notice. He must write to the other owner(s) and state
that the tenancy is severed. There are no particular words
prescribed. The courts have held that the notice is effective if
it is received at the other's address, even if he does not read it,
even if the sender, having changed her mind, picks it up and
throws it away, even if the dog eats it. This is equity favouring a
tenancy in common. That statutory provision preserves methods
of severance invented before 1925, which means in effect that
Williams v Hensman remains the law. It sets out three methods:
severance can be done by one joint tenant dealing with his own
share; by 'mutual agreement'; and by a course of dealing. 'Dealing' means selling or mortgaging one's share; which is why it
was said above that both forms of joint owners can do this. It
points to the unreality of saying that joint tenants do not have
'shares' in the land. Bankruptcy is another 'dealing' that severs
the joint tenancy. Agreement is self-explanatory; but it can be
inferred from behaviour and so can merge with the other
method, a course of dealing. In one of the leading cases[9] two
people bought a house as beneficial joint tenants; the man
intended that they would get married, and the lady did not.
When the misunderstanding became apparent, the man agreed
to buy his friend out; but then she withdrew from that arrangement. Next, the man died; so now of course the lady argued that
their discussions did not amount to severance. Did she take his
share by survivorship? It was held that the course of dealing and/
or agreement was sufficient to sever the joint tenancy. Note that
the agreement does not have to be a valid contract. There is a
large body of case law about attempts to sever; a fertile ground
for dispute is the commencement of divorce proceedings; does a
request for financial provision on divorce sever a joint tenancy?

---

[8] (1861) 1 John & H 557.
[9] *Burgess v Rawnsley* [1975] Ch 429.

Moreover, this rather limited body of thinking must now be split wide open by the approach taken by the Supreme Court in *Jones v Kernott*;[10] a wide range of dealings with property and indeed of fluctuations in the personal relationship of the parties over the period of joint ownership may have the effect of creating a common intention constructive trust and so of changing the beneficial entitlement and therefore of severing a beneficial joint tenancy.

A final and very effective way to sever a joint tenancy is homicide; if you murder your joint tenant, you will not take his share by survivorship: this is provided by the Forfeiture Act 1982. Where the homicide is manslaughter rather than murder, there is the possibility of relief from forfeiture; the court may decide that severance is not fair. It may be very unfair if the killer was a battered wife, for example, as happened in one case.

Severance by will, as already stated, is impossible. There is something to be said for making it possible; the argument against it is that severance is not only unilateral but unknown to the other party. This is a poor argument in view of the courts' policy of finding severance by other methods wherever possible. But severance by will, which would presumably take effect on the death of the testator, would be peculiarly one-sided. It would leave the testator with the chance of benefiting by survivorship, while claiming the independence gained by severing in case he died first. This is perhaps the unwelcome aspect of this method of severance. The essence of joint tenancy is that it is a gamble, and to weight the dice in this way would not seem right.

Policy

The difficulty with the joint tenancy is that it takes a choice away. And folk are not always aware of its effect. They may not remember what their solicitor explained to them (if indeed he did); they may find that survivorship operates in an unwelcome way after a relationship has broken down; they may be surprised to find that joint tenancy means that the two owners must take an equal share of the sale proceeds, no matter what their

---

[10] [2011] UKSC 53; again, see Chapter 4, p 94.

contribution to the purchase price—usually the survivorship point gets explained and this aspect is omitted. If joint tenancy becomes unwelcome, people may be unsure how to sever. Litigation may be needed to determine whether or not severance has taken place. And if a joint tenancy is severed, the resulting tenants in common hold the land in equal shares unless they explicitly agree otherwise; they do not hold in proportion to their contributions to the purchase, and this may be an unexpected, and unwelcome, feature of the joint tenancy. Moreover, the recent developments in the law relating to common intention constructive trusts mean that a beneficial joint tenancy may be found to have been severed, and the shares adjusted, in accordance with intentions inferred from the parties' conduct or indeed attributed to them by the courts, in a way that will not be equally welcome to both.

Against those arguments are two in favour of its continued availability. The joint tenancy is known as the 'poor man's will': one rather weak argument in its favour is that it saves making a will. There is much to be said, on the other hand, for encouraging the tidy habit of doing so. If this became standard whenever property was purchased, equitable joint tenancy would be needless. The stronger argument is the rather fuzzy ideological one, that joint tenancy is appropriate to an intimate partnership arrangement. Recent research into community of property in Europe has shown that in those countries where community of property is more comprehensive—particularly The Netherlands—there is a strong feeling that it is fitting for married couples to share their property as deeply as possible. We do not have community of property; but joint tenancy has been described as a 'thorough and most intimate union of interest and possession'.[11] And it is worth noting that in California a new form of community of property has been introduced by statute: Community of Property With Right Of Survivorship.[12] In a jurisdiction where community of property is available and normal, there was popular demand for it to be

---

[11] W. Blackstone's *Commentaries on the Laws of England* (London, 1st edn, 1765–1769) Vol II, p 182.

[12] California Civil Code 682.1.

strengthened by the addition of the characteristic of a joint tenancy.

THE STATUTORY FRAMEWORK
FOR TRUSTS OF LAND

From a formal issue affecting only concurrent co-owners, we turn to a structural matter relevant to all forms of joint ownership: the nature of the trust of land. This is the domain of the Trusts of Land and Appointment of Trustees Act 1996, known as 'TLATA'.

TLATA's first task was the reform of the structure of the trust of land. From 1925, there was always a trust when land was owned jointly, whether deliberately or not; and prior to 1996 the vast majority of them took one of two forms: the 'trust for sale' or the 'Settled Land Act settlement' (also called the 'strict settlement'). The default form was the latter; the preferred form was the former.

The trust for sale was adopted as a management tool by the 1925 legislation, borrowed from nineteenth-century investment practice and designed for cases where land was bought as an asset and not as a home. It operated in all cases of concurrent joint ownership—our cases one, two, and four above—and in express trusts when expressly chosen, that is where the will or other trust document used the words 'upon trust for sale'. The legal estate in the land was held by trustees, who might or might not be identical with the beneficiaries, and who had the power to manage and control the property. The trustees were under a duty to sell the land, but had power to postpone sale. Where there was no agreement on postponement, the trustees had to sell.

Such a trust was ideal for our case four. It seems very strange indeed for the other cases, particularly where the property was a family home; and indeed, this was not the case that the 1925 reformers particularly had in mind, since at that date only a small proportion of homes were owner-occupied and joint ownership by couples was unusual. But provided the trustees—the joint owners themselves—agreed to exercise their power to postpone rather than their duty to sell (and in their ignorance of the existence of a trust for sale, of course, they would in effect do so), the trust for sale was a perfectly good structure for long-term co-ownership. Its theoretical basis was that the beneficiaries had interests in the sale proceeds rather than in the land, and it was not until *Williams and Glyn's Bank Ltd v Boland*[13] that the courts forced a change. Recall that the bank was taken by surprise by the enforceability of Mrs Boland's interest in that case.[14] Among the reasons for this was the fact that even if a wife might have an unexpected equitable interest, and even if, despite being a mere wife, she could be regarded as being in actual occupation of the property, she was not regarded as having an interest *in the land*. The House of Lords held that the theory of the trust for sale had to give place to the reality of modern joint ownership, and that of course she did have an interest in the land; but it was not until TLATA in 1996 that the doctrine of conversion—the converting of a beneficiary's interest into money—was formally abolished.

The Settled Land Act 1925 regulated a form of trust with a very different structure. Until 1925, and to some extent afterwards, the strict settlement was the normal vehicle for the settlement of land within a family. It worked like this. Take a gift of land by will to A for life, with remainder to B in fee simple. A gift in those terms before 1996, which did not use the words 'upon trust for sale', would create a settlement in which the legal estate was held by A. A, the tenant for life, had the power to manage and control the land. The settlement would have trustees, whose task was not to hold an estate in land, but to receive the proceeds of sale if the land was ever sold, and then to distribute or reinvest them (and, of course, to be the vehicle for overreaching, which occurs when purchase money is paid to at least two trustees).

The strict settlement was the vehicle intended by the 1925 reformers for our case three, the deliberate settlement; it would also arise automatically in some quite unusual cases, for example an attempted conveyance of land to a minor. It involved some difficult conveyancing documentation. In time, the fact that the

---

[13] [1981] AC 487.   [14] Chapter 3, p 61.

trustees of the settlement did not actually hold the legal estate in the land became very counterintuitive, as did the principle that the tenant for life rather than the trustees managed the property. The fact that a gift by will 'upon trust for my wife for life with remainder to my son' generated a strict settlement became very unpopular.

So TLATA provides that no more strict settlements can be created; that all trusts of property that consist of or include land are, simply, trusts of land; and that a trust of land only involves an obligation to sell if the trust document says so. Trustees of land have all the powers of an absolute owner, subject to any restrictions imposed by the settlor of an express trust; those restrictions may include a requirement that they obtain someone's consent before selling, or may even take away the power to sell altogether. Statutory provisions dealing with joint ownership are all amended so that they speak of trusts of land, not trusts for sale.

So we can no longer enjoy the baroque twistiness of the distinctions between the two forms of trust of land, nor the pleasures (genuine, in this writer's view) of Settled Land Act conveyancing. But in the interests of plain speaking, the trust of land can only be an improvement. We now need to look at the provisions of TLATA that govern the operation of the trust of land.

THE INTERNAL MANAGEMENT
OF TRUSTS OF LAND

How does joint ownership work on a day-to-day basis?

Our first case, the deliberate joint purchase, ought to self-regulate. In most cases trustees and beneficiaries will be identical. The parties have chosen joint ownership; whether the context is business or the home, they have to work out how to share. In our second case, co-ownership is asserted, or discovered, at the end of the relationship, and has had no effect on everyday life. In our fourth case, the trust will end soon after it begins. But in our third case, ownership may be complex. The trust has brought together trustees, with responsibilities, and beneficiaries with ownership rights which may conflict. There is bound to be a formal conflict of interest when there is successive co-ownership; and even when all the interests are technically identical, there may be an actual conflict. Where there are three beneficiaries with a life interest in possession, for example, who is to live in the property?

TLATA provides a framework for the management of trusts of land. The balance of power is weighted heavily in favour of the trustees, as they have all the powers of an absolute owner, so that there is no limit on, for example, the length of lease they can grant or the activities they can permit at the property. The Act acknowledges that a settlor may limit the trustees' powers, or may impose a requirement to regulate certain activities, for example by providing that a particular individual must consent before the land can be sold—it is easy to see how useful this is when land is left to a widow for life, with remainder to an adult child. The Act also gives some specific rights to beneficiaries, albeit rather heavily qualified. It states that 'in the exercise of any function relating to the land subject to the trust' the trustees must consult adult beneficiaries who have an interest in possession in the land, and give effect to their wishes—or to the majority's wish—'so far as is consistent with the general interest of the trust'. It also gives such beneficiaries a right to occupy the land, 'if the purposes of the trust include making the land available for his occupation' (think of the widow again), provided the land is not 'unavailable' or 'unsuitable'. The Act does not say what these words mean, and we have no case law to give guidance. The Act enables the trustees to exclude or restrict this right to occupy if two or more beneficiaries have it, and to impose conditions on occupation, such as payment to compensate another beneficiary, but not actually to evict anyone without a court order. A more leisurely account could construct a lot of stories to illustrate these provisions, found in sections 11 to 13 of TLATA. The Act also makes provision for the trustees to delegate their functions; and for the retirement of trustees and appointment of new ones.

The point of principle to take away from this is that for an ongoing settlement where trustees and beneficiaries are not identical, TLATA does a lot of work. It lays the ground rules for the power balance, tilting it towards the trustees without being entirely one-sided. Yet by far the most common instances of trusts of land are ordinary joint ownership cases where trustees and beneficiaries are the same people and no one has given any thought to the existence of a trust. To these people, the detailed management provisions in TLATA are irrelevant. Either they will sort things out by themselves, using whatever is their personal power balance, or they will need outside help. Equally, the personnel, in our case three, may find that TLATA's management provisions do not solve their disagreements.

DISPUTE RESOLUTION FOR TRUSTS OF LAND

TLATA provides as follows:

14.—(1) Any person who is a trustee of land or has an interest in property subject to a trust of land may make an application to the court for an order under this section.

(2) On an application for an order under this section the court may make any such order—

(a) relating to the exercise by the trustees of any of their functions (including an order relieving them of any obligation to obtain the consent of, or to consult, any person in connection with the exercise of any of their functions), or

(b) declaring the nature or extent of a person's interest in property subject to the trust,

as the court thinks fit.

15.—(1) The matters to which the court is to have regard in determining an application for an order under section 14 include—

(a) the intentions of the person or persons (if any) who created the trust,

(b) the purposes for which the property subject to the trust is held,

(c) the welfare of any minor who occupies or might reasonably be expected to occupy any land subject to the trust as his home, and

(d) the interests of any secured creditor of any beneficiary.

So the solution offered for intractable disputes is the court, and the court is given examples of matters to which it is to 'have regard'. Examples of the sort of dispute that might be brought before the court under these sections are: one owner wants to sell and another does not; the trustees wish to sell but the beneficiary whose consent is needed is being difficult; the beneficiaries disagree with the trustees about the need to sell or mortgage the land, or the desirability of a letting arrangement. Persons with an interest in the land may include folk who are neither trustees nor beneficiaries. Any joint owner—concurrent or successive—can treat his share in the land as a separate asset, and this may involve extra personnel in the trust. He can mortgage his beneficial interest in it, for example; and in order to repossess the property, the mortgagee will have to apply to the court under section 14 for an order for possession and sale.

How does the court resolve these disputes? Sections 14 and 15 take over the job formerly done by section 30 of the Law of Property Act 1925, intended for use for trusts for sale. Section 30 gave no guidance to the courts at all, and for a few decades after 1925 the courts worked on the principle that the default option in a trust for sale was to sell. If the parties could not agree, sale was the answer. By the 1960s, however, a more subtle approach developed; the court looked at the *purpose* of the trust. If its purpose was over—for example because the house was bought as a home by a couple who had now split up—then the land had to be sold.[15] But if its purpose was to be a home for the growing children of the family, who still needed to live there, then the answer would probably be that the house must remain unsold until the children grew up.[16] It can be seen that this approach has found its way into the legislation. There is still very little case law on the operation of these sections. What we still do not know is how a case will be resolved when the purpose of the trust has changed, for example where the house was bought as a home for the couple, but now granny has come to live with them. We can expect some pragmatic reasoning, driven as much by need as by principle.

When the application is made by a creditor of the joint owner it seems that the courts are occasionally willing to look at the

[15] *Jones v Challenger* [1961] 1 QB 176.
[16] *Re Evers' Trust* [1980] 1 WLR 1327; more recently, *Edwards v Lloyds TSB Bank plc* [2004] EWHC 1745 (Ch).

purpose of the trust and postpone sale, but not unless the creditor is compensated for the wait; and the general trend is to favour the creditor in such a case. As will be seen, the position when application is made by the trustee in bankruptcy is rather different; and any leniency to a debtor's family under section 15 would only serve as an incentive to creditors to petition for the joint owner's bankruptcy.

One unusual tool for dispute resolution is partition. This means literally dividing the property up, physically, between the owners. Before 1925 it was the only order available to the courts in these cases, however inconvenient a physical split might be. Now, TLATA specifically empowers the trustees to partition the property with the beneficiaries' consent. Equally, the court may order partition.[17]

So: a sensitive and useful provision for dispute resolution? To some extent. Again, we meet the point that joint owners come in different forms; and not all will find that TLATA goes far enough for their needs. For joint owners who are couples, most cases of dispute about ownership happen in the context of relationship break-downs and are not primarily *about* the property or the joint ownership.

So when a couple fall out, their first port of call might well be the provisions of Part III of the Family Law Act 1996, which enables the court to make occupation orders—swift, emergency-type orders removing one joint owner from the property, temporarily or even permanently. Typically they are needed because of domestic violence, where the dispute is not *about* the property but about the relationship and the parties' safety. But such an order will precipitate a property dispute. For a married couple, the solution then lies not in TLATA but in the Matrimonial Causes Act 1973, and for civil partners in the Civil Partnerships Act 2004. For under TLATA the court can regulate whether or not the property is to be sold; but it cannot vary the ownership shares in the property. It can do nothing by way of adjustment of the parties' capital; and it can make no provision for support for either partner, or the children, in their

---

[17] A rare case in which the possibility was considered, but dismissed, is *Rodway v Landy* [2001] Ch 703.

day-to-day needs. It is well established that TLATA should not be used when the Matrimonial Causes Act 1973 is available, and the same must go for the civil partnerships legislation; these tailor-made statutes can adjust the parties' capital entitlements[18] and make flexible orders for the postponement of sale.[19]

So married couples involved in divorce proceedings, and civil partners bringing their partnerships to an end, are not going to use TLATA. Cohabiting couples, on the other hand, may do so, whether or not they have the need to use the domestic violence legislation first.

However, all couples have a further option if they have children, although only unmarried couples will use it: Schedule 1 to the Children Act 1989. This makes provision for property to be transferred or settled for the benefit of children. Married couples will not use it because the Matrimonial Causes Act 1973 will do all that the Children Act 1989 can do and more, as part of a package of provision for the whole family. Unmarried couples may choose the 1989 Act, which is available to non-owners as well as joint owners, and can be used to require the owner, or joint owner, of land to settle it for the benefit of his or her child or children. Settlement in this case does *not*, according to the courts, mean changing the beneficial ownership of the land. It may involve the suspension of beneficial ownership—or of most of the rights in the bundle—for some years, while the house is held on trust for the use of the child concerned. This will enable one of the parents, typically the applicant, to live there with the child. It will always be followed up by a provision that the house is to be returned to its owner once the child is grown up; or sold, and its proceeds divided, if it is jointly owned. It will not lead to permanent capital provision for the child; ownership of the property will not be changed or transferred.

In effect, what the courts do under Schedule 1 to the Children Act 1989 is going to be the same as what is done under TLATA; but the Children Act will always be used if the house is

<hr />

[18] *White v White* [2001] AC 596.
[19] *Mesher v Mesher* [1980] 1 All ER 126, CA.

not jointly owned, or if the aim of the application is to get the respondent to *buy* a house or to provide the money for purchase.

If this feels like a digression, it is. There are a number of pathways to the resolution of disputes about jointly owned property, and TLATA is not always an appropriate way to travel.

TRUSTS OF LAND IN BANKRUPTCY

In one case, however, the family-friendly provisions of section 15 of TLATA are actually a forbidden route. Here we must introduce a fifth case of joint ownership: it occurs when one of the co-owners is adjudicated bankrupt. At that point all his property vests in (ie now belongs to) his trustee in bankruptcy, who becomes a joint owner in his stead.

Inevitably the trustee in bankruptcy wants a sale; the other joint owner(s) may not; and so there will be an application to the court to resolve the issue. Section 15 of TLATA states that in this instance its provisions are not to be used. Instead, section 335A of the Insolvency Act 1986 operates on the section 14 application:

(2) On such an application the court shall make such an order as it thinks just and reasonable having regard to—
    (a) the interests of the bankrupt's creditors;
    (b) where the application is made in respect of land which includes a dwelling house which is or has been the home of the bankrupt or the bankrupt's spouse or former spouse—
        (i) the conduct of the spouse or former spouse, so far as contributing to the bankruptcy,
        (ii) the needs and financial resources of the spouse or former spouse, and
        (iii) the needs of any children; and
all the circumstances of the case other than the needs of the bankrupt.

(3) Where such application is made after the end of the period of one year beginning with the first vesting under Chapter IV of this Part of the bankrupt's estate in a trustee, the court shall assume, unless the circumstances of the case are exceptional, that the interests of the bankrupt's creditors outweigh all other considerations.

Thus, there are two differences from section 15 of TLATA: one is that the bankrupt's own needs are irrelevant; the other is that one year after the bankruptcy, the creditors' needs become paramount. The courts have been fierce in their operation of this provision: except in exceptional circumstances, where the trustee in bankruptcy wants a sale, after that one-year period has passed, a sale will be ordered. If this means that the family becomes homeless, so be it. That, the courts have said, is what 'debt and improvidence' involve.[20] Why the severity of this rule?

It would be unfair and unrealistic to attribute it to a determination to see the family home as a capital asset in preference to its other functions, or to the law's preference for dynamic security and the wish for a fluid property market. What has drawn the legislation, and the courts, away from sympathy with the bankrupt's family is an awareness that the mortgage industry is an essential support for the supply of homes. Any reluctance to sell the family home in response to the demands of the family's creditors may, on the one hand, lead those creditors into debt and hardship; or it may, on the other hand and of wider significance, boost the costs of borrowing and make home ownership less accessible, as mortgagees try to share around the cost of the risk they incur. So the operation of section 14 on the bankruptcy of a joint owner is far more complex than a straight contest between small homeowner and big bank. Nevertheless, concerns have been voiced about the human rights implications of section 335A of the Insolvency Act 1986 and the courts' approach to it. It has been suggested that the policy of postponing sale only in exceptional circumstances may be an illegitimate interference with the bankrupt's and his family's right to respect for their private and family life and for their home. A High Court decision noted this argument, without finding that it influenced the outcome of the case before it.[21] Later cases have considered the point again. The approach that seems to be emerging is that, on the one hand, section 335A captures the balancing of interests that Article 8 of the European Convention

---

[20] *Re Citro* [1991] Ch 142.
[21] *Barca v Mears* [2004] EWHC 2170 (Ch).

on Human Rights requires but, on the other hand, the implication of Article 8 must be that hardship to the bankrupt's family *could* amount in itself to exceptional circumstances so that *Re Citro* may not be the last word on that point. So while no clear change in the law has been prompted by human rights considerations in this area, the issue remains a live one and will continue to be argued.

EQUITABLE ACCOUNTING

It may be that TLATA has rendered unnecessary the business of equitable accounting. This is the name given to a set of principles built up by the courts over the years, by which joint owners may be required to make payments to each other, after sale of the property, as a result of what has happened during their joint ownership. Equitable accounting is a matter of personal obligations, not of property rights.

Equitable accounting covers four broad principles. Let us assume co-owners M and F, who own the property in the respective proportions two-thirds and one-third. First, if M has financed an improvement to the property which has increased its value, after sale and after division of the sale proceeds F must in addition pay to M one-third of the increase in value. Second, if for any period M took sole responsibility for the mortgage payments, again after division of the proceeds F must pay him one-third of the total mortgage payments that he made. Third, if M lived alone in the property at any stage, he *may* be obliged to make a payment to F of two-thirds of the market rental value for that period. The old principle that rent was payable only if F had been forced out (because, of course, both co-owners are entitled to possession of the whole) has given place to a more flexible approach which regards relationship breakdown as a more realistic trigger for an obligation to pay rent. In practice, items two and three above are generally regarded as cancelling each other out. Finally, if one joint owner received rent from the property without sharing it, he can be made to account to the other. So if M let the property out for part of the time while he had sole use of it, he will have to pay one-third of the rent received in that period to F when the house is sold.

The operation of equitable accounting principles is known as 'taking accounts' between the parties. It is time-wasting when some payments will cancel each other out. It is not relevant in divorce proceedings, where the court's discretionary jurisdiction is broad enough to make equitable accounting superfluous. It is scarcely necessary in any event, since TLATA gives trustees the power to impose conditions on beneficiaries as a term of their being allowed to occupy the property, and the court can make an order in the same terms under section 14. The courts' approach in recent years has been to resolve financial inequities by adjusting the beneficial interests. It is arguable that equitable accounting might be a neater way of managing this, and would avoid the inroads recently made into trust law principles for the sake of achieving fairness between separating cohabitants.

THE EXTERNAL FACE OF
THE TRUST OF LAND

Finally, and squarely for the first time in this chapter, we turn to the pervasive conflict in land law: static versus dynamic security. Joint ownership has to exist behind a trust for the sake of safeguarding purchasers. How thoroughly has the law achieved this end?

Some safeguards are very simple. As has already been said, the number of trustees of the legal title is limited to four; there is a physical limit on the number of signatures a purchaser must find.

Along with that requirement goes another limitation: joint holders of a legal estate in land must be joint tenants. They cannot be tenants in common, and a legal joint tenancy cannot be severed. This is another tidying-up measure, motivated by the different tendencies of the two forms of joint ownership over time. Tenancy in common tends to proliferate, as individuals deal with their shares or pass them on to their children. Where there are originally two tenants in common, there might be four after a number of years, and so on. The number of personnel involved will not get smaller unless one joint owner buys another out. Joint tenancy, however, has the opposite tendency. Every time one joint tenant dies, there will be a unification. A pair will become a singleton by survivorship.

Four joint tenants will eventually become one, unless transfer is effected by the survivors at any point to themselves plus another. So joint tenancy is compulsory for the legal estate, in order to ensure that legal estates get simpler over time, rather than more complex.

But we do not want legal estates to get too simple. For if land is jointly owned, two trustees are needed in order for a purchaser to be sure that any beneficial interest he does not know about will be overreached. And here lies a difficulty; faced with a single legal owner offering to sell or mortgage land to him, how does a purchaser know that the seller is not a sole trustee?

This is to a large extent material that we have covered already; we have discussed the fact that social change, and the rise of the implied trust, mean that it is no longer possible to be sure that a sole owner is not a trustee. It *is* possible for a purchaser to be caught out, although conveyancing practice, in particular the enquiries routinely made about adult occupiers of the property, mean that instances are rare. Specifically to this chapter belong one safeguard, and one pitfall.

The safeguard relates to registered land. When joint owners purchase as beneficial tenants in common, the registrar must enter, against the register for the property, a restriction. A restriction is a direction to the effect that certain dispositions of the property cannot be registered. A restriction is entered, for example, when a bankruptcy order is made, at which point a restriction is entered forbidding the entry of any disposition; and in practice of course no purchaser will embark upon a disposition that cannot be validated by registration. The joint ownership restriction states that no disposition is to be registered if the transaction was carried out by a sole survivor of the tenants in common.

The point of this is to ensure a purchaser is warned that he must ensure that the legal estate is sold or mortgaged to him by two trustees because overreaching will be needed. This is important because tenancy in common does not involve the right of survivorship. When one of two tenants in common dies, his share *may* vest in the survivor; but equally it may pass to someone else: Fred, say. Either way, of course, the survivor becomes the sole legal owner, because the legal estate was held on joint tenancy. Because there *may* be a Fred, the purchaser must make sure that overreaching happens. (This is very easily done; the transfer to the purchaser does two jobs, first appointing an additional trustee of the legal estate, and then transferring the property.) By contrast, when the death of a beneficial joint tenant leaves a sole survivor, legal and equitable interests are united in that survivor. Thus there is no need for a joint ownership restriction, because there can be no Fred.

This does not quite work. The pitfall is that methods of severance of a beneficial joint tenancy, discussed above, mean that a beneficial joint tenancy can turn into a tenancy in common, without there being any dealing with the Land Register; so a restriction, which is now necessary, will not be entered. The corresponding problem in unregistered land—where the deeds will make clear that the seller is the survivor of beneficial joint tenants—is solved neatly by section 16 of TLATA, which (put simply) states that if there is no evidence of severance the purchaser can safely, and must, assume that the tenancy was unsevered. The draftsman failed to notice that the problem remains unsolved in registered land. To date, there are no reported disasters.

AFTERWORD

If this chapter feels messy, that is unavoidable. What we can see is the law's attempt to create a unitary format for trusts of land, regulated by TLATA. The attempt does not produce a tidy body of law, for a number of reasons. First, TLATA—in line with a great deal of English legislation—is not a codification. It does not try to state the whole of the law, and only partially abolishes older law. What was not deemed to be broke was not fixed, and so we still have to look at quite elderly case law for the rules about severance, for example, or about equitable accounting. Another reason is that TLATA is not the answer to every form of trust. Where a trust of land runs into crisis because of family breakdown, the parties have to jump ship into the Matrimonial Causes Act 1973 and associated legislation designed with the flexibility needed for family breakdown. And in some cases the picture is untidy because of a simple mistake, as in the case of the hidden severance of a joint tenancy in registered land. A further reason for the untidiness of the picture is that provisions in TLATA are incomplete: the court is not actually told what to do on section 14 applications, merely given things to think about.

That last point is a very positive one; it is that incompleteness that gives hope for TLATA. Because the statute is not entirely prescriptive, there is room for it to adapt to different forms of co-ownership, and also to the new tide of thinking that is growing out of the Human Rights Act 1998. This is likely to be the source of major debate in land law over the next decade and beyond, particularly in the area of joint ownership, family breakdown, and the balance between a joint owner's creditors and family.

BIBLIOGRAPHY

H. Conway, 'Co-owners and Equitable Accounting: A Comparative and Commonwealth Analysis' in E. Cooke (ed), *Modern Studies in Property Law, vol III* (Oxford, Hart Publishing Ltd, 2005).

E. Cooke, 'Community of Property, Joint Ownership and the family Home' in M. Dixon and G. Griffiths (eds), *Contemporary Perspectives on Property, Equity and Trusts Law* (Oxford, Oxford University Press, 2007) 39.

J. Dewar, 'Land, Law and the Family Home' in J. Dewar and S. Bright (eds), *Land Law, Themes and Perspectives* (Oxford: Oxford University Press, 1998).

6

MORTGAGES

In his book *The Mystery of Capital*, Hernando de Soto asserts that the key to the prosperity of the West is our ability to unlock the capital value of our wealth. Capital, he explains, is wealth whose full potential is exploited; it is put to work rather than hoarded. If he is correct—and his book is convincing and has been extremely influential—then, after ownership rights, mortgages are the most important property right discussed in this book. They may be the key to wealth, and are certainly the key to current patterns of home ownership, in this country. We might say that the great discovery about real property in the twentieth century was this: that the home we cannot afford can itself be security for the loan that makes it affordable. However, not all loans really are affordable by those to whom they are advertised, and debt is not a reliable route to prosperity. The bitter lesson of the early years of the twenty-first century has been that to build financial systems on a trade in debt that cannot be repaid is to court disaster.

A mortgage is a security interest. We have said a lot about mortgages already, and mortgages are now (though they were not in 1925) very much part of the vocabulary and concerns of most adults. But most people use the word incorrectly, speaking of something like 'getting a mortgage for a house' to mean getting a loan to finance a purchase. In fact a mortgage is what is given in exchange for the loan. It is a property right, given to the building society or other lender, which makes the house liable and available to pay the loan. If the loan is not repaid on time, the lender can sell the house and take as much of the proceeds as he needs in order to recover his money. He can do this because he holds a mortgage.

Familiar to most homeowners but perhaps not to all law students are the different kinds of mortgage, depending upon their purpose and the way they are repaid. Acquisition mortgages are part and parcel of a purchase: a loan is made to a buyer, who transfers the money lent to the seller. Two things then happen: the land (whether freehold or leasehold) is transferred to the buyer, and the lender (who made the purchase possible) acquires a mortgage as the security for his loan. A post-acquisition mortgage is when an already-owned property is used as security for a loan, whose purpose could be one of several. It could be a refinancing of the acquisition mortgage (known as a re-mortgage), consolidating one or more earlier loans, perhaps at a better rate of interest. It could be to pay for an improvement of the land, such as an extension. Or it could be for something quite different, the most common example being a loan to finance a business. And a business loan may be raised on the security of the business premises, or of the businessman's home. The most important element of the mortgage contract (since a mortgage, like a lease, is a property right and also a contract) is the arrangement made for paying off the loan. A repayment mortgage provides simply for the repayment of the loan in instalments, so that the first month's payment will be very nearly all interest while the last will be all capital. An interest-only mortgage provides for the purchase, alongside the land, of an investment calculated to pay off the loan when it matures at the end of the term of the mortgage—perhaps twenty years ahead. Meanwhile the borrower only pays off interest. The borrower may get a windfall if the endowment policy is larger than needed when it matures, but will be in serious difficulties if it does not grow as anticipated.

Finally, a property may be mortgaged several times, simultaneously, and so a mortgage may be a first mortgage or a subsequent one. Where a home costing £200,000 is purchased with the aid of a loan for £150,000, there is potential for the property to be used again as security for a further loan. In theory, there may be one or more subsequent mortgages for anything up to another £50,000. Suppose there is a second mortgage in return for a loan of £30,000, and a third mortgage for another £10,000. It is easy to see that the first mortgagee is much more secure than the second or third, and that therefore the cost of borrowing rises as the limits of the property's value are reached.

THE MECHANICS OF MORTGAGES

Before 1925, a mortgage was achieved by the borrower conveying an ownership right to the lender, on terms that the latter would convey it back when the loan was repaid. In early medieval times the estate conveyed was a lease; from around the fifteenth century onwards the borrower had to convey the fee simple (or whatever his own estate was) to the lender. Draconian rules that kept people to the very letter of the contract—so that if the money was one day late the property was lost to the borrower—were mitigated over the years by the courts of equity, but even so the transaction was objectionable. It was a legal fiction, which is undesirable in itself. Worse, it left the borrower with no legal estate in his own land. Yet the reformers of the early twentieth century found the problem difficult; there was no such thing as a mortgage, in the sense of a pure security right, and they were reluctant to invent one. Had they done so, it is unlikely that conveyancers would have been willing to use it. There was considerable difficulty, as it was, in getting conveyancers to trust the new mechanisms. Many of them insisted for some years on continuing, pointlessly, to use pre-1925 conveyancing documentation alongside the new material.

The 1925 legislation solved the mortgages problem by using a different legal fiction. Instead of the mortgagee (ie the lender, to whom a mortgage is granted) being given the fee simple, he would be given a lease (not an entirely new idea, of course). Moreover, there were two ways of doing this. He could be given a 3000-year lease on terms that it would terminate when the loan was repaid; this was known as a 'mortgage by demise'. Alternatively he could be given a 'charge by way of legal mortgage', or legal charge, which meant that he had exactly the same rights and remedies as if he had a 3000-year lease whose terms stated that it would terminate when the loan was repaid. A mortgage of a lease, similarly, takes the form of a sub-lease, or gives the lender the rights and remedies of a sub-lessee. What is the difference between the two forms? If property rights are indeed bundles it is hard to see that the content of a 3000-year lease is any different from a bundle consisting of all the rights one would have if one had a 3000-year lease.

A lease was not what a lender wanted or needed, any more than the fee simple had been. But the new fiction had some advantages. The main one was that the mortgagor (the borrower, who grants the mortgage) could keep the fee simple. He therefore retained a property right superior to that of the lender, which was how it should be. The lender got something less than what the borrower kept. For another, the possibility of using concurrent leases meant that second, third, etc mortgages could be added into the structure without their having to be in completely different form (as was the case when the first mortgagee took the fee simple). And for another, the matter was dealt with in a way that looked as if the reformers had done it without inventing a new property right (even though they had, because this was not a conventional lease). The new conceptualization of a mortgage also enabled a lot of the old theory to survive; in particular, just as a pre-1925 mortgagee had the right to take possession of the property by virtue of having a fee simple, so today's mortgagee has the right to possession of the mortgaged property by virtue of having a lease, or of having a lessee's rights.

The mortgage by demise, however, met its own demise in the Land Registration Act 2002, which states that a registered estate cannot be mortgaged by demise, only by a charge. This is the one restriction on an owner's powers that the 2002 Act specifies, and it means that we no longer have to accept that a mortgagee is the lessee of the mortgaged property. But we do have to regard him as having the same rights and remedies, which is just as uncomfortable and inappropriate. The registered mortgage of a registered estate is known as a 'registered charge'; and, of course, a mortgage of a registered estate is not a legal one unless it is registered (this is the effect of section 27 of the Land Registration Act 2002).

One challenge with which the law has yet fully to engage is the practice in some communities of using leases and other transactions that are not, on their face, mortgages, when what is intended is in fact a security right; the practice is widespread, and arises from religious prohibitions on lending, but it is not yet clear how the law treats such transactions.

As to formalities, it can be deduced from what has been said already about other estates and interests in land that for a mortgage to be legal (and it is one of the legal estates listed as possible in section 1 of the Law of Property Act 1925) it must be created by deed and must be registered; failure to register generates an equitable mortgage. An equitable mortgage will also arise if the borrower himself has only an equitable estate; or where one of two or more joint owners mortgages just his own equitable interest.

Since the Middle Ages mortgages have not really been self-regulated. The courts of equity became involved at an early stage in legal mortgages, in order to protect the borrower from the consequences of having to make the wrong deal—to transfer ownership, rather than just a security right. The major intervention was in the creation of the 'equitable right to redeem'. For the common law ruled that repayment of the loan had to be made on the date set in the mortgage contract. If the borrower paid late he lost the land, but still owed the debt. This was so obviously inequitable, on any meaning of that word, that the courts of equity preserved the borrower's right to pay back the loan after the due date. This remains important; in any domestic or commercial mortgage the date for redemption is set very shortly after the commencement of the mortgage—six months into the mortgage term, or even just one month. Most mortgages provide, in addition, that if one interest payment is missed, the whole debt falls due. This is done so as to make available to the mortgagee some of his statutory rights which can only be exercised when the legal date for redemption has passed, in particular the power of sale. A homeowner taking on a domestic mortgage for a twenty-five-year term would be startled to be told that, strictly speaking, he must pay all the money back in a month's time, and that his having twenty-five years in which to pay is merely a concession. This is another aspect of mortgages where what is wanted is achieved by a fiction (because if all is going well, *neither* party wants the loan to be paid off in a month's time).

Equity's involvement in the mortgage relationship was so significant that the term 'equity of redemption' is used to describe the sum total of the mortgagor's rights while the mortgage is in existence, including the equitable right to redeem; and this is so even post-1925 when the mortgagor's ownership remains intact subject to the mortgage. The word 'equity' is used in everyday language to describe the value of the property that is not accounted for by the mortgage debt, so that a property worth £200,000 purchased with the aid of a loan of £150,000 has an equity of £50,000. If the market falls and the property is worth only £140,000 it is said to be in 'negative' equity, which is a serious problem for both parties because the sale of the property will leave a debt outstanding.

So once we get into the more technical aspects of mortgages we become aware of a number of tensions. One, already touched upon, is that the way the law describes mortgages is rather different from the layman's understanding. Another is the prevalence, even today, of legal fictions: leases and contractual deadlines are used in an unusual way. And already we are seeing aspects of the need to protect one party from another. For the mortgagee is in a very powerful position. The mortgagor is dependent upon the mortgagee, often for the purchase of his land and, in all cases, for the continuance of his ownership. And so a lot of the law of mortgages is about the protection of the mortgagor—the borrower—who may be very much the underdog in the relationship. But this protection exists in tension with the fact that a mortgagee takes an interest in land in exchange for money and so is a purchaser. The preference of the 1925 reformers and of the twentieth-century courts was for the protection of a purchaser: and a mortgagee qualifies for all the purchaser protections incorporated in modern land law and particularly in registered land.

This means that where the law is dealing with mortgagor and mortgagee, as a duo in a continuing relationship, much has been done to protect the mortgagor, to enable him to keep his property, and to prevent the mortgagee from exploiting the power imbalance between them. But if we turn the mortgagee outwards from that duo, to face the rest of the world, he becomes a favoured and protected species. Thus when the mortgagee really has acquired the ability to sell the property— when all the protections for the mortgagor have failed—the courts have taken care to enable him to sell freely, and have restricted the mortgagor's ability to dictate the terms or the timing of the sale. And when the mortgagee encounters third parties—co-owners or tenants, in particular—whose interest in the property threatens to dilute or destroy his security, the courts have done everything possible to enable the mortgagee to walk away from them with a clean and marketable title. This gives rise to some hard cases, because there are contests between innocent parties; mortgagees, on the one hand, and, on the other, individuals whose home or property is threatened by someone *else's* failure to repay a loan; their landlord, or their lover.

The policy of land law is to protect the market. Protecting mortgagees and reducing the risk they undertake stimulates the market by keeping the cost of borrowing down. That is not a heartless commercial aim. The mortgagee is a bank, but he finances, and stands for, countless underdogs: ordinary people buying their homes. This is easily forgotten. Difficulties have arisen when the courts' sympathy for the lover or the tenant makes it hard to see the nameless millions represented by the mortgagee; but in most cases subsequent decisions or legislation have come to the rescue and capitalism, in the sense described by de Soto, has triumphed.

It does not have to be this way. Land ownership is not a human right, although having a home is or should be; and land ownership is not the only way to have a home and may not be the best way. But our current society as a whole has taken some sort of collective decision that this is the right way for us, and mortgages have made it possible. The law's firm policy of protecting mortgagees as purchasers is consistent with this decision.

RIGHTS, REMEDIES, AND PROTECTIONS IN THE MORTGAGE RELATIONSHIP

The law's approach to the mortgagor/mortgagee relationship has been to ask which elements are necessary as part of the giving of security, and to be restrictive in allowing anything non-essential to that relationship. Thus the mortgagee may control the mortgagor's use of property insofar as that is necessary to preserve the security, but the courts will declare void any contractual term that appears to take an unfair advantage; and when the mortgagor is in default, the law is particularly careful to give him every possible chance to put things right rather than lose the property.

Controlling the mortgage relationship

A mortgage, like a lease, is a contract, and contains extensive terms regulating the behaviour of both parties, but principally the mortgagor. Most mortgage contracts, certainly the domestic ones and to a considerable extent commercial ones too, are 'off the peg': they are standard deals, available on a take-it-or-leave-it basis with no scope for negotiation. But the terms of that standard deal are framed in the context of centuries of control of mortgages by the courts; they are made in the shadow of the law and of what the law will allow.

Most mortgages provide that the borrower is not allowed to let the property without the mortgagee's consent, overriding the provision in section 99 of the Law of Property Act 1925 that gives the mortgagor a limited power to grant leases. That contractual prohibition is backed up by a provision that there shall be a restriction on the register, preventing the registration of any dealing with the property without the mortgagee's consent. The point of this is that if the mortgagor defaults, the mortgagee will want to sell, and of course will get a better price if the property is not burdened by leases. Accordingly, the cost of borrowing when a property is 'bought to let' is higher than for a normal domestic mortgage.

How far can the mortgagee go in restricting the use of the mortgaged property? A large body of law has been built up around the doctrine of 'clogs and fetters'. This is the antiquely named principle that there should be no 'clogs' or unnecessary restrictions on the equity of redemption, nor any fetter on the mortgagor's right to redeem the mortgage, early if he wishes to. Much of the case law in this area concerns nineteenth- and early twentieth-century commercial contracts, often for mortgages of public houses. Such properties are generally subject to the very obvious restriction of being tied houses: one particular brand of beer is to be sold. Where the brewery is also the mortgagee, there is potential for exploitation. So a mortgage contract that provided for the pub to sell the mortgagee's beer during part of the mortgage term was acceptable to the court. By contrast, a term that the pub was to be tied forever, even after the debt was repaid, was not, because the mortgagor has to be able to retrieve his security in an unencumbered form. More recent cases have looked at this sort of problem as one of restraint of trade, preferring to use this more up-to-date doctrine rather than the old equitable principle. The courts have been particularly fierce about deals that give the mortgagee the right, in the form of an option, to buy the mortgaged property; this is not allowed unless it can clearly be seen as part of a separate deal—even if it does not obviously disadvantage the borrower. Terms preventing the redemption of the mortgage for several years have also been declared void.

Most of these cases are remote from today's domestic borrower. Building societies do not take options to buy the property, and they do not force commercial deals upon their borrowers. What they do force upon them is the ordinary, non-negotiable mortgage contract, which provides for the rate of interest—usually the most important, perhaps the only important, element of the deal for the borrower. It may also impose penalties for early redemption, perhaps of something like three month's interest if the mortgage is redeemed within the first three years. Surprisingly, the latter type of provision does not seem to have been attacked under the 'clogs and fetters' doctrine, even though it obviously fetters the ability to redeem. Perhaps it survives because building societies keep such penalties within affordable bounds; perhaps because domestic borrowers are unwilling to risk litigation with financial giants. The courts *will* in theory intervene to strike down an inordinately high lending rate, but they have not done so in standard, 'off the peg' domestic mortgage deals. The equitable doctrine of unconscionable bargain has been used to outlaw excessive rates in commercial mortgages, but only where the parties have clearly been in an unequal bargaining position. Sections 137 and 138 of the Consumer Credit Act 1974 enable the court to adjust an 'extortionate credit bargain'; but the

provisions have rarely been used. They do not apply to building societies or to local authority lenders; and where they have
been invoked, the difficulty has been that the borrowers have
been in a precarious financial situation at the time of the deal,
with the result that a high interest rate was seen as justified in
the light of the risk the mortgagee was undertaking. Thus
borrowers who are financially secure and a good risk will not
need protection; it tends to be those who are in financial
difficulties who resort to expensive mortgage deals, and the
courts are therefore unwilling to intervene. The individual is
allowed to go under, in the interests of maintaining a mortgage
market for the majority.

Controlling remedies for default

The mortgagee has a whole battery of powers, all aimed at
getting his money back. Most obviously, the loan contract itself
enables him to sue the debtor; and that right survives even after
sale of the property, if the sale has not discharged the loan. But
the whole point of a mortgage is to enable the mortgagee to take
the property in satisfaction of the debt; and so he has a wide
range of powers for use, in effect though not always in form,
when something has gone wrong.

The most notorious of the mortgagee's rights is his right to
possession of the property. This is anomalous, for it is a right, not
a remedy. It arises, as one old case put it, 'as soon as the ink is dry
on the mortgage'. Historically this made sense, because the
mortgagee was in fact the owner of the property. In practice
the mortgagee is normally only going to want possession in
order to sell. In the case of commercial premises, he might
want possession in order to manage, and perhaps let, the property in order to maximize income from it, or to preserve its
value, if the mortgagor is failing to manage it properly and
where immediate sale is not a good option.

The difficulty with taking possession in order to manage the
property is that the mortgagee is put under a very heavy duty of
care and is strictly answerable for the profits of his possession. If
he does not make as much money out of the property as he
could have done, he is liable to the mortgagor. Therefore he is

likely to rely not on his right to possession, but on his statutory right to appoint a receiver under section 109 of the Law of Property Act 1925. This works rather differently in that the receiver is deemed to act as the agent of the mortgagor, and is not so strictly liable for any failure to make a profit. The appointment of a receiver must be in writing, and can only be done if the mortgagee's power of sale has become exercisable (see further below).

Where the property is domestic the right to possession is far more strictly circumscribed. The mortgagee will not take possession of occupied property without a court order, because of the potential for violence and the risk that the mortgagee will commit an offence under the Criminal Law Act 1977. And if he wants a court order, the provisions of section 36 of the Administration of Justice Act 1970 and of section 8 of the Administration of Justice Act 1973 state that proceedings must be adjourned or suspended if it appears to the court that the mortgagor is going to be able to clear the arrears within the term of the mortgage.

That is the combined effect of those two sections; there are two of them, because the 1970 version was inadequately drafted and appeared to state that the mortgagor must catch up his arrears within a relatively short time in order to escape an order for possession. The effect of this was dramatic where a mortgage included a provision that if two monthly instalments were missed, the whole loan became due. Repayment within, say, six months is impossible in these circumstances. Hence the 1973 qualification, extending the catching-up time to the whole mortgage period. Sections 36 and 8, taken together, probably save the right to possession from a human rights challenge because they do allow the mortgagor a lot of leeway and ensure that the most the mortgagee can demand is the repayment of the loan within the intended term of the mortgage.[1]

However, when arrears do build up it is not uncommon for a mortgagor simply to give up, move out, and give the keys of

---

[1] As to the use of human rights arguments as a defence to possession proceedings, see Chapter 7, pp 201 ff.

the property to the mortgagor. In these circumstances no court order is needed for possession, and the statutes and case law on the permissibility of possession are irrelevant. Whether or not this is a deprivation of possessions or an interference with the borrower's right to respect for his home is debatable; surely not, since the action is a voluntary one on the borrower's part. More troubling is the situation where the mortgagee takes possession when the property is in fact vacant, without a court order, but in circumstances where the property was not vacated for that purpose. This is lawful, and section 36 of the Administration of Justice Act 1970 has no application in these circumstances; but there are proposals to restrict a mortgagee's ability to take possession of a vacant property without a court order.[2]

The sequel to possession, then, is generally sale. It has been suggested that the mortgagee's current right to possession throughout the mortgage term, anomalous as it is, be replaced with a right to sale with vacant possession, subject to the court's discretion to postpone the sale on terms. That would then restrict possession to those cases where it is truly appropriate. As things stand, there is nothing to prevent the mortgagee from selling, in cases where he has the right to do so, without first obtaining possession. This is not generally done because, in general, the mortgagee will not find a buyer; a purchaser would be unwilling to 'buy a lawsuit', as we say. However, in a recent case the mortgagee did successfully sell, and the purchaser succeeded in proceedings for possession, a human rights-based challenge being unsuccessful.[3]

But when does the mortgagee have the right to sell? This is perhaps an odd question because *this* response to default may be seen as the whole point of the mortgage. Nevertheless it is not automatic.

In fact, two things must have happened before the mortgagee can sell. The power of sale must have arisen; and it must have

---

[2] *Ropaigealach v Barclays Bank Plc* [2000] QB 263; and see the Consultation Paper on this point issued by the Ministry of Justice in 2009: CP 55/09.
[3] *Horsham Properties Group Ltd v Clark* [2008] EWHC 2327 (Ch).

become exercisable. So there are two stages, and two things to check in any practical scenario.

For the power of sale to arise, the mortgage must be by deed, and the loan must be due for repayment. The latter requirement is the main point of the contractual date for redemption, fixed artificially early even in a long-term mortgage. An equitable mortgage will normally not be made by deed, of course, and the mortgagee would instead have to seek a court order enabling him to sell as if he were a legal mortgagee. For the latter, the power of sale arises without the need for an order, if both these conditions are met (ie the mortgage is by deed, and the loan is due for payment). But that is not enough. The power must also have become exercisable, which happens on the occurrence of any one of three things; either notice requiring payment of the mortgage money has been served on the mortgagor and he has not paid in full within three months of service of that notice; or some interest under the mortgage is in arrears and has been unpaid for two months or more; or there has been a breach of some other provision in the mortgage, for example the prohibition on letting. The twin requirements that the power of sale must have arisen and must have become exercisable are protections for the borrower, because they will deter a purchaser from dealing with a mortgagee who is not entitled to sell. If the power of sale has not arisen, the purchaser will take only the mortgagee's own interest; and if the power has not become exercisable, the mortgagor may be able to set aside the sale if he can show that the purchaser had notice of the problem.

Once the protections have all failed and sale is inevitable the mortgagee is able to take control of proceedings. He must sell the property for the best price reasonably obtainable, taking proper care to advertise it and suchlike, and he may not sell to himself or to his agent or employee; but the timing of the sale is up to the mortgagee. He need not, for example, wait for a rise in the market. This is another balancing; all the mortgagee wants and can have is his loan repaid, but he is not allowed to sell at a knock-down price that would just cover the loan and his costs. What the mortgagor wants is as much of a surplus—the financial equity—as possible; and the mortgagee's duty goes most of the way to ensuring this. Nevertheless, repossession sales do have a certain flavour; properties are likely to be cheaper than others, and there will be no 'chain' involved, but they are notorious for being in poor condition. There is no proud and anxious householder to show buyers round. The theoretical basis of the mortgagee's duty is that it lies in equity rather than in tort; the 'duty of care' is not the same as that invoked in the negligence cases. But the practical consequence of this distinction may be minimal.

Once the sale is completed, the mortgagee must apply the proceeds in a specific order; and this determines where any shortfall will lie. He must first apply the proceeds to redeem any securities prior to his own; he might, of course, not be the first mortgagee, and the first mortgagee gets first cut. Then he pays the costs of sale, and then his own loan. Next, any still remaining proceeds go to repay any subsequent mortgagees; and finally, the surplus goes to the borrower.

Far more Draconian than sale is foreclosure. Foreclosure is the mortgagee's ability to bring the equity of redemption to an end by taking property and extinguishing the borrower's ownership. This requires a court order, vesting the mortgagor's ownership right—the fee simple or the lease—in the mortgagee (whereas before 1925, of course, no order was needed as the estate was vested already). The mortgagee may then keep the property or sell it, but there will be no surplus for the mortgagor, who loses everything. For this reason, the court order is made in two stages, allowing the mortgagor a six-month period in which to repay the loan. Foreclosure is rare today, and the court has power, on an application for foreclosure, to order sale instead; and it is hard to imagine the court not doing so. This may be why the mortgagee's right to forfeit has not yet been the subject of a human rights challenge. If challenge comes before abolition of the right to forfeit, it may well be that section 91 of the Law of Property Act 1925 may be found incompatible with Article 1 of the First Protocol to the European Convention on Human Rights; for the legislature here is giving the lender a right that amounts to confiscation of property, in a manner disproportionate to the purpose it serves and without compensation—the more so because the alternative remedy, sale, is available and makes proper provision for the borrower to get whatever value is left for his own estate after the sale.[4]

THIRD PARTIES AND THE PROTECTION OF MORTGAGEES

Priorities: mortgagee sells the title he took

The tale of the law of mortgages is rather like a piece of music whose harmonic climax is the sale of the property and the consequent redemption of the loan—even though most mortgages are paid off in an uncontroversial manner and never involve an exploration of the rules relating to sale. And because this is the anticipated climax, a great deal of law is devoted to ensuring that the mortgagee has a clean title which he can pass on to a purchaser. This he will have if, and only if, he took a clean title at the point when the mortgage was granted. This takes us back to issues examined in Chapter 3. Anything enforceable against a purchaser at the point of the mortgage will bind the mortgagee and will therefore bind any purchaser who buys from the mortgagee. By contrast, any interest created by the borrower subsequent to the mortgage, and without the mortgagee's authorization, will have no effect on the purchaser who buys from the mortgagee. The mortgagee's purchaser takes what the mortgagee took.

This means that at the point of sale, if there is any dispute about burdens on the title, it is necessary to look back to the point when the mortgage was granted so as to see what is the title that the mortgagee is able to transmit.

Put like that, the answer is simple. If the mortgagor's title is registered and the charge is registered, the mortgagee is bound by any burden whose priority was, at the point when the mortgage was granted, protected by section 29 of the Land

---

[4] Equally, foreclosure could be challenged on the basis that it is incompatible with the mortgagor's right to respect for his home, pursuant to Art. 8 of the European Convention on Human Rights. That would seem in this context a less reliable basis for challenge than Art. 1 of the First Protocol; see further Chapter 7.

Registration Act 2002;[5] that is, by anything on the register, by any overriding interests in existence at that point, and by the obligations contained in the lease if the mortgaged property is leasehold.[6] If the mortgagor's title is unregistered, the mortgagee will be bound by any interests registered under the Land Charges Acts, and in addition by all unregistrable legal interests, and by any unregistrable equitable interests of which he has notice.

Some examples may help, both in seeing how the mechanics work and also in seeing what is the practical effect of a mortgagee being bound, or not being bound, by a given interest (we shall limit the discussion to registered titles). Indeed, these issues bring together a number of principles that have been discussed already in earlier chapters, so what follows may be useful as consolidation. The B Building Society (BBS) took a registered charge over Whiteacre in 2000, in return for a loan to the owner, O, to finance O's business (O is the registered proprietor of a 999-year lease; but it does not matter, for any of these examples, whether he is a long leaseholder or the freeholder). Now, O is in default and the BBS is selling. It sells, obviously, O's lease; and section 29 of the Land Registration Act 2002 makes it clear that the purchaser will be bound by all the tenant's obligations in that lease. But the A Building Society (ABS) took a first legal mortgage of the lease in 1998 when O purchased it. BBS therefore took its registered charge subject to the prior registered charge in ABS's favour, and ABS gets its loan repaid first. Moreover, in 1999 O granted to his neighbour an easement over part of Whiteacre; perhaps a right of way over the

---

[5] It is perhaps worth mentioning a small complication in parenthesis here. A mortgage, being an interest in land, can be transferred; X Building Society can transfer its interest—its debt, and the security for it—to Y Building Society (YBS). If this happens, then the title that YBS takes is determined by s 30 of the Land Registration Act rather than by s 29. However, it is easy to see from a comparison of the two sections that the end result is the same.

[6] Another complication, again in parenthesis: if the mortgagor's title is registered but the mortgage is not registered then s 29 is of no assistance, and moreover the mortgage is merely equitable. The effect of s 28 of the Land Registration Act 2002 in such a case would be that the mortgage would take effect subject to all legal interests in the property and to any equitable interests in existence at that point.

end of the garden. It was a legal easement, created by registration in accordance with section 27 of the Land Registration Act 2002, and so as a registered burden in 2000 it bound BBS in accordance with section 29. Therefore BBS sells the land subject to the easement. We can play with variations on this theme: if the easement was acquired in that year by informal means, for example by long use,[7] there may be nothing on the register, but the easement is legal and is therefore an overriding interest under paragraph 3 of Schedule 1, and the result is the same. But if the easement is equitable it probably did not bind BBS because it is unlikely to be noted on the register and cannot be an overriding interest—because paragraph 3 is only for legal interests, and it is unlikely that the holder of an easement would be in actual occupation of the property so as to benefit from paragraph 2.

If the property is sold by ABS rather than by BBS, then whether or not ABS is bound by the 1999 easement would depend on whether or not the grant was authorized by ABS. If it was authorized, then sale is subject to the grant; if it was not authorized, then the easement disappears at the point of sale—or, rather, at the point of an order for possession of the property—and ABS can sell the property free of the easement. The effect of the easement on the value of the land is of course a factor in a mortgagee's decision whether or not to permit the grant of the easement.

Similar examples can be constructed if the interest created in 1999 is a lease. The outcome depends upon whether or not the mortgagor's statutory power to lease the property has been excluded by ABS as it normally would be; an unauthorized lease in 1999 will not bind ABS, but it remains valid between O and the tenant, and will bind BBS if it is a legal lease appearing on the register or, being too short for registration, is an overriding interest under paragraph 1 of Schedule 3 to the Land Registration Act 2002. Even an equitable lease will bind BBS if the tenant is in actual occupation so that the lease falls within paragraph 2 of Schedule 3.

---

[7] For the law on prescription and other informal methods of acquiring easements, see Chapter 8.

That example moves us on from the preceding, relatively uncomplicated, ones which did not involve third party claimants in actual occupation of the property. Actual occupation causes, or at least has caused, greater problems, as we have seen. It is problematic because the interests of those in actual occupation tend to be substantial—they may have a long lease, or a beneficial interest under a trust, so that the effect of their interest having priority may be disastrous to the value of the security. Where the occupier has a beneficial interest, it is likely to be undocumented, and the occupier may be unaware of the nature of his interest until the matter is litigated much later. In all cases, the interests of those in actual occupation may be unnoticed by the purchaser if he does not inspect properly (few of us do!) or at all (mortgagees rarely do). And the legislation itself is defective in that it does not cater for all possible circumstances, although the 2002 Act does better than did the Land Registration Act 1925. Let us look at some of the permutations.

Priorities: actual occupation interests

Again, O bought Whiteacre in 1998 with the aid of a loan from ABS, and took a further loan in 2000 from BBS, each loan being secured by separate mortgages. Let us suppose that O got married in 1999. Mrs O had some savings, and when they got married she paid off some of the acquisition mortgage. We are instantly in difficulties. Did she do this as a wedding present? Or not, so that we can say she takes a beneficial interest under a resulting trust? It is possible to construct facts and conversations that could be interpreted as giving rise to a common intention construction trust or even proprietary estoppel. At any rate, let us suppose that by one of these means, in 2000 when O is negotiating his second mortgage, Mrs O already has a 40 per cent beneficial interest, while 40 per cent of the property's value is still accounted for by the acquisition mortgage. She cannot register her interest,[8] and it may not occur to her that she has it. But she has an actual occupation overriding interest under

---

[8] Land Registration Act 2002, s 32; see Chapter 3, pp 50–1.

paragraph 2 and BBS will be bound by it, as was Williams and Glyn's Bank by Mrs Boland.[9]

This brings us straight back to the subject matter of Chapter 3. The *Boland* scenario was unforeseen by the 1925 legislators, as they did not regard an equitable co-owner as having an interest *in the land*, only in the sale proceeds. It took a re-conceptualization of these property rights in the 1970s to create the problem. It is worth pausing to consider, in more detail than we did in Chapter 3, the context in which Mrs O's claim comes to light and the difficulties it causes. Mrs O will make her claim when BBS takes possession proceedings against O. She is saying: 'you took your mortgage subject to my interest; and whereas you thought that the whole of the equity was available to you as security (60 per cent of the value), your security is only 20 per cent of the value of the property'. The consequences of this are, first, that in order to get an order for sale at all, BBS has to explore the provisions of sections 14 and 15 of the Trusts of Land and Appointment of Trustees Act 1996, because BBS holds a mortgage of only one co-owner's share and therefore has to obtain an order for sale of co-owned property against the will of the other owner.[10] If it does obtain such an order, it is likely to find the security inadequate to discharge the loan.

That, as we saw in Chapter 3, is why *Boland* was seen as such a disaster for the mortgage industry and therefore for home owning in general. The interest is substantial, and although it is visible (because paragraph 2 of Schedule 3 to the Land Registration Act 2002 says it must be, thus straightening out a confusion under the 1925 Act), it is unseen, because mortgagees do not usually inspect; and it wrecks the security.

However, things were not as bad as they seemed. The obvious first point to make is that the occupying beneficial owner is only a problem to a purchaser, including of course a mortgagee, if he deals with a sole owner. If there are two or more trustees of the legal estate, any other beneficial interests are overreached

---

[9] *Williams and Glyn's Bank Ltd v Boland* [1981] AC 487; see Chapter 3, p 61.
[10] See Chapter 5, pp 124–5.

and will not trouble the purchaser. A mortgagee taking a charge from joint owners has nothing to fear from *Boland* (although, as we shall see, there is a different hazard to face where there are joint mortgagors).

For those who deal with a sole owner (and there is no standard practice of insisting on the appointment of a second trustee of a legal estate, although that would be a simple solution to the problem under discussion), small points have been tidied up to make the operation of the actual occupation principle cleaner. The 2002 Act states that occupation must be obvious, which will rule out some claimants. And it states that where the occupation is of only part of the property (perhaps a separate flat) the occupier's interest is overriding only in relation to that part. Moreover, it puts on to a statutory footing a decision made by the courts under the 1925 Act, namely that the time for determination of actual occupation status is the making of the disposition (what the layman calls 'completion': the day when people move house) and not registration. This is not the case for other overriding interests. Thus if a Tree Preservation Order takes effect as a local land charge between completion and registration, the mortgagee is bound by it (because local land charges are a separate category of overriding interests). But if the owner's partner moves into the house and acquires an equitable interest in it between completion and registration, the mortgagee is not bound. Underlying this rule is a decision (made initially by the courts and now enshrined in legislation) about the sort of interests that *ought* to bind a mortgagee. If and when electronic conveyancing becomes a reality the rule will become otiose because there will be no gap, at least in theory.

However, the effect of *Boland* today is best seen in the contrast between acquisition mortgages, where interests like Mrs Boland's cannot (on the current state of the authorities) bind a mortgagee, and post-acquisition mortgages. In the latter case the combined effect of case law and conveyancing practice is that a mortgagee will nearly always be safe. Here is how the law arrived at this position.

The response to Boland

(1) Acquisition mortgages and the effect of *Cann*

The charge in *Boland* was not an acquisition mortgage; the mortgagee came on the scene when both Mr Boland's legal estate and Mrs Boland's equitable interest were in place, and the precise time when those two forms of ownership came into effect did not matter. But what happens when property is bought by a sole legal owner, with the aid of a contribution from another who therefore takes a beneficial interest in the property? Can an acquisition mortgagee be bound by the equitable co-owner's interest? Initially it was thought that this could indeed happen because the logical sequence of events is as follows: first, the buyer completes his purchase; second, the equitable co-ownership takes effect, through a resulting or a common intention constructive trust; third, the mortgage takes effect. If, and only if, during this sequence of events the beneficial co-owner is in actual occupation of the house (by design, because of an agreement that the buyer should take possession early, or by accident, because keys were released too early) then his interest is given overriding status by that occupation and takes priority to the mortgagee. The mortgagee loses priority to a third-party right arising from a deal that the mortgagee could not prevent and could not detect, and taking effect in the theoretical interval between purchase and mortgage—known, famously, as the *scintilla temporis*, which means a very brief moment, or the twinkling of an eye.

Facts following this pattern reached the House of Lords in *Abbey National Building Society v Cann*.[11] George Cann bought a house for his mother, Daisy, to live in. She paid most of the purchase price, but he raised the balance, £4,000, as a loan secured by a mortgage to Abbey National. When he defaulted on the mortgage repayments, Daisy resisted the mortgagee's possession proceedings on the basis that her interest, combined with her actual occupation of the house for about 35 minutes before completion, took priority to that of Abbey National.

---

[11] [1991] 1 AC 56.

The House of Lords' solution to this problem was, first, to rule that Daisy was not in actual occupation, given the particular facts. She was not there in person, although her furniture was being moved in. This solved the mortgagee's problem in this particular case. But, secondly, the Lords solved the problem for the future by declaring that in any event the gap between purchase and mortgage simply does not exist. There is no *scintilla*. The buyer acquires a fee simple already burdened by a mortgage, and after that double and simultaneous event there is time for third party rights to be created.

The decision in *Cann* dramatically reduces the wrecking potential of *Boland* by making it virtually impossible for an acquisition mortgagee to be bound by an unforeseen equitable interest in the property. The *Cann* solution will only fail if there is so long a gap between the purchase of the fee simple and its mortgage that the denial of the existence of the *scintilla* loses credibility. How big a gap that might be has yet to be seen (24 hours? 24 days? 24 minutes?).

Cann is a heavy-handed piece of judicial law-making, a denial of logic and of practical reality motivated by what are euphemistically called policy considerations but could perhaps be more accurately labelled sociopolitical manipulation. Contrast the many cases where the courts have refused to change the law on the basis that that would be to usurp the role of Parliament.[12] Among their Lordships' reasons for the decision was the assertion that when George Cann acquired the freehold, purchased with the aid of a mortgage, he never acquired anything more than the 'equity of redemption'. This is untrue, and a harking back to pre-1925 days. He did indeed acquire a fee simple, to be burdened not eliminated by the mortgage. Insofar as the first mortgage did not exhaust the equity in the property he could mortgage that fee simple again. And he could, in theory, have failed to execute the mortgage. He would of course have been in breach of contract with the mortgagor, liable in unjust enrichment, and possibly also criminally liable.

---

[12] The example seen in this book is the reluctance to use estoppel as a way of rescuing informal contracts; see Chapter 4, p 105.

The fact that this is very unlikely to happen, because the conveyancing will be in the hands of a solicitor acting for the mortgagee as well as for the mortgagor, does not weaken the logical point. The decision also ignores the fact that Cann had an equitable interest in the property before completion day, by virtue of his contract to purchase.[13] If Daisy's money went into the deposit (it is not clear from the law report whether or not it did) her interest in the property would surely have taken effect when contracts were exchanged. If that were the case, then the slaughter of the *scintilla* did not affect her priority, provided she was in actual occupation before the mortgage took effect.

Cann is simply a decision, couched in the language of reasoning, that *Boland*-type interests cannot bind an acquisition mortgagee. It fits so firmly into the political and economic ethos of the late twentieth century that it is unlikely to be reversed.

(2) Post-acquisition mortgages and the effect of *Prestidge*

Boland is therefore only really a problem to post-acquisition mortgagees, where there is clear time in which beneficial co-ownership can arise. In these circumstances, the waiver system evolved in the wake of *Boland* is the mortgagee's first line of defence, and it will almost always be effective. This has been discussed earlier,[14] and it will be recalled that mortgagees routinely inquire as to the adult occupiers of the property and secure from each of them a waiver of their rights, if any, vis-à-vis the mortgagee. The system appears to work, in the sense that its effectiveness in straightforward cases has not been challenged; and this in spite of the fact that it assumes that a mortgagor will tell the truth, and despite the fact that the available remedies if he does not do so will be worthless. The system continues despite the fact that solicitors are very reluctant to advise clients on giving such waivers (the fee chargeable being out of all proportion to the potential liability for getting it wrong), so that those who give them may well be doing so without proper advice.

---

[13] See Chapter 2, p 33.   [14] See Chapter 3, p 96.

Sometimes waivers are not obtained, and there is a second line of defence. It relies on the case of *Equity and Law Home Loans Ltd v Prestidge*,[15] which in turn derives from the decision in *Bristol and West Building Society v Henning*.[16] *Henning* was a pre-*Cann* decision and it said this: that when a house is being purchased with the aid of a mortgage, a co-owner who knows that the mortgage is necessary to the purchase is deemed to consent to the mortgage. Although there are difficulties inherent in saying that someone consented when they did not consciously do so, there is certainly a problem with a beneficial co-owner insisting that his beneficial interest in a property take priority to a mortgage, when without the mortgage the beneficial interest (at least in *that* property) could not have existed. The deemed consent acts in the same way as an express waiver, ensuring that the mortgagee can claim possession and realize its security as if the co-owner did not exist.

Now, after *Cann* the decision in *Henning* is not needed. But *Henning* was extended by *Prestidge*, which established the principle that where the property is re-mortgaged (ie a replacement mortgage granted to secure a loan used, and intended by all parties, to pay off the acquisition mortgage) then the co-owner's deemed consent to the acquisition mortgage is transferred to the re-mortgagee.

There is some logic in this. The co-owner may know nothing about the re-mortgage; but she should not obtain priority to the mortgage (in this scenario there is only one) just because the legal owner changed lenders without telling her. There are also some problems in the application of *Prestidge*, and it should not be applied unthinkingly, as if consent to the re-mortgage could be constructed automatically. If the terms of the re-mortgage are particularly harsh (and recall the comments made early in this chapter, to the effect that it is those in financial difficulties who tend to have to accept expensive loans) the cohabitant might well have refused to consent if asked. The *Prestidge* analysis does not work for a second mortgage, that is, an additional mortgage to secure an additional loan. A second mortgagee who does not

---

[15] [1992] 1 WLR 137.   [16] [1995] 1 WLR 778.

protect himself by the waiver system should not be able to use this alternative protection. It is not clear whether it should work for a mortgage intended as a second mortgage, where the borrower chooses instead to use the loan to pay off the acquisition mortgage—this has been called the 'accidental re-mortgage'. Where *Prestidge* is appropriate the theoretical basis of its operation is unclear; there is a suggestion that it is a form of subrogation.

Subrogation is a technique used when someone who does not own the property pays off the mortgage. He is said to 'be subrogated to' the rights of the mortgagee, which means that he stands in the mortgagee's shoes and takes on the mortgagee's rights. It is easiest to see the sense in this if we imagine an unconnected individual paying off someone else's mortgage, not as a gift but as a way of—perhaps—assisting a friend who would otherwise suffer repossession or a very high interest rate, although such a scenario is rather implausible and has a nineteenth-century flavour to it. But that, without the element of philanthropy, is just what a commercial lender does when he makes a loan in order to pay off the first mortgage. Normally this lender's rights are secured by a mortgage, but if for some reason that mortgage does not take effect, the law is that the lender is subrogated to the rights of the first (now paid-off) mortgagee, since otherwise the borrower would be unjustly enriched at the lender's expense.

The reasoning can be transferred to the *Prestidge*-type case, this time reversing the unjust enrichment of the co-owner, who would take a windfall benefit if she took priority to the re-mortgagee. There is no direct judicial authority for this analysis of *Prestidge*, but if correct it would appear to give a sound doctrinal basis to the case as well as to give the courts some discretionary control over these cases (in line with restitution decisions in general).

As a final point: some jurisdictions seek to avoid this type of difficulty by legislating that a sole owner of the family home cannot dispose of it—by sale, gift, mortgage, or whatever—without the consent of his or her spouse or (in those jurisdictions where they exist) registered partner. The non-owning partner is therefore given a veto. Such protection does not exist in this country unless the spouse has registered her right of occupation so that the purchaser simply will not go ahead unless she withdraws her registration, again producing a kind of veto.[17] It exists as nearby as Ireland and in many European jurisdictions. The consequence of proceeding without consent is that the transaction is void or voidable—the details vary. It would be possible to enact such a system in this jurisdiction. But if that were to happen, another problem would arise; what of the spouse who gives consent, but then suggests that she did so because she was lied to or pressurized? The problem would then merge with the next one we have to tackle, which concerns joint mortgagors.

JOINT MORTGAGORS AND THE PROBLEM OF PRESSURE

This final section deals, again, with the title the mortgagee is able to sell and, therefore, with the quality of title that he took when he granted the loan and purchased his security interest. Like the problem of priorities, it is discussed at this end of the chapter because it will be litigated when the mortgagee comes to enforce the security and so belongs with the climax of the mortgagee's tale.

The problem is this. Greenacre was bought in 2000 by Pat and Chris. In 2005 Pat needed a business loan, and a joint mortgage was executed in order to secure a loan to Pat from the bank. Whether or not there was a prior acquisition mortgage does not matter for the purposes of this example. Pat's business goes under, the mortgage payments are not kept up, and the bank seeks possession of the property prior to sale. And at this point Chris objects to the mortgage and claims not to be bound by it.

There are two principal dangers for the bank here. The first is that Chris' signature may have been forged by Pat. This is unusual but not unknown; and on the principles applicable in unregistered land it will mean that the apparent legal mortgage is void—because Pat did not have the ability to mortgage the legal

---

[17] Chapter 4, p 88.

estate—although Pat's own equitable interest will be charged to
the bank. The bank must therefore look to the principles in
sections 14 and 15 of the Trusts of Land and Appointment of
Trustees Act 1996 for a decision as to whether or not the land
can be sold. The position where the title is registered is rather
different. A legal mortgage will be created once the bank's
charge is registered: this is the effect of section 58 of the Land
Registration Act 2002.[18] Normally, however, the victim of
forgery will be able to have the register altered so as to remove
the legal mortgage and replicate the position in unregistered
land so that only a charge of the forger's equitable interest
remains.[19]

The effect of forgery in registered land is complex, as we saw
in Chapter 3. It is the less common of the two dangers in joint
mortgages.

The second and more common problem is where Chris
claims not to have understood or really intended the transaction:
specifically, that Pat lied to Chris about the effect of the mortgage, or that Pat pressured Chris into it. Chris is claiming to be
the victim of misrepresentation or of undue influence. Either of
these wrongs would make a transaction between Pat and Chris
voidable; that is, it is not void, and remains valid until Chris
claims otherwise. But Chris can apply to the court to have the
transaction set aside, so that things will be as if the transaction
had not happened.

So much for dealings between Pat and Chris; at first sight
this does not seem to be a problem for the bank. But it is,
because the courts have held that in some circumstances the
bank can be regarded as involved in Pat's misconduct, so that the
mortgage executed by Chris is tainted by Pat's misrepresentation
or undue influence and can be avoided by Chris. This means
that the mortgage is void, and the register will be altered so as to
remove the bank's registered charge.[20] All the bank has at that
point is its debt, which can be enforced against Chris. Ultimately, it can be enforced by a charging order—a form of
compulsory mortgage, which will make Chris' share in the

---

[18] Chapter 3, p 65.   [19] Chapter 3, p 66.
[20] Chapter 3, pp 65 ff.

property liable for the debt. The effect is then, again, very like that of *Boland*. The bank is going to have trouble realizing its security because of the involvement of a co-owner whose share is not charged with the debt, and in any event, Chris' share in the value of the house may be an inadequate security.

A considerable body of law has built up as the courts have struggled to develop guidelines about three issues. First, how can undue influence be proved? Misrepresentation is much simpler (simpler to do, and simpler to prove), being about statements rather than pressure, and the account that follows concentrates on undue influence, although issues two and three are equally relevant to misrepresentation. Second, when is a bank tainted by, or involved in, its client's undue influence, so as to make the mortgage voidable even though the bank did not do anything to Chris? Third, how can a bank protect itself from this problem, by taking action in advance?

In the leading case on this area of the law, the House of Lords devoted a great deal of attention to issue three, because from the bank's point of view this is the most important. If the safeguards prescribed in that case are put in place by the bank, issues one and two will not trouble it. The safeguards will, incidentally, in some cases protect persons in Chris' position from entering an unwise transaction; but the purpose of the safeguards is to protect the bank. This should be no surprise from what we have seen already. It should be stressed that it would be simplistic to regard this as a preference by the courts for financial interests rather than those of individuals. At the heart of this area of the law is the courts' awareness of the financial needs of businesses. To be avoided at all costs is a situation where the family home is not acceptable for use as business security:

If the freedom of homeowners to make economic use of their homes is not to be frustrated, a bank must be able to have confidence that a wife's signature of the necessary guarantee and charge will be as binding upon her as is the signature of anyone else on documents which he or she may sign. Otherwise banks will not be willing to lend money on the security of a jointly owned house or flat.[21]

---

[21] Lord Nicholls of Birkenhead in *Royal Bank of Scotland v Etridge (No 2)* [2001] 4 All ER 449 at 35, HL.

As that quotation makes clear, the 'victim' in most of the many cases of this type that have reached the courts has been the borrower's wife; one of the challenges for the courts in developing this area of the law has been the need to ensure that it is gender-neutral, and that protection does not depend—as it used to—on the parties being married. An approach to this kind of case was developed in a number of cases prior to 1994. That approach was to some extent disapproved, and a new approach enunciated, in the House of Lords' decision in *Barclays Bank Plc v O'Brien*.[22] *O'Brien* helped lenders enormously, but generated some theoretical and practical controversy. The current law is as set out in *Royal Bank of Scotland v Etridge (No 2)*.[23] Accounts and analysis of the law are therefore beset by the need to explain how these two decisions of the House of Lords have each changed what went before them, and a layered effect is created. What follows is an endeavour to state the current law on the three issues identified above, with an explanation where necessary of how it reached its current state.

Proving undue influence

Proving undue influence has caused huge difficulty because of its subtlety. Whereas misrepresentation is a matter of making an untrue statement, undue influence involves statements, tone of voice, implication, and above all a relationship. What Pat says to Chris about the mortgage might cut no ice with me, but be irresistible to Chris. And of course we are all influenced by our friends, family, colleagues, and children; and the law accepts this, intervening only when influence is undue in the sense of being excessive and unconscientious. Undue influence may range from threats and coercion, through bullying to pressure. The leading case suggests that there is undue influence where A trusts B to manage things for the two of them, and B 'prefers his interests to hers and makes a choice for both of them on that footing'.[24]

---

[22] [1994] 1 AC 180.   [23] [2001] 4 All ER 449.

[24] Lord Nicholls of Birkenhead in *Royal Bank of Scotland v Etridge (No 2)* [2001] 4 All ER 449 at 33, HL.

The courts have developed two ways of proving undue influence. The obvious way is for the victim to satisfy the court of what was said and done so as to demonstrate that undue influence did in fact take place. But this will not always be possible because of the subtlety of the problem and the role played by the parties' relationship. So the courts have held that if the victim can show *both* that he had a relationship of trust and confidence with the other party *and* that the transaction calls for explanation, then it will be held that there was undue influence unless the other party can provide an explanation which shows that undue influence did not take place.

The term 'relationship of trust and confidence' is unfortunate, in that it should be true of all good relationships. In this context it means something more, and something perhaps less wholesome, than the words would normally imply. It derives from earlier case law, and denotes a relationship where one party is likely to do as the other tells him or her, without enquiry or independent thought. It has been held that some relationships always have this characteristic: doctor and patient, priest and penitent, lawyer and client. Others may do in individual circumstances, and in particular, a married or engaged couple may or may not interact in this way.

So 'trust and confidence' in this context is an unexpectedly pejorative attribute of a relationship. All it demonstrates is the potential for abuse, however; it does not tell us that anyone did anything wrong. The next step towards proving that (and recall that this operation only takes place where *actual* undue influence cannot be shown) is to show that the transaction calls for explanation; that is, simply that there is something unusual about it. The fact that a member of such a couple—the one potentially abusable—has given the other a birthday present, for example, does not call for explanation. The fact that one has given the other his entire wealth does. This phrase avoids the need to show that the person claiming undue influence has done something specifically disadvantageous—something required in the pre-*Etridge* case law. That requirement was unhelpful because when a wife mortgages her share in the family home in order to support her husband's business she may well do so as much for her own benefit as for his. Obviously a transaction to which the two were equal parties—where the borrowing was to finance a joint venture such as a holiday, or a business in which both are equal and active partners—does not call for explanation.

Once these two things have been proved (the nature of the relationship and the fact that the transaction is unusual or unexpected) then the position is this: that unless the other person actually provides that explanation, explaining away the unusual nature of the transaction, the court will find that undue influence was exerted. This method of proof is therefore known as *presumed* undue influence, rather than actual. It is so called because it involves a shifting of the burden of proof. The person alleging undue influence need not go all the way; he or she need only take these two prescribed steps, and will then be taken to have arrived unless the defendant can show that undue influence was not exerted.

This analysis is the product of the decision in *Etridge* and is simpler than that advocated in *O'Brien*, although not radically different from it.

Entangling the bank

The more important change made in *Etridge* is in the analysis of the circumstances in which the bank will be held to have been entangled in its client's misdeed, so that undue influence exerted by Pat over Chris will render voidable the transaction between Chris and the bank. The law here has gone through some distinct stages, and it is perhaps a measure of the artificiality of what is going on here that it has gone through a number of obviously incorrect analyses before hitting upon the current acceptable one.

Before *O'Brien* the courts attributed Pat's misconduct to the bank by regarding him, in obtaining Chris' cooperation, as the bank's agent. This worked technically, by providing a way to force the bank to take responsibility for Pat's actions, but was unrealistic. Pat is the prime mover in the transaction and it is he who wants the loan; for his own sake he secures Chris' co-operation.

Conscious that this analysis was not convincing, the House of Lords in *O'Brien* said this: that the bank is bound by notice of

Pat's undue influence; and that it would have notice of the undue influence if it failed to take prescribed steps to ensure that Chris received independent legal advice.

This too was unconvincing. The use of 'notice' as a tool of analysis is misleading; it is appropriate where a party to a transaction is or should be aware of a right arising through a previous transaction. But here there is just one deal. The wife's rights, against anyone, have not arisen at this stage; there is nothing to have notice of.

Etridge makes it simpler again. In all cases where the relationship between the borrower and the fellow mortgagor is non-commercial, the bank is 'put on inquiry'. And if the bank is put on inquiry, it is liable for the mortgagor's undue influence, if any, unless it takes certain steps. This means that the bank is potentially entangled in the borrower's wrongdoing in a huge range of cases—all those where the fellow mortgagor is not a business partner. It avoids any inquiry into relationships or into emotional matters. It avoids any reference to gender or to marital status (contrast the pre-*O'Brien* cases where it was said that equity has an 'especial tenderness' for wives, which nowadays seems endearing but inappropriate). It is not seen as a particular hardship for the lender, because the latter can protect itself simply and unambiguously by following the procedure set out in *Etridge* for its protection in cases where it is put on inquiry.

Protecting the bank

So in certain cases the bank is 'put on inquiry'. This sounds as if it should ask questions, and in particular, 'why'? Why is this person going to be liable for the other's debt? Why is Chris doing this for Pat? But those questions are too personal and are not going to produce the truth. Instead, when it is 'put on inquiry', the bank will nevertheless *not* be liable for any misrepresentation or undue influence on the part of the borrower if it has taken the steps prescribed in *Etridge*.

What must the bank do to be saved? It must ensure that the fellow mortgagor, to whom the loan is *not* made, has been advised by a solicitor about the implications of executing the mortgage. The advice to be given is rather thorough; it must include a breakdown of the borrower's financial situation (which therefore the bank must disclose) and a full explanation of the level of the loan, the possibility, if any, of the borrower drawing down further funds, and the consequences of its not being paid. The solicitor—who may be the solicitor acting for the borrower—must certify to the bank that he has done all this. The bank need not check that he has done so. The existence of that certificate is a complete protection for the bank.

Notice that the bank itself does not have to do anything with or for Chris. It does not have to interview or advise Chris (as suggested in *O'Brien*; banks simply will not do it and the requirement was wisely dropped by the House of Lords in *Etridge*). The onus of protecting Chris falls on the solicitor, and it is the solicitor, not the bank, who is at risk of litigation if the advice given was inadequate. The consequence for banks is one-stop litigation: the bank need have no involvement in the issues of whether or not there was undue influence or misrepresentation, it need only produce that protecting certificate from Chris' solicitor, which is then a complete answer to any involvement by the bank in proceedings arising from Chris' complaints that he was pressurized.

Notice that none of this is relevant if the loan was made to both mortgagors. In that event there is nothing to put the bank on inquiry. If there is no question of a business loan and the borrowing is claimed—truthfully or otherwise—to be taken on in order to pay for a holiday or a conservatory, then there is no place and no need for the *Etridge* rules.[25]

Outcomes of the problem of pressure

So what is the position of a post-*Etridge* Chris, who is not happy about the security? If the bank can produce a certificate to show that *Etridge*-compliant advice was given to Chris, then the mortgage is valid in its entirety. Chris' options are to sue Pat for undue influence, which is unlikely to be useful; or to sue the solicitor for negligent advice. The solicitor, of course, is insured.

[25] *CIBC Mortgages v Pitt* [1994] 1 AC 200, HL.

In the event that the bank cannot show that it followed the *Etridge* rules despite being put on inquiry, the mortgage is voidable. But the debt, from Pat to the bank, remains due. If Pat does not pay it back the outcome may be bankruptcy, and Pat's trustee in bankruptcy will be able to ensure a sale of the house so that Pat's share in it can be applied to pay the debt. Chris's share will be unaffected.

What we have to hope is that the *Etridge* procedure will produce real protection for borrowers, at least to the extent of making them aware of risk. It is unlikely to prevent many people from taking risks; and it is well-established that the pressure, or pleasure, of an intimate relationship makes people far more willing to take financial risk than they would otherwise be. This is one of the things that capital enables people to choose to do. What *Etridge* is certainly designed for is to prevent people from taking deliberate risks, and then, when it goes wrong, seeking to escape by saying that they did not mean it, or did not know what they were doing, or were not told. The bank is given a way of proving that the risk was taken deliberately.

MORTGAGES, CAPITAL, AND RISK

So: real property is a form of capital, and one of the sources of our prosperity is the ability to use it as such. The mortgage is essential to this. And a mortgage is a risk, as just remarked. The law has developed a web of protection, for lenders and borrowers. It is not all entirely logical or consistent; some of what looks like protection for the borrower is in fact protection for the lender. Much of the legal shape of this area of the law is determined by what individuals and institutions are prepared to take on, in a particular era. The evolution of the law of mortgages reflects different risk-aversions at different periods. Where an earlier age was concerned about commercial strings attached to mortgages, today we are willing to accept the standard form contracts imposed by banks, and are more worried about the pressures exerted by individuals. At the time of writing, we cannot yet see the full effects of the financial crisis that besets Europe and the world; but the law relating to mortgages may be the subject of further development in the wake of that crisis.

BIBLIOGRAPHY

H. de Soto, *The mystery of capital: why capitalism triumphs in the West and fails everywhere else* (London, Black Swan, 2001).

B. Fehlberg, *Sexually transmitted debt* (Oxford, Oxford University Press, 1997).

J. Houghton and L. Livesey, 'Mortgage Conditions: Old Law for a New Century?' in E. Cooke (ed), *Modern Studies in Property Law I* (Oxford, Hart Publishing Ltd, 2001) 163.

M. Oldham, 'Mortgages' in L. Tee (ed.), *Land Law: Issues, debates, policy* (Cullompton, Willan, 2002) 169.

G. Watt, 'The Lie of the Land; Mortgage Law as Legal Fiction' in E. Cooke (ed.), *Modern Studies in Property Law IV* (Oxford, Hart Publishing Ltd, 2007) 73.

L. Whitehouse, 'A Longitudinal Analysis of the Mortgage Repossession Process 1995–2010: Stability, Regulation and Reform' in S. Bright (ed.), *Modern Studies in Property Law I* (Oxford, Hart Publishing Ltd, 2011) 151.

7

LEASES, LICENCES, AND COMMONHOLDS

Much of what we have discussed so far has been about sharing, and relationships, and balances of power and of interests. So is this chapter. It is concerned principally with leases, but also with licences and commonholds. The law relating to leases is largely the tale of the law's endeavours to control the power imbalance between landlord and tenant. Licences are often hard to distinguish from leases, but a reason for wanting to grant a licence rather than a lease is to avoid the legal controls imposed on the landlord-and-tenant relationship—a dodge that the courts have been keen to frustrate. Commonhold was created out of exasperation with the power imbalance and the wish to create a better ownership structure for interdependent properties.

This chapter looks first at the definition of a lease, and contrasts it with the licence. We then look at legal characteristics and content of leases in general, and at some important case law relating to the human rights implications of the ending of the landlord and tenant relationship. We look at statutory regimes designed to mitigate some of the problems of leasehold tenure; we see how security of tenure has disappeared; and we consider the development of leasehold enfranchisement and of commonhold.

LEASES

A lease is the grant of exclusive possession of land for a defined length of time. The payment of rent is not a necessary ingredient, although a lease is normally granted in exchange either for a 'market rent', representing the value of the property in income form, or for a low or nominal rent plus an initial capital sum (often called a 'premium'). A lease can be of whatever length the parties want; but whereas a freehold estate is of uncertain duration (no one knows when a life estate or a fee simple will come to an end), the length of a lease (known as its 'term') has to be defined at the outset. The grant of exclusive possession, and the defining of the term, are part of the contractual relationship which lies at the heart of the law of leases, or, as we also say, of the law of landlord and tenant.

The lease has its origins, like so much of land law, in medieval times. Alongside the feudal system, in which land was granted by the social superior to the inferior to be held in return for services, the use of land could also be managed by contract in return for the payment of money. The lessee, or tenant (now in the modern, landlord-and-tenant sense and not in the sense of a feudal tenant who held a freehold), did not originally have a property right in the land. He had simply a contract with his landlord, which would lose its force if the landlord sold the land. The arrangement was seen as purely commercial.

In time this changed. The lease was given increasing protection by the courts, and so it came to be regarded as a property right; like a freehold estate it came to confer ownership-type rights including the power to alienate and to exclude others. Initially it was merely personal property, so that—in contrast to real property—the remedy for dispossession was money rather than the land itself. This too changed. The lease came to be described as 'chattels real', that is, as a hybrid between real and personal property—and the distinction was very important when it came to inheritance rules, which were different for real and personal property. This distinction, too, has passed.

Leases are regarded as real property. They are a form of ownership in that most lessees (or tenants—the terms are interchangeable) can say that their leasehold land is *theirs*; a lease is tenure, because it is a way of holding land, and it is an estate, because the lease determines how long the land is held for. As we have already seen, the lease is now one of the only two legal estates in land permitted after the 1925 legislation; section 1 of the Law of Property Act 1925 defines these as the 'fee simple absolute in possession', and the 'term of years absolute', normally known as a lease. It will be recalled that leases will be legal, rather than equitable, if the requirements for the creation of a legal estate are met; the requirements are discussed further below.

Let us put this into an everyday context: an estate agent's window will often advertise properties by reference to their tenure, labelling them leasehold or freehold. For reasons already indicated, and to be discussed, flats will normally be leasehold. Belinda and Ben are looking for their first home; they spend a while deciding between a freehold terraced house and a lease-hold flat. Both cost £120,000. Eventually they decide upon the flat. They find, on looking at the details, that it is held on a 125-year lease, granted in 2005 to Simon, who is now selling it. When they buy it, they take on Simon's contractual relationship to the landlord, including the obligation to pay rent and service charges; equally, they become the joint holders of a leasehold estate, derived from the landlord's freehold. The rent will be nominal, perhaps £25 per year, as the lease was granted to Simon in exchange for a premium (that is, a price not far off what he would have paid for a freehold), which is why he is selling it now for a capital sum. When Ben and Belinda buy, Simon's name is removed from the register of title for the lease, and the names of Belinda and Ben are substituted. The lease will end in 2115, 125 years after its commencement. Between now and then, Belinda and Ben can live in the flat, sell it, mortgage it, dispose of it by will—just as they could have done the freehold house. One important difference is that although the lease represents a major investment for the tenant, it will depreciate rapidly, as a capital asset, towards the end of its term. This would not be a problem if the term had been 999 years.

The habit of regarding leases as tenure grew up long after the statute Quia Emptores in 1290. It will be recalled that this statute prevented the maintenance of the feudal system by forbidding any further feudal grants; but it did not and could not apply to leases, which were not at that stage a form of tenure. They are now, and there is nothing in the nature of a lease to prevent leaseholders granting leases—although a particular landlord and tenant may agree, in their lease, that this is not allowed. Thus Belinda and Ben could grant a sub-lease to Caroline, provided that the sub-lease is timed so as to end, at the latest, immediately before the expiry of their own lease. Caroline, too, can sub-let, unless her lease forbids this. She might choose to grant a periodic tenancy—a lease which lasts only a week, or a month (whatever is agreed) at a time. This well-known and convenient arrangement in practice goes on, week after week or month after month, until it is brought to an end by one party giving notice to the other that the tenancy is to terminate at the end of the next contractual period.

These then are the very basics of a description of leases. There is a little more to say about the definition of leases before we discuss some details.

LEASES DEFINED

A lease is defined as the grant of exclusive possession of land for a term. This definition is the product of a number of decisions of the highest courts in recent years.[1] The various exercises in definition tend to take the form of an alleged landlord arguing that *even though* this looks like a lease, it is not. The other party argues that certain conditions, which are met, are *sufficient* conditions for the existence of a lease even though other factors, previously thought to be essential, are absent, or still other factors, thought to be fatal to the existence of a lease, are present. Thus a grant of exclusive possession is a lease even if the parties have stated, in the written agreement between them, that it is not. It is a lease even if no rent is paid, and even if the landlord did not own the land. The issues have arisen, typically, where a tenant is claiming one of the add-on benefits that arise, not from the relationship of landlord and tenant itself, but from statutory protection given by the legislature to enhance the security or well-being of the tenant—in particular, security of tenure, or the landlord's statutory obligation to repair. Ironically, for most homes since 1989 security of tenure for tenants is a thing of the past, and the landlord's obligation to repair is very limited indeed unless the lease itself imposes this upon him. But these apparently peripheral issues have been used as a testing ground on which the definition of the lease has been worked out.

The most recent of these developments was the House of Lords decision in *Bruton v London and Quadrant Housing Trust*.[2]

---

[1] *Street v Mountford* [1985] 2 All ER 289; *Ashburn Anstalt v Arnold* [1989] 1 Ch 1; *Bruton v London Quadrant Housing Trust* [1999] 3 WLR 150.

[2] [1999] 3 WLR 150.

A housing association had been allowed to use a block of flats, owned by the local authority, as temporary accommodation for homeless people pending redevelopment of the block. Homeless people were, in turn, given permission to live there. Permission to occupy land is known as a 'licence'; a licence may be given freely, as when you invite a friend into your house, or it may be contractual. I have permission, derived from my contract of employment, to work in an office at the University of Reading. Mr Bruton was granted a licence to live in one of the flats. Redevelopment was postponed, and he lived there for some years. Eventually, he claimed that the housing association was obliged to repair the flat, pursuant to the obligation laid upon landlords by the Landlord and Tenant Act 1985. For that argument to work, the association had to be a landlord and he a tenant, and the issue went all the way to the House of Lords.

The Lords' answer was something of a surprise. We had grown so used to regarding leases as tenure and estate that we were rather shocked to be told that neither characteristic was part of the definition of the lease. A landlord who has an estate in land will, if he grants exclusive possession for a term, have granted a lease which is itself an estate; and *that* tenant can, again, grant an estate to a sub-tenant. But a licensee, like the housing association in *Bruton*, can grant a lease. Such a lease will not itself be a property right, and it will have no effect on anyone other than the landlord - because someone who does not have a property right cannot grant one. To be proprietary, a lease must be derived from—scooped out of—the grantor's property.

Hence the careful phrasing of the paragraphs describing leases, above. We have indeed 'come to regard' leases as estate and 'got into the habit' of seeing them as tenure. And usually they are. It is very rare that someone who does not himself have a lease or a freehold will grant a lease, except by accident or, even more rarely, fraudulently. *Bruton* re-states the lease's contractual origins and asserts that, although a lease is usually proprietary, it does not have to be. The privileges of a tenant (in this case, getting repairs done) are available to all who have been granted exclusive possession of land, even where the grant is purely a personal one, enabling the tenant to shut the door on the landlord but not on, say, the true owner of the land (the local authority, in *Bruton*). The local authority's reaction to the House of Lords decision was to remove the housing trust from its land, so as to enable it then to remove the *Bruton* tenants. In the ensuing litigation, the courts have stressed the tenants' non-proprietary status. Arguments that they have any rights in the land, or any security vis-à-vis the freeholder, have been firmly rejected.[3]

Leasehold law is thus a law of sufficient conditions. The grant of exclusive possession for a term is sufficient to constitute a lease; such a grant, made by a landowner, is sufficient to create a proprietary lease; compliance, in addition, with the formalities required for the creation of a legal lease (if any; as we have seen, there are none for short leases) is sufficient to create a legal lease. What the parties actually *want* to do is irrelevant. This is intentional. Few areas of land law have been so thoroughly regulated by the courts and by Parliament. To enter into a landlord-and-tenant relationship is to take on a large number of involuntary obligations and restrictions, and of course this characteristic has meant that people—especially landlords—have tried to define or stipulate their way out. It is very tempting to try to create a relationship that gives them the advantages of being landlord and tenant, without actually being such. The courts have been determined that this should not work. They have been concerned about the inequality of bargaining power between landlord and tenant. The fact that a landlord does not want to grant a lease will mean that he labels the deal a 'licence', regardless of what the prospective occupier wants. Accordingly, the courts have worked on the principle that the reality should be determined by conditions that are independent of the parties' expressed intentions.

The wisdom of this is greater in some contexts than in others. Given a political decision to have security of tenure for residential tenancies, it was obviously important for the courts to operate an anti-avoidance regime, and the courts' policy must be judged alongside the political decision. The issue is in fact nearly dead for residential tenancies, except for those in the public sector. The

---

[3] *Kay and others v London Borough of Lambeth, Leeds City Council v Price and others* [2006] UKHL 10. As to the security of public sector tenancies, see pp 200 ff.

decision in *Bruton*, by contrast, is worrying. It was not driven by precedent; it runs counter to centuries of development that regarded the lease as a property right. Before that decision, a lease was defined as *an estate in land generated by* the grant of exclusive possession for a term—even if, on most occasions, we forgot to say the italicized words. *Bruton* affects very few situations but, where it does, the decision may be disastrous for those whom the licence agreement was intended to help. There is a world of difference between a landlord trying to avoid giving his tenant security of tenure, and a housing association trying to help as many people as possible. The precedent for the decision is unclear (the more orthodox account of leases given in the Court of Appeal decision in *Bruton* is much more attractive). The knock-on effect may be that more people sleep on the street.

Bruton affects only a tiny minority of leases. For the rest of this chapter we consider the normal paradigm where leases are proprietary, being both contract and estate. Yet another preliminary to the detail of leases is the contrast with licences, with which leases can so easily be confounded.

LEASES CONTRASTED
WITH LICENCES

A licence is a permission to be on someone else's land. The friend who pops in for coffee has a 'gratuitous licence', given for free. More usual is the contractual licence, such as you grant to the man who comes in to lay the carpet, or (perhaps) to the student who rents a room and shares your kitchen. The contractual licence is usually given in exchange for payment, as in the case of a hotel room booking, or is part of a larger deal (as with the carpet man, or between me and my employer who provides an office). Least frequently encountered is the idea of a 'licence coupled with an interest'. A right to fish on someone's land, for example, is a property right in that land, and carries with it a permission to enter the land to do the fishing.

A gratuitous licence can be withdrawn at any time; you can ask your coffee friend to leave now. If a contractual licence is withdrawn there may be a breach of contract—as when my employer ceases to provide an office, or the theatre manager does not recognize your ticket and let you in. The remedies for breach of contract are damages and, occasionally, an injunction—that is, an order to the landowner to let the licensee enter. Despite this, and despite confusion in a line of cases during the twentieth century, a licence is not a property right. It is a personal right, corresponding only to a personal obligation of the landowner. It cannot normally be transferred (that is not invariable; consider theatre tickets) and it will not bind a purchaser of the land. If the theatre management sells the theatre before the performance for which you have a ticket, your right to sit in a particular seat next Thursday need not be honoured by the new owner of the land, but you can claim damages from the theatre management. Similarly, if Reading University sells its land tomorrow, the new landowner will not be obliged to let me continue to use 'my' office. Very occasionally—and the law on this is complex and not properly worked out—a licence will be enforced against a purchaser on the basis that he has undertaken an obligation to honour the licence, and therefore holds the land upon a constructive trust to that extent.[4] And a licence may be continued because the landowner is estopped from withdrawing it, because he has made assurances which the licensee has relied upon; this is part of the law relating to informal acquisition of land, since the continuance of a licence is one of the possible responses to estoppel.[5] But in normal cases, a licence is just a personal permission.

The difficulty arises with contractual licences and their closeness to leases. Look again at the student, Fred, who rents a room in a family house. He pays rent; he has a key to the house, but not to his room; but the homeowner does not enter his room. He has the shared use of the kitchen and bathroom. Is this a licence, or is it a lease: exclusive possession for a term? A term is easily derived from the intervals at which rent is payable, and so the issue boils down to one of exclusive possession. If Fred has it, he is a tenant. If not, he is a licensee, and this type of licensee is known as a 'lodger'.

The traditional lodger is easy to identify. He is like Fred, with the additional feature that the owner of the house provides clean linen, cleans the room for him, and makes him one or more

---

[4] *Ashburn Anstalt v Arnold* [1989] 1 Ch 1; see Chapter 3, p 54.
[5] See Chapter 4, p 96.

meals each day. The owner needs access in order to provide these services, and so Fred does not have exclusive possession. But the lodger is rather old-fashioned and actually quite unusual these days. Fred cleans his own room, does his own laundry, and makes his own meals. His agreement with the owner is headed 'licence agreement', and gives the owner the right to enter the room, but the only time the owner goes in is when he is decorating and needs access to paint the window frame. Is Fred a tenant or a licensee? The owner does not actually want to grant him a lease but, as we have seen, intention is irrelevant and Fred may in fact be a tenant of his room. No amount of clever drafting in the agreement changes this, because the courts look at the reality of the parties' behaviour.

Even more difficult is multiple occupancy, where a house or flat is rented by more than one person. Do they collectively have exclusive possession of the house and a joint tenancy, or are they each licensees, bound to share the house with whoever the owner puts in it? There is no fixed formula for determining this, but consider two contrasting cases. One is the house purchased as a 'buy to let' investment in a university town, with four bedrooms let out to a group of students. They are a floating population; when one leaves, the other three have no choice about who comes in to occupy the spare room (although they may decide among themselves who is to take over the vacated room before a new occupant arrives). They have separate agreements, and are responsible for separate rental payments. Contrast the couple renting a flat. They arrive together, they sign separate 'licence agreements', and are each responsible for half the rent. They share a bedroom. Neither would have moved in without the other. The agreement gives the landlord the right to enter, and may state that he is entitled to move another person into the flat. But he does not do so. The couple are tenants, despite the documentation; the four students are licensees.[6]

Much of the heat has been taken out of this debate because of the disappearance of security of tenure, discussed below. Whether or not Fred is a tenant, the landlord can remove him

---

[6] cf *AG Securities v Vaughan; Antoniades v Villiers* [1990] 1 AC 417, HL.

when he needs to. A landlord would probably prefer to rent a house to a group of four students as joint tenants than to deal with each individually because if they are joint tenants then each is responsible for the whole of the rent, and the landlord need not take any action if one of them moves out. We are perhaps fortunate that a good crop of cases was decided before security of tenure became a non-issue.

There are just a few formal exceptions to the rule that exclusive possession for a term gives rise to a lease. They are: when the occupier is allowed to live in the property as an act of charity; when he is a service occupier, required to live in the house as part of his job; and when he is a purchaser who has contracted to buy the property and is allowed in, pending completion. These are cases where the courts actually give effect to the parties' intention.

Now we turn back to leases, and look at the characteristics common, in one way or another, to them all.

TYPES OF LEASE

Leases can be split up formally—by length, and manner of creation; or functionally—into commercial, residential, and agricultural, or alternatively into short residential, long residential, and commercial (including agricultural). A commercial lease is a world away from a tenancy of a house, and for some purposes it is better to use function as the basis of classification. However, there are both periodic and fixed-term leases in all use-types, and the penalties for uncertain duration are the same whatever the function of the property, and so on; and in this basic account we shall have more to say about these distinctions than about specifically functional ones. So the more traditional method of classification is more helpful in this context.

Perhaps the most fundamental distinction between types of lease is that between periodic and fixed term. A fixed-term lease lasts for one defined length of time, specified in the contract between landlord and tenant. In the absence of specific statutory intervention (and we shall see that the law of landlord and tenant is riddled with this) the lease comes to a halt when that one period expires. By contrast, a periodic lease—or tenancy, as this type of lease is usually called—is defined by reference to a relatively short period of time. There is no theoretical limit to the size of the period, but a week, a month, or a year is usually chosen. Payment of rent is specified by reference to the period: so much per week, per month etc. The duration of the tenancy operates by default: the tenancy carries on until one of the parties gives notice to the other, timed to expire at the end of a period. When the notice expires, the tenancy comes to an end. The length of notice needed may be defined contractually, but if there is no express agreement there are rules: a week for a weekly tenancy; a month for a monthly one; but six months for a yearly one. The most familiar instance of the periodic tenancy is probably domestic, where one pays rent for a house, a flat, or a room on a monthly basis, but business and agricultural tenancies may equally be periodic. The yearly tenancy has traditionally been most useful to farmers. An important qualification to the notice rules for periodic tenancies is that the Protection from Eviction Act 1977 requires that a minimum of four weeks' written notice be given to residential tenants.

It would be an oversimplification to say that a fixed-term lease is always granted, and assigned, for a capital sum and imposes a nominal rent, whereas a periodic tenancy imposes a rent—normally at a level known as the 'rack rent' or 'market rent' for that particular property. Certainly that is the case in general, and the distinction needs to be borne in mind if one is to understand how leases function financially; but a fixed-term lease for a few years might well impose a rent without a capital price.

Bear in mind what was said about the conditions for a lease: exclusive possession for a term. This means that whenever there is a periodic arrangement for the exclusive use of land (eg I have sole use of your factory, or your house, in return for a payment every month) then in the absence of special circumstances there is a periodic tenancy, whether the parties want it or not. That was the basis of the decision in *Bruton*, as we have seen.

Some other, less common types of lease are again defined by reference to time. A reversionary lease is one that gives the tenant possession of the property not at the point when it is granted, but at an agreed future date: for example, next

Monday. A reversionary lease which gives possession more than twenty-one years ahead is void: but there is nothing to stop you making a contract now to grant a lease in twenty-five years' time. This is an example—and we shall see others—of a rule which may have a purpose (in this case, to avoid land being tied up for generations so that it cannot be traded) but which is ill-formed and can easily be evaded. A lease for life is another form of forbidden lease: an attempt to grant a lease to someone for their lifetime is transformed, by statute,[7] into a ninety-year fixed-term lease, which can be brought to an end by notice after the death of the tenant. Another statutory transformation is effected in the case of perpetually renewable leases: such a lease is for a fixed term, but contains a clause obliging the landlord to grant a fresh one, on exactly the same terms, when it expires, if the tenant so requests. It is easy to see that such a lease is perpetually renewable, unless the clause contains the words 'on the same terms as this one *but excluding this option*' or similar. The penalty for granting a perpetually renewable lease is that it is transformed into a 2000-year lease.[8] Such a lease, being a single fixed term but on the same terms as the initial one, will probably not contain an adequate rent review clause (ie a clause enabling the rent to be raised in line with inflation) and is therefore disastrous for the landlord. The aim is to impose a deterrent to prevent such arrangements, because of the fear that they make the land commercially sterile. But if the parties really want a lease that continues forever at the tenant's option (why?), they need simply grant a 999-year term with generous 'break clauses', that is, provisions enabling the tenant to serve notice to bring the lease to an early end.

A tenancy at sufferance is what happens when a landlord has given notice to bring a periodic tenancy to an end, the notice has expired, and the tenant has not left yet. Such a tenant is really a trespasser and can be removed, by force if necessary—though the only safe way (legally and physically) to remove a tenant by force is to obtain a court order, which can be enforced by the

---

[7] Law of Property Act 1925, s 149(6).
[8] Law of Property Act 1922, s 145; one of the few bits of this Act that actually worked and remain in force.

court's bailiffs. A tenant who 'holds over', as we say, after the expiry of a lease with the landlord's permission has a 'tenancy at will'; this is a very strange entity that arises when someone occupies land as a tenant on the basis that either party may determine the arrangement at any time. It is not at all clear how this squares with the requirement of certainty of term, or how it is to be distinguished, in practice, from a licence. It is unlikely that the concept would survive sustained analysis if it were to prove crucial in a case before the higher courts.

THE NEED FOR CERTAINTY
OF TERM

As we have already seen, running through the rules about types of leases is a worry about timing—the idea that a lease must not go on forever. Put more precisely, leases must be for a certain term. Leases granted in the early 1940s 'for the duration of the war' were void, but because they were such sensible arrangements they were specially validated by the Validation of Wartime Leases Act 1944. An agreement in a periodic tenancy that one party cannot ever give notice is void. A lease expressed to continue until the occurrence of an event which may never happen is void.

Since the war there have a been a number of cases that have appeared to compromise the certainty rule, and in *Prudential Assurance Co Ltd v London Residuary Body*[9] the House of Lords reasserted it. The London local authority granted Prudential a lease of a strip of pavement, back in the 1930s, to last until the land was required by the authority for road widening. In due course, the local authority became the GLC, and later, when the GLC was abolished, it became clear that the road widening was not going to happen. The landlord was now the London Residuary Body. The rent, set up in the expectation of a very short term, was now hopelessly inadequate even for such a narrow strip of commercial property in central London. The landlord therefore claimed that the lease was void because it was for an

---

[9] [1992] 2 AC 386, HL.

uncertain term, and succeeded. The outcome was that the land was indeed still let to Prudential, but on a periodic tenancy: Prudential still had exclusive possession of it and was paying an annual rent, so the necessary conditions for a lease were present. But the periodic tenancy was terminable by notice and, presumably, after the litigation the matter was resolved by a threat in the form 'pay more rent or we give you notice to quit'.

From what has been said so far it will be seen that it is therefore very easy to let out a piece of land until you happen to want it for road widening, residential development, a go-karting track, or whatever. Grant a 3000-year lease, include sensible rent-review provisions, and add a clause that states that if the landlord requires the land for [whatever it was] he may terminate the lease on giving, say, six months' notice. The lease would provide for the correct form of notice and would also, presumably, provide for some way of verifying that the land-lord's requirement was genuine: for example, the production of a grant of planning permission.

Moreover, it is very difficult to persuade oneself that a peri-odic tenancy complies with the certainty rule. As a matter of fact, no-one knows when a periodic tenancy is going to end. The arguments that it consists of a series of fixed terms tacked together, or that it is one single fixed term, which expands by the space of one period every time a period comes to an end without notice being given, are just word-games. So what is the point of the certainty rule given that it is child's play to evade it, and that periodic tenancies breach it in fact if not in form? It cannot be justified as a prevention of injustice, since it is indis-criminate in its benefits: the landlord was saved from an uneco-nomic deal in *Prudential*, but the tenant would have benefited if the lease had contained an upwards-only rent review clause (such clauses have been very common, and are extremely nasty to a tenant in times of recession).

The requirement seems to be linked with a philosophical debate about the nature of a lease. Is it mostly an estate in land, with some contractual features; or is it mostly a contract, with some of the attributes of an estate in land? Academic discussion of *Prudential* at the time of the decision was surpris-ingly passionate, and seems to have been linked closely with the various writers' conceptions of the nature of a lease. *Bruton* has taken much of the steam out of that debate, confirming the essentially contractual nature of the deal. That being the case, the certainty rule seems all the more arbitrary and pointless.

The Supreme Court in *Berrisford v Mexfield Housing Co-operative Ltd*[10] confirmed the certainty rule, while echoing the many concerns expressed over the years about its unsatisfactory nature and calling for its reform. The lease in question was uncertain because it purported to be a monthly tenancy but the landlord did not have the right to serve notice to quit. The case added one more twist to the story: where the tenant of an uncertain term is an individual, ancient common law rules convert it into a lease for the life of the tenant, on the basis that that is what the parties are supposed to have intended (whether or not in fact they did so intend); and that in turn is converted, by section 149(6) of the Law of Property Act 1925, into a 90-year term. It is therefore a valid fixed term lease; 'curiouser and curiouser', as Lady Hale put it.[11]

CREATION AND REGISTRATION OF LEASES

The practical requirements for the creation of leases follow from what has been said already about the requirements for the creation of legal and equitable interests, and for contracts to create or transfer interests in land. If a lease is basically a contract then at a minimum it must comply with the requirements for land contracts in section 2 of the Law of Property (Miscellaneous Provisions) Act 1989: all the terms expressly agreed (contrast those implied by law) must be written down, documentation must be signed, etc. All leases, whether or not they are estates in land and whether or not they are recognized at law rather than merely in equity, must comply with this rule. But the rule contains an exception: leases for a term of three years or less, and granted for a market rent, need not be made in writing. They can simply be oral. Within the

---

[10] [2011] UKSC 52.

[11] *Berrisford v Mexfield Housing Association Ltd* [2011] UKSC 52 at [93]; Lady Hale is of course quoting *Alice in Wonderland*.

exception are leases for fixed terms of anything from one
minute to exactly three years, and all periodic tenancies
(provided the period is three years or less; and in fact in
practice the maximum period is one year).

A contract for exclusive possession for a term is therefore a
lease, and if it is granted by a person with an estate in land then
the lease will itself be an estate in land. But if it is to be a *legal*
estate then further requirements must be met. If it is for a term of
more than three years it must be granted by deed; and if it is for
more than seven years it must be registered (whether or not the
landlord's estate is registered).[12] Otherwise it remains merely
equitable. Once registered, a lease has its own title number and
its own individual register, so that where both landlord and
tenant have a registered title, there will be two registered titles
for one piece of land, and if there are sub-leases there may be
more than two. Leases for seven years or less are not registrable,
but are nonetheless legal estates in land. Leases for three years or
less need not be created by deed, nor even in writing, but, again,
are nonetheless legal estates if a market rent is being charged.[13]
Until the Land Registration Act 2002 the registration requirement was for leases of more than 21 years, so the new limit
represents a significant reduction.

As well as being estates in land, leases are rights that burden
the landlord's title. What makes leases enforceable against a
purchaser of the landlord's estate? This, again, takes us back to
what has been said earlier. In most cases today, the landlord's
title will be registered, and in that event the enforceability of the
lease will depend upon section 27 of the Land Registration Act
2002. It will bind purchasers from the landlord if it is registered,
or if it is an overriding interest. Where a lease is registered with
its own title (because it is for a term of more than seven years, or
because it falls within one of the categories of shorter leases that

---

[12] See Chapter 4, p 79. A few leases for a term shorter than seven years are
also registrable, including most reversionary leases: Land Registration Act 2002,
s 4(b), (d)–(f).

[13] It is therefore quite unusual to find an equitable periodic tenancy if a
market rent is being paid; but one would arise if the landlord himself had only an
equitable estate in the land.

have to be registered nevertheless),[14] it will also be registered as a burden on the landlord's title, as a result of cross-checking within the Land Registry and whether or not the parties have requested this. If it is not registered, either because it is an equitable lease or because it is too short to be registered, it will bind the landlord if it is an overriding interest. Most unregistered leases will be overriding interests: legal leases for seven years or less are an independent category of overriding interests, and others will often be overriding interests by virtue of actual occupation. Where the landlord's title is unregistered (whether a lease or a fee simple), anyone buying it will take it subject to any legal lease the landlord has already granted. If he has granted an equitable lease, a purchaser will be bound by it if it has been registered under the Land Charges Act 1972, as this is one of the rights that requires registration.[15]

The picture of enforceability is thus complex, but can be worked out steadily from principles. The point of the rules is to ensure that purchasers are not caught out by unexpected leases; but of course what makes them enforceable is not the fact that the purchaser knows about them, but the fact that they appear on the register or are overriding interests.

LEASEHOLD COVENANTS

The content of the lease

A lease is a collection of obligations generated by contractual promises, known as 'covenants', made by the landlord and tenant in the lease. These are undertaken by both landlord and tenant, and are crucial to the functioning of the leasehold relationship. Some are express, being written in the lease itself, and the more the professional involvement in the grant of the lease, the more express covenants there will be. Some are implied, which means that statute or case law have declared that they are among the contractual obligations set up by the lease even though neither party intended this; and these may be very important in correcting an imbalance of power. Some

---

[14] See n 12.   [15] See Chapter 4, p 55.

implied covenants are common to all leases, some only to particular types.

Thus all leases are deemed to contain covenants by the landlord to allow the tenant 'quiet enjoyment' of the property (nothing to do with noise levels or pleasure) and 'not to derogate from his grant', which means that the landlord must enable the tenant to retain possession of the land without harassment from the landlord or from his other tenants. A tenant covenants to pay the rent imposed by the lease, if any, to pay any taxes on the property, and not to deny his landlord's title, for example by paying rent to someone else. These covenants, as their terminology implies, are ancient. Further covenants may be implied in particular leases on the contractual principle of necessity: thus leases of flats in a block have been held to contain a covenant by the landlord to give access to the stairs.

Residential leases of seven years or less contain a covenant by the landlord, implied by statute, to carry out certain repairs.[16] These are carefully defined, being: to keep the structure and exterior of the property in repair; to keep in working order the installations for the supply of gas, water, electricity, and sanitation; and to keep in working order the space heating and water heating. It is easy to see how important this is in short residential leases. A tenant in such cases is very unlikely to have a capital investment in the property (the vast majority of these leases will be at the very short end of the category, being periodic tenancies) and really should not have to pay for items such as structural repair and the installation of central heating. But without the statutory implied covenant, there is nothing to stop the landlord imposing this obligation if he has the bargaining power. When a lease falls outside the scope of the statutory covenants, the only arrangements for repair will be those made expressly. They are vital to almost every lease, but may be non-existent or inadequate. They need to be particularly complex in a shared building: a block of flats or offices. Sometimes a landlord sets up a management company to take over the landlord's obligations; where there is a group of residential flats there is a statutory right

---

[16] Landlord and Tenant Act 1985, s 11.

considerably better than the open-ended liability in pre-1996 leases. There is no automatic release for landlords from their contractual obligations, but the Act enables the landlord to apply to the tenant for that release. The statute does not prevent the parties to a lease from agreeing a more generous rule. A clause that states that the original landlord or tenant's obligations will cease when either assigns his estate is valid, because the statute is intended to provide an additional escape route from liability, and not to prevent the parties from agreeing their own, whether for the tenant's benefit or for the landlord's.[23]

TERMINATION OF LEASES

At first sight there can be little to say here. Periodic tenancies end when notice is given, fixed-term leases expire at the end of their term. But there are qualifications to this simple picture, all arising from the basis of the lease in the landlord-and-tenant relationship.

First, a fixed-term lease may make its own contractual provision for early termination by the inclusion of a 'break clause', enabling one or both parties to give notice and bring the lease to an end. Usually there is some stipulation of the time when this is allowed: perhaps after a defined period or on the occurrence of a specified event. We noticed, at p 184, the usefulness of this as a way of controlling the length of a lease without falling foul of the rule about certainty of term. Second, a lease may be forfeited by the landlord for breach of covenant (ie breach of an obligation in the lease) on the tenant's part; we shall have more to say about this shortly. A further contractual feature is that a lease may be frustrated. This will occur very rarely when something happens to destroy the whole basis of the letting; for example, destruction of the premises by fire or landslide.[24] This is a relatively recent development and is an assertion of the contractual rather than the proprietary nature of the lease. So is the other 'discovery' that a landlord's breach of covenant may be so fundamental as to amount to a repudiatory breach so that

---

[23] *London Diocesan Fund v Avonridge Property Company Ltd* [2005] UKHL 70.

[24] *National Carriers Ltd v Panalpina (Northern) Ltd* [1981] AC 675, HL.

the tenant is justified in leaving the land and ceasing to pay rent.[25] Neither of these developments has unleashed a flood of cases, and they seem more to be a reaction to individual fact patterns rather than any radical new thinking.

One very counterintuitive rule is that a periodic tenancy held by joint tenants can be brought to an end by notice given by one tenant alone.[26] This means that one can render the other homeless. It feels odd because both tenants' signatures would be required, for example, to assign the tenancy, or to mortgage or assign a lease. It is justified by the theory that a periodic tenancy goes on from one period to another because the tenant has chosen not to give notice. Not giving notice is regarded as a positive act, in which both tenants must participate. If one of the two gives notice, it is clear that the pair do not choose to continue the tenancy and it must end. The same rule does not apply to the exercise of a break clause, by notice, to make an early end to a fixed-term lease, because *that* type of notice is indeed a positive act in which both must participate.

A final qualification to the rules on termination relates to security of tenure. As has already been indicated,[27] there are instances where the law requires the lease to continue, if the tenant wants it to do so, despite the giving of notice or the ending of the term. Of the host of legal interventions in the landlord and tenant relationship, this is the most drastic. It is, however, very much a creature of politics and economics. A couple of decades ago a significant proportion of leases were subject to security of tenure, including many residential tenancies and almost all commercial and agricultural leases; but since then most of the statutory structure has been dismantled and security is very much a minority phenomenon. Security of tenure is discussed further below.

What of the argument that the termination of a lease, or for that matter of a licence, is a violation of an occupier's human rights because it takes away one of his possessions, and interferes with his home and his private life, contrary to Article 8 of the

[25] *Hussein v Mehlman* [1992] EGLR 87.
[26] *Hammersmith and Fulham LBC v Monk* [1992] 1 AC 478.
[27] Chapter 2, p 25.

European Convention on Human Rights and to Article 1 of its First Protocol?

In principle, there is no violation of human rights. The relevant provisions of the Convention were intended to protect individuals against arbitrary interference with their possessions and their homes, in the aftermath of war in Europe. The courts have held firmly to the view that where proceedings are taken to remove someone from land in which he does not have any property or other right, that is an interference in the public interest. It is done in accordance with the law and for the protection of the rights and freedoms of others.[28] Where a lease has been ended, in accordance with its own terms and with those of any legislation extending it, human rights legislation does not give the tenant any additional rights. The only small dent made by human rights considerations in this armour of legal certainty belongs in the context of secure public sector tenancies, which is discussed below.

STATUTORY REGIMES FOR THE PROTECTION OF THE TENANT'S HOME AND INVESTMENT

The idea of power imbalance has been a theme of this chapter. Perhaps the ultimate imbalance in leasehold law is that the tenant, in paying rent, or in buying a lease in return for a premium, is investing in property which ultimately—in the long or the very short term—belongs to the landlord. In return the property is the tenant's for a while, perhaps for many years, or perhaps for a few years or a few weeks. There are a number of points of view as to whether or not this is fair, and points of view in this context tend to be political. Whatever one's views, it is easy to see the hardship for the residential tenant whose total payments of rent, over most of an adult lifetime, amount to the value of the freehold; or the business tenant who takes a ten-year lease of a shop (because that is the longest the landlord would grant him), builds up the business, and then has to walk away after ten years; or for Belinda and Ben who bought a

---

[28] Reference is made to the wording of the relevant provisions of the Convention; see Chapter 1, p 11.

125-year lease, right at the beginning of this chapter, for something close to the price of the freehold of a similar house, and find that 60 years later it is unsellable, because unmortgageable, because the end of the lease is in sight.

The law has found ways to protect the tenant's investment in the leasehold property. For most of the twentieth century this took the form of security of tenure, turning a short-term use right into a long one. Recent politics have frowned upon this because of its adverse effect on the landlord's investment. More recently, the tenant's right to buy, in public sector housing, and the right to leasehold enfranchisement in the private sector, constitute new ways of protecting—perhaps rescuing—the tenant by giving him a capital asset.

SECURITY OF TENURE

Most people have heard the expression 'sitting tenant'. It signifies a tenant who cannot be got rid of, so that his landlord is not able to sell the property with vacant possession. In legal terms, such a tenant has security of tenure, and for much of the twentieth century he may have been residential, agricultural, or commercial.

Security of tenure for residential tenants in the private sector was generated by the Rent Acts, which operated on lettings of houses below a certain rateable value, but where the rent was above two-thirds of the rateable value. Thus long leases granted for a premium were excluded, as was the upper end of the market, and the Acts bit primarily on periodic tenancies of relatively low value. They restricted, stringently, the circumstances in which the landlord could remove the tenant. The landlord's notice would indeed terminate the contractual tenancy, but transformed the tenant into a 'statutory tenant' with a personal (not proprietary) right to remain there. If he paid his rent and observed all the tenant's covenants he might stay there for his lifetime. The legislation even allowed members of his family living with him to take over the statutory tenancy after his death. Similar protections in the Housing Act 1985 operate to protect public sector tenants—in particular, those renting council houses. The Rent Acts applied only to tenancies and not to licences, and were therefore the source of the litigation that thrashed out the sufficient conditions for the existence of a lease. The other role of the Rent Acts was control of rents. The idea was to restrict rents for certain properties—limited by rateable value—at a level below what could be obtained on the open market. Rent control remains today for the remaining Rent Act tenants (see further below), but in a much diluted form that is scarcely a disadvantage to the landlord.

Security for business tenants—again, licensees were excluded—derives from the Landlord and Tenant Act 1954. It took a rather different form: it prevented the ending of a business tenancy except in accordance with the terms of the 1954 Act. So whether the tenancy was periodic or fixed-term, it would not come to an end in the normal way, by expiry or by the giving of notice; it could be ended if the tenant so desired, or by the tenant's application for a new tenancy, or by the landlord's giving notice and establishing one of the grounds for possession set out in the Act. These grounds included breach of the tenant's obligations, and a limited range of possibilities for the landlord to recover possession of the land in order to redevelop it or to occupy it himself. The Act sets out a minefield of procedural requirements for the various notices. It enables the court to determine the provisions of a new tenancy, if either of the parties so requests. These will depend to a considerable extent on those of the old one, but the maximum term is fourteen years. There was provision to have a lease excluded from security, subject to the approval of the court, but the Act provided no criteria for the court's approval or otherwise of exclusion. Thus whether or not the lease was excluded from security came to depend largely upon the bargaining power of the parties.

Meanwhile quietly in the background successive Agricultural Holdings Acts gave security of tenure to agricultural tenants and licensees, converting most of them to yearly tenancies, requiring at least a year's notice to quit, and ensuring that they could not be ended against the tenant's will except on the basis of one of the grounds specified in the Act.

Today, security of tenure has largely been dismantled. Residential security went first. It made investment in property to let extremely unattractive, and was of course inimical to Thatcherite politics. The Housing Act 1989 enabled landlords to choose whether to grant an assured tenancy, which gave the tenant security, or an assured shorthold tenancy, which gave the landlord full rights to terminate the lease on notice after the expiry of a short initial fixed term (usually six months). Following the Housing Act 1996, residential tenancies are assured shorthold tenancies in the absence of specific provision to the contrary, and it is hard to think why a landlord would voluntarily adopt the secure regime. Thus residential security is no more, in the private sector, for tenancies granted from 1989 onwards. Its death was virtually unnoticed by the Press and seems to have attracted no protests.

Existing secure tenants have not lost their rights in this sequence of reforms: it is just that there will be no new secure tenants in the private sector. There are, of course, Rent Act tenants still; they and their successors will be around for another generation yet. They have been a godsend for family law and human rights. Out of litigation to decide who was a 'member of the tenant's family' and who has been 'living with [the tenant] as his or her husband or wife' have come decisions as to the nature of the family and the value of partnerships, and the recognition that a same-sex partner, unable to marry the deceased, is nevertheless to receive the same succession rights as the tenant's spouse. The draftsmen of the Rent Acts did more good than they could have dreamed of.

Business and agricultural security took rather longer to die. The Agricultural Tenancies Act 1995 designates all agricultural tenancies granted thereafter as 'Farm Business Tenancies', without security of tenure. For other business tenancies, a regulation made in 2003 enables landlord and tenant to contract out of security for leases granted after that date, provided the landlord has met the requirement to give a notice to the tenant explaining the security he is foregoing. Thus unless a tenant has exceptional bargaining power, business security is no more.

The one context where security of tenure is alive and well is that of public sector residential tenancies, that is, those where the landlord is a local authority or other public sector landlord. Such tenancies are regulated by the Housing Act 1985, and do give security. It is possible, nevertheless, for such a landlord to grant a very short-term 'introductory tenancy' in order to assess whether or not a tenant should be retained. The difference is obvious; the whole point of the provision of housing by such landlords is the provision of housing, and not the making of an investment or the receipt of income. It has been suggested that this is what marks out public ownership of land from private ownership: the right, or the absence of it, to act in a self-seeking way and the obligation, or the absence of it, to act in the public interest.

And so we come to the impact of human rights on housing law. This was first felt in a decision of the European Court of Human Rights, *Connors v United Kingdom*.[29] Here a local authority evicted gypsies who had lived as licensees on a site for 14 years, in summary proceedings. The law gave the gypsies no security and no defence. The European Court found that the gypsies' Article 8 rights had been infringed. It was swayed by their special status and needs as a minority, as well as by the fact that had the gypsies been camping on a private site they would have had some limited security.[30] But even so, no proprietary rights were being conferred. The decision focused on the lack of procedural safeguards for the gypsies. The direct result was the amendment of the Caravan Sites Act 1968 to enable the court to adjourn possession proceedings in such cases for up to twelve months, so ensuring that in appropriate cases the gypsies would have time to make arrangements for a move.

A more far-reaching effect of the gypsy saga was the House of Lords' examination of the potential effect of human rights upon possession proceedings in *Kay and others v London Borough of Lambeth, Leeds City Council v Price and others*.[31] Their Lordships accepted that it cannot be the case that the enforcement of a right to possession in accordance with domestic property law will never be an interference with someone's home, or will *always* be justified under Article 8(2) of the Convention. However, by a majority they held that a human rights defence to possession proceedings can *only* be mounted on the basis that the legislation concerned is incompatible with the Convention. There could be no defence purely on the basis that the occupier's own circumstances make this exercise of the owner's

[29] Application No 66746/01 (2004).
[30] Under the Mobile Homes Act 1983.
[31] [2006] UKHL 10.

rights a breach of the occupier's human rights.[32] Their Lordships made clear their view that the various legal regimes under which possession proceedings might be taken (depending upon the type of lease or licence involved) would be human rights compliant. Many involve consideration by the court of the individual's behaviour or circumstances. Even where the claimant has an unqualified right to possession, the legislation will have undergone scrutiny by Parliament with a view to the public interest and in the light of the need to protect the rights and freedoms of the various parties involved. A landowner's right to recover his own property is important. In the case of a public authority landlord, a powerful consideration will be the needs of others for housing, in a context where there is not enough local authority housing or land to go round.

This was a restrictive interpretation of the Strasbourg Court's decision in *Connors*. The decision meant that human rights could only be raised in the form of a challenge to legislation, so that unless the court could interpret the provision concerned in a way that was compatible with the Convention, the outcome on the human rights point would be a transfer of the case to the High Court and a declaration that the legislation was incompatible with the Convention. This would not affect the issue in the individual case—and so there would be very little incentive for the individual to plead Article 8 in answer to possession proceedings. The decision was to a considerable extent motivated by the perceived need to prevent the wholesale complication of simple county court possession proceedings by the involvement of human rights considerations, as well as by the view that the European Convention does not force a local authority to house or accommodate someone who would not otherwise be entitled to such assistance.

The law as enunciated by the House of Lords in *Kay v Lambeth* did not stand for long. The Strasbourg Court in a series of decisions made clear its view that it is not permissible for an order for

---

[32] The decision in *McPhail v Persons Unknown* [1973] Ch 447 is thus upheld, and that in *Harrow LBC v Qazi* [2003] UKHL 43, [2004] 1 AC 983 modified slightly, by the concession that legislation might be subject to challenge, but not overruled.

possession of property to be made in favour of a public authority without the occupier having the opportunity to put to the court his personal circumstances in order to enable a decision to be taken about proportionality. And in *Kay v United Kingdom*[33] the European Court of Human Rights held that the Article 8 rights of the tenant in *Kay v Lambeth* had been violated because there had been no opportunity in that case for a decision about proportionality.

The implications of this were examined by the Supreme Court in *Manchester City Council v Pinnock*.[34] To understand the background of the case we have to observe that a secure tenancy under the Housing Act 1985 (that is, a public sector tenancy where the landlord is a local authority) cannot be brought to an end without a breach of one of the tenant's obligations or some other consideration—set out in the statute—which will indeed involve consideration of the particular circumstances of the case. However, the Anti-Social Behaviour Act 2003 introduced new provisions giving the court power to make a 'demotion order'. Mr Pinnock held a 'demoted tenancy'. This meant that he had already been found by a court to be in breach of its terms, and now held his home on the basis that, for one year from the making of the order, the local authority could bring the tenancy to an end at any point without further consideration of the tenant's merits or difficulties. The court's only role was to check that the proper procedure had been followed. If the tenant survived that year's precarious occupation, he reverted to his standing as a secure tenant.

The Supreme Court made it clear that in cases where there has been no demotion order a consideration of the proportionality of the possession order will take place as a matter of course, because there will be an assessment of all the circumstances as a part of the establishment of grounds for possession. But it accepted that an order for possession of a demoted tenancy without scrutiny of the circumstances—which the statute appeared to authorize—would be an unlawful interference with the tenant's right to respect for his home. The court must therefore have the opportunity to hear the tenant's

---

[33] Application No 37341/06 (21 September 2010).
[34] [2010] UKSC 45.

representations on the merits and proportionality of the order. That said, success for the tenant would be rare, because the circumstances would already have been examined when the demotion order was made. The Supreme Court duly heard argument on behalf of Mr Pinnock and concluded that the making of the possession order was a proportionate step taken in the public interest.

This is not a major legal development. It is expressly limited so as to apply only to public sector tenancies. It imposes a check on proceedings by ensuring that important factors relating to the tenant cannot be ignored at the point of possession. But it makes no real change to the local authority's ability to recover possession of its housing stock or to control the behaviour of its tenants; nor does it make any change in the nature of property rights, held by landlords or by tenants. It highlights the fact that we have the right to respect for the home, not a right to a home.

THE RIGHT TO BUY AND LEASEHOLD ENFRANCHISEMENT

The Housing Act 1980 introduced the 'right to buy', that is, the right for public sector tenants to compel their landlord to sell their house to them, at a discount determined by the number of years the tenant has been paying rent. The motivation behind this legislation is complex. It arises to some extent from the feeling that it is unfair for someone to pay rent without getting a capital return, but also from the very political view that it is in some senses 'better' to own than to rent.

The right applies only to periodic tenants and, of course, only to public sector tenants. Private landlords can be subjected to a similar form of expropriation, but only in the case of long leases. The Leasehold Reform Act 1967 gave to tenants holding leases of houses of over twenty-one years, which they occupy as their homes, the right to 'enfranchise', that is, to covert their leasehold tenure to freehold tenure (to 'enfranchise' is to 'make free') by buying the property from the landlord. The 1967 Act is of no assistance to tenants of flats, who cannot become freeholders because of the impossibility of enforcing vital covenants. The Leasehold Reform, Housing and Urban Development Act 1993 tackled this by giving tenants of flats, acting together, a right of collective enfranchisement by acquiring the freehold of the block. If they do so they can grant themselves leases so long as their expiry is not an issue. They can then, together as owners of the freehold, take over the management or, rather, adopt the usual structure of delegating this to a management company. The Act also allows individual tenants to purchase a new lease of their own flat—relevant where a majority of tenants cannot be found to enfranchise collectively. The system has been further reformed by the Commonhold and Leasehold Reform Act 2002, which removed the residence qualification from the right to enfranchise, and also enabled collective enfranchisement by 50 per cent of qualifying tenants.

The price for enfranchisement is subject to two different regimes. Tenants of low value houses under the 1967 Act are able to pay a very low price, supposed to be the site value without the building. Others—tenants of higher value houses, and tenants of flats—pay a higher price, including (unless the lease has more than 80 years to run) one half of the property's 'marriage value', that is, the additional price payable on the open market by *this* tenant because he lives there and is the only one capable of merging the lease with the freehold. This results in something near to a market price, and represents a less Draconian deal for landlords.

Leasehold enfranchisement—the private sector version of the right to buy—has been subjected to challenge on the basis of human rights; and the European Court of Human Rights ruled, in the case of *James v United Kingdom*,[35] that enfranchisement legislation did not contravene Article 1 of the First Protocol 1 to the European Convention, because its goal was to remove social injustice. Injustice is a notoriously moveable concept, but at the root of the enfranchisement legislation, in its private law context, is the idea that one should not be paid twice for something. A landlord who receives a premium for a long lease should not be allowed at the end of that lease to regain possession and do it again. The right to buy is the public law parallel, and here the motivation is much more benevolent: it is not merely that

[35] (1968) 8 ECHR 123.

a landlord should not be paid unfairly but rather that a public sector landlord should be actively facilitating home ownership by the tenant, giving a discount on capital price as a response to rent paid.

COMMONHOLD

Commonhold is a response to the same problems that enfranchisement addresses; and it solves the problems that beset enfranchisement in the case of flats. It is a form of freehold ownership for interdependent properties, where leasehold is objectionable both because of the wasting nature of the lease as an asset, and because of the potential for oppression, in the form of poor management, by landlords. Conventional freehold ownership is impossible in such cases because it is imperative to have enforceable positive obligations between owners. Commonhold is not restricted to flats, but is available to any group of properties: houses on an estate; business units, whether divided horizontally or vertically; or a pair of maisonettes.

Commonhold was created by the Commonhold and Leasehold Reform Act 2002. It consists of, first, a number of unit holders (two or more) and, second, a commonhold association. The latter is a limited company, of which all the unit holders are members. Title to the whole of the land involved must be registered. Unit holders hold their own unit, and the association holds the common parts of the property (staircases, roofs, car parks, etc—the parts that would be retained by the landlord of a block of leasehold flats). The obligations of all are regulated by the commonhold community statement—registered along with the property holdings—which sets out a 'local law' for the group. Some of its contents are prescribed by statute, including the repairing and maintenance obligations. Others are variable by the association, including rules about the use of the property and the rights of holders to grant leases. As to the latter, there are severe restrictions by statute. The theory of commonhold is that it should be a system of self-regulation by occupiers, and therefore unit holders may not grant leases of more than seven years, nor may they grant a lease in return for a premium. There may be further restrictions in a particular commonhold association.

Obligations, negative and positive, run with the unit, and enforcement of covenants is not a difficulty. Unit holders will pay a maintenance charge to the commonhold association to pay for the upkeep and management of the common parts.

This apparently simple and obvious arrangement has a great many parallels in the law of apartment ownership worldwide, and there has been a corresponding industry in comparative academic analysis. The key to comparison, however, has to be the fact that in this jurisdiction the leasehold structure has been the norm, whereas in other jurisdictions this may not be an option. The introduction of commonhold had to be done in a form that was at least as attractive to developers, and to potential mortgagees, as leasehold, and the devising of such a form proved controversial and time-consuming. What we have now has not, so far, been a success; at the time of writing, only 17 commonhold schemes have been registered at the Land Registry. Commonhold has not proved attractive to developers or their lawyers; there is anecdotal evidence that it is regarded as too complicated. Moreover, existing leasehold developments can only convert to commonhold if all the holders of leases over twenty-one years consent; but unanimity may be hard to organize and, without it, conversion cannot happen.

CONCLUSIONS AND REFORM

It is perhaps possible to work one's way through an account of leasehold tenure and conclude that nobody wants it, particularly in the light of the development of rights to enfranchise, and of commonhold. But that would not be a safe conclusion. There is certainly a dislike of inequality, and of unequal sharing, which makes the landlord-and-tenant relationship problematic. And the purchase of a lease as a capital asset is almost a contradiction, since it is a wasting asset. But given our society's use of land as capital, leasehold tenure is an ideal structure both for landlords wanting to maximize the potential of their land, and for tenants who do not have and cannot raise capital. Business and agriculture cannot function without the ability to rent land or office space, and almost a third of the population of England and Wales rent their homes.

So leasehold tenure is essential to our economy and as a way of housing people. Given that, perhaps the greatest problem with it is the multitude of ways in which successive governments have tried to help with its admitted disadvantages. Successive security regimes in the public and private sector have left us with far too many different types of tenancy—protected, statutory, assured, assured shorthold, introductory, and so on, with a number of different succession regimes, and with parallel regimes coexisting because legislation has not been retrospective. The law is widely recognized to be a mess. The Law Commission has made recommendations for a new scheme for those who rent their homes; its plan would involve sweeping away the current multitude of types of tenancy and replacing it with two forms: public sector and private sector, the former carrying security of tenure, the latter not, but both involving some succession rights. Most radically, the terms of these two types of occupation agreement would be prescribed by statute, rather than left to individual negotiation (and therefore to individual bargaining power) as at present. It would be possible to vary prescribed terms, but only in favour of the occupier. The Commission's recommendations have, for the most part, been rejected by the government so far as the law of England is concerned, although the Welsh Assembly has made a more positive response. But for the moment there is no prospect at present of any large-scale reform and simplification of leasehold law, nor even of its unsatisfactory details, such as the rule about certainty of term.

BIBLIOGRAPHY

S. Bright, 'Uncertainty in lease: is it a vice?' (1993) 13 *Legal Studies* 38.

D. N. Clarke, *Commonhold, The New Law* (Bristol, Jordan Publishing Ltd, 2002).

A. Goymour, 'Private Property, Housing and Human Rights', in D Hoffman (ed), *The Impact of the Human Rights Act on Private Law* (Cambridge, Cambridge University Press, 2011) 249.

Law Commission *Renting Homes: The Final Report* (Law Com No 297) London, The Stationery Office, 2006).

N. Roberts, 'Two cheers for commonhold' (2002) 152 NLJ 338.

P. Routley, 'Tenancies and estoppel—after *Bruton v London and Quadrant Housing Trust*' [2000] 63 MLR 424.

J. Seitler and L. Crabb, *Leases, Covenants and Consents* (London, Sweet and Maxwell, 2009).

8

APPURTENANT RIGHTS

This chapter is mostly about appurtenant rights; that means rights that are held along with ownership rights. Three such rights are explored: easements, which are rights to do something on someone else's land, profits à prendre, which are rights to take something from someone else's land; and restrictive covenants, which are rights to prevent someone doing something on his own land.

An example of an easement is a right of way. A grazing agreement or a right to hunt may be a profit à prendre. And a transfer of part of A's land to B may impose upon B a restrictive covenant that he may not use the land for business purposes.

The chapter is *mostly* about appurtenant rights because, of those three types of right, a profit à prendre may be held by itself, without the holder also owning land in fee simple or leasehold. In that case the profit can be registered with an independent title; it can be bought and sold as a standalone right. Nevertheless, most profits are appurtenant to owned land. And really 'appurtenant rights' is the best we can do for a single term that describes all three rights. They can be referred to as non-ownership, non-security rights, which is true but clumsy; we sometimes call them third-party rights, which is a bit mysterious. Americans call them servitudes, but the Scots reserve that term for what we call easements. It might have been convenient to call them land obligations, but the Law Commission has used that term for a new interest in land which would, if the Commission's recommendations are accepted, replace restrictive covenants for the future.

Note that the covenants with which this chapter is concerned are often referred to roughly as freehold covenants; they are not covenants made between landlord and tenant and contained in leases, which follow very different rules and were discussed in Chapter 7. Note also that the three rights fall into two distinct categories. Easements and profits arise from a grant, made by a landowner, of a right over one's own land; and that right can be (and will be if the correct formalities are observed) a legal interest held by the grantee in the grantor's land. By contrast a covenant is a promise, given to another landowner, to do or not to do something on one's own land. The promisee (that is, the one to whom the promise is made) thereby has an equitable interest in the promisor's land, but the promise cannot give rise to a legal interest. This gives rise, as we shall see, to unwelcome complexity.

In June 2011 the Law Commission published its report, *Making land work: easements, covenants and profits à prendre.*[1] This was a major study that is likely to flavour discussion of these interests for some time to come, whether or not its conclusions are accepted by government. The title of the report reflects the fact that appurtenant rights are very often a way of ensuring that land is put to good use, and is a reminder of the interdependence of the separate plots of land that we own.

In this chapter we look at the law relating to easements, noting as we go along the reforms that the Law Commission has recommended in respect of each. No separate consideration is given to profits, which in general follow the same rules. We then look at restrictive covenants, and finally at the Commission's more radical proposals which would prevent the future creation of these hybrid property/contractual rights and instead make available a legal interest in land to support obligations both positive and negative.

EASEMENTS

What is an easement?

Easements are to some extent familiar already. We have mentioned the right of way as an obvious example of a non-ownership right over someone else's land, and we know that an easement is one of the few possible legal non-ownership rights.[2] An easement is usually a right to do something specific on

---

[1] Law Com No 327, 2011.
[2] Law of Property Act 1925, s 1.

another person's land, for example to walk across a path, or to drive down a roadway, to enter the land for a particular purpose such as repair of one's own property or access to pipes, to use storage space, or to park a car. The right might not involve personal presence: it might be the right to have one's drains or sewers run underneath a neighbour's garden. Most easements, and all those just described, are positive: they give a positive right to the owner of another piece of land to do something, directly or otherwise. A negative easement is a right to prevent the owner of the burdened land from doing something. So an easement of support, such as the right for my semi-detached house to lean against my neighbour's, prevents my neighbour from demolishing his building, and an easement of light prevents him from obstructing my window (but note that an easement of light must be a right for light to pass through a defined aperture; there can be no right to a lovely view).

Similar to easements are profits à prendre. A profit, as it is briefly called, is the right to take something from someone else's land, typically fish, sometimes other game or crops. Profits behave, technically, very similarly to easements in the way they are created and in their enforceability, and this chapter has very little to say specifically about them.

Any formal definition of an easement tends to start with the old case of *Re Ellenborough Park*,[3] in which the court worked out what sort of right *could* be an easement if correctly created. Strictly speaking the case was about the nature of a legal interest in land, rather than about easements specifically, but the right in question was an easement if it was anything. The case concerned the garden in the middle of a square of houses, which the residents in the square were able to use for recreation. Did they therefore have an easement over the garden? The court came up with four conditions for an easement. First, there must be a dominant and servient tenement. A tenement means a piece of land. The dominant one has the benefit of the easement, and the servient one is the object of the right. This is perhaps unexpected, because it means that it is not quite true to say

---

[3] [1956] Ch 131.

that my neighbour has a right of way over my back yard. Rather, *his land* has the benefit of a right of way, so that he and anyone who buys the land from him can walk across my yard. The right of way is a property right, but it is not separable from the ownership of my neighbour's land. Not all jurisdictions have this rule. In civil law countries an easement, or its equivalent, can be held 'in gross', that is, separately from the ownership of another piece of land. That is not possible for easements in England and Wales; but it *is* possible for profits à prendre. As we have seen, the benefit of an easement should be noted on the Land Register as part of the description of the property, ie in the property register of the dominant tenement. It should also appear on the 'Charges' section of the servient tenement, as a burden on that title. Easements thus have a debit and a credit entry, one on each of the two titles involved.

Second, the right must be one which 'accommodates the dominant tenement'. This links the easement more closely with neighbouring ownership, because it means that the easement must be a right which makes the dominant land a better property. Typical is the English terrace of houses, where there is no access from back garden to front without going through the house, which is inconvenient for someone wheeling a bicycle or a lawnmower. A terraced house is a better property if it comes with a right of access across the neighbours' back gardens to the end of the terrace.

Third, the two pieces of land must be in different ownership. If a servient owner buys the dominant tenement, in theory the easement is extinguished. This gives rise to some practical difficulties. The Land Registry does not automatically remove the note of the benefit and burden of the easement from the two titles, which means that the validity of the easement is still guaranteed—thus creating a mismatch between the common law and the law of registered land.

The Law Commission recommended no change to the first two *Ellenborough Park* rules. But it did recommend that where title to both the dominant and servient land is registered, the fact that both are in the same ownership should not prevent the existence of an easement. That would eliminate the mismatch just noted. It would also mean that where a large area of land is to be developed, easements could be created to benefit and burden the individual plots before they were transferred to purchasers, which would cut out a great deal of potential for error.

Turning to the fourth of the *Ellenborough Park* rules, finally and infuriatingly the Court of Appeal ruled that an easement must be 'capable of forming the subject matter of a grant'. It is unfortunately difficult to say that this means anything except that the right must be 'the sort of thing that can be an easement'. This fourth condition seems simply to leave the courts leeway to rule out something which does not feel like an easement. We can give it substance by pointing out examples of things which have been held *not* to be so capable. Anything that requires the servient owner to spend money, for example the right to draw on a hot water supply—although, anomalously, an obligation to maintain a fence may be expressed as the grant of a right to the neighbour, in which case it is an easement. If the obligation to fence is expressed as a promise to do so, it is a covenant—the behaviour of the right depends upon the wording used in its creation. Anything that amounts to taking exclusive possession of the servient land and preventing the servient owner from using it will amount to 'the wrong sort of thing'. This last one is tricky and has generated some inconsistent decisions about storage spaces and parking rights, and one of the Law Commission's recommendations clarifies the position in this context. Of course, if a particular right cannot be an easement, it can still be granted by one landowner to another; but it remains a contractual right, not an interest in land, so that it should not appear on the Land Register and cannot be alienated, nor be enforced against anyone other than an original party.

So the rules we have as to the nature of easements are rather complex, and not entirely logical. A few anomalies have been mentioned already. Another is the easement of support: the owner of land has a natural right to have his land—ie the earth itself—supported by his neighbour's, but not to have his buildings supported. Thus while he has bare land, his neighbour may not dig up against the boundary, but as soon as he builds on it, he effectively loses that right because there is nothing to prevent his neighbour digging so as to threaten the building, until it has stood for twenty years and acquired an easement of support by prescription (see further below).[4] This has been a difficulty in the law for a long time, but in recent years it seems that the neighbour who undermines a building will be liable in tort, and equally that the Party Walls Act 1996 will give neighbours a degree of protection from each other's activities. Another tricky area is rights of access to neighbouring land for the purpose of repairing one's own land, or for inspecting services. Some properties have it, by express grant when they were divided by a single owner; some have not. All benefit from the Access to Neighbouring Land Act 1992, which imposes a pragmatic solution to this common problem by setting up a system of notices, access, and compensation. Again, the law of easements has not been tidied up in order to take account of this development in the law.

Creation of easements

(1) Express creation

How do easements happen? The theory in all cases, and the reality in most, is that they are granted deliberately by one landowner to another. Usually easements are created when part of a landholding is sold; and they may be either granted to the buyer, or reserved for the seller. This is easy to imagine for a pair of houses, originally owned together. When one is sold off, the seller grants the buyer a right of way over his half of the shared driveway, and reserves for himself a right of way over his new neighbour's half. Occasionally an easement is granted as a separate deal, without a sale. In either case, because an easement is an interest in land, the grant must be in writing in accordance with section 54 of the Law of Property Act 1925. If an easement is to be legal it must be granted by deed (section 52) and registered against the servient owner's title (unless that title is unregistered). Easements that fall short of these requirements— for example, only created in writing, without a deed—will be equitable provided that they meet the requirements of section 2

---

[4] *Dalton v Angus* (1881) 6 App Cas 740.

of the Law of Property (Miscellaneous Provisions) Act 1989; so will any easement granted by someone who only has an equitable ownership right.

Creation by a written grant, usually followed by registration, is conceptually easy. More difficult is the fact that there are so many other ways in which easements can be created. They fall into two groups: creation by implication and creation by prescription.

(2) Creation by implication

We have met a number of contexts now where the law implies things: for example trusts of land or covenants in leases. When this happens the law is saying that the parties did something, even though they did not. Similarly, an easement is implied when the parties did not create one expressly but the law says that they have done so. An easement will be implied 'by necessity' when A buys part of B's land and then finds that he cannot get access to it because it is completely landlocked. This is going to be rare, and probably accompanied by an action in negligence against the conveyancer. It will not work if access is possible but difficult, for example if the land is bordered by a public road, but there is a natural barrier such as water or a cliff face in the way; the law is not generous about necessity. Another category of implication is 'by common intention', when it is clear that the parties must have intended there to be an easement when land was sold off. The example usually given is of the ground floor of a building, let for use as a restaurant. A leaseholder claimed that he had an easement enabling to him to fix a ventilation shaft to the upper part of the building so as to allow cooking smells to escape; because the owner of the building had leased the land specifically for this use, the court held that there was an easement arising from the intention they must both have had, that the requisite ventilation shaft be fixed to the wall, since without it the tenant would not have had health and safety clearance for the restaurant.[5] (This latter case is a useful example of the fact that a tenant may have an easement over his landlord's land or,

---

[5] *Wong v Beaumont Property Trust* [1965] 1 QB 173.

equally, over a neighbour's land.) As in most cases where the law implies something because of the parties' intentions, it is a complete fiction; the best that can be said is that the law is filling in what the parties *would* have intended if they had thought of this situation and sorted it out in good faith. But perhaps the owner of the building *did* think about it, and consciously did not want the ventilation shaft, and did not care that the tenant would not be able to operate his restaurant without it? After all, he remains liable for the rent. Implied intention, in these cases, is really a matter of what the parties *ought* to have intended, regardless of whether they did or not.

A further context for the implication of easements is where two areas of land have been owned together, but have to some extent functioned as two separate properties, whether just by being physically divided (two fields next to each other with a fence between) or in a more complex way, for example where one area has been in the possession of a licensee or tenant while one person remains freehold owner of both. In such situations it may *look as if* there are two 'tenements' and an easement, even though that is not possible because the land is in the same ownership. For example, a farmer always drives across his own, fenced, field to get to the main road; or a person running a shop (whether a tenant or a licensee) always uses the yard at the back to get to the service road; or a lodger hangs out his washing in the garden. Problems arise when part of the land is sold, where, before the sale, it looked as if it had the benefit of an easement, although it did not. Should it *actually* benefit from an easement when it passes into separate ownership? If the shop manager takes on a lease of the shop (a new lease on the expiry of an old one, perhaps, or a lease instead of an earlier licence) he might want to carry on using the landlord's yard for an extra means of access. Ideally he would negotiate for this and get it written into the lease. If he forgets, or did not persuade the landlord, will the law let him have the easement nevertheless?

The law does so, making use of a statutory provision that was not designed for this purpose. Section 62 of the Law of Property Act 1925 states, roughly, that certain words are written into conveyances by magic. 'Conveyances' means any deed creating or transferring a legal estate in land: a transfer of registered land, a lease, a mortgage. The magic spell says that the deed 'shall be deemed to include and shall . . . operate to convey, with the land all buildings, erections, fixtures, . . . fences, liberties, privileges, easements, rights and advantages whatsoever appertaining or reputed to appertain to the land . . . or, at the time of the conveyance, demised, occupied, or enjoyed with . . . the land'. Section 62 derives from a nineteenth-century statute. The intention was, first, to ensure that with the land is conveyed the house that stands on it, and the garden shed—hardly necessary, given the statutory definition of land,[6] but the draftsmen were careful souls. In addition, it ensured that if the land had the benefit of an easement, that benefit was transferred to the buyer, without the need for the conveyance to include a paragraph to say so. Also, where a buyer had, for example, been allowed access across the seller's other land during the period between contract and completion, the section was supposed to convert such informal permissions into easements for continued use after the sale. The latter was the most intrusive of the section's purposes, as this might not have been the seller's intention; but if it was not, he was of course free explicitly to exclude the operation of the section from the conveyance.

However, section 62 has been used by the courts to go two steps further. First, it operates where the two pieces of land, although in common ownership, are occupied by different people before the 'conveyance', as we have imagined with the shop manager or the lodger, and has some sort of permission to use the owner's other land. In that case, section 62 will write that permission into the conveyance. If it is the sort of thing that *can* be an easement (ie we have to look at the *Ellenborough Park* requirements first) then by dint of being (magically) set out in a deed it will become a legal easement. The shop manager's lease will have an easement over the landlord's yard; if the lodger formalizes his situation by taking a lease of part of the house, he will acquire with it an easement to hang washing. So will anyone to whom he transfers the lease.

[6] Chapter 1, p 7.

Second, section 62 operates where both plots of land are owned and occupied by the same person, but there is visible evidence of something that looks like an easement, benefiting one plot by the use of the other. The obvious example is a path; moorings for boats might be another. The name for this is a 'quasi-easement'—something that would be an easement if the two plots had different owners. When the owner sells what we can call the 'quasi-dominant' land, section 62 will write into the conveyance the 'liberty' or 'advantage' of being able to walk across, or moor boats on, the other plot of land, or whatever, and if it is a right that *can* be an easement (as can those just mentioned), it will be. This trick with quasi-easements can also be achieved using the authority of the case *Wheeldon v Burrows*[7] in the few fact-patterns where section 62 will not work (eg where the 'quasi-dominant' plot is sold or leased, but the interest granted is equitable rather than legal).

The Law Commission has recommended the amendment of section 62 so that it could no longer be used to create easements or to transform permissions into easements. It also recommends reform of the law relating to the implication of easements; for the future, easements would be implied where they are 'necessary for the reasonable use' of the land transferred—intended as a generous test of reasonable necessity, to be assessed by reference to a list of statutory factors that would enable the courts to replicate the rational and useful instances of implication under the current law including those cases where the operation of section 62 is helpful rather than arbitrary.

(3) Creation by prescription

Prescription is the acquisition of easements by process of time. Roughly, if you walk across your neighbour's back yard once a day, for twenty years, without her permission, you will have a legal easement. This may sound very like the process of acquisition of title to land by adverse possession (discussed in Chapter 9), and the two processes do indeed look alike, but to the lawyer they are conceptually distinct.

---

[7] (1878) 12 Ch D 31.

Adverse possession works on the basis that possession of land gives title (ie a species of ownership); the longer possession goes on, the stronger it gets; once the limitation period expires the person dispossessed loses his title. At that point the squatter's is the best title there is and so he is the owner of the land. By contrast, for the whole of the twenty years during which you walk across your neighbour's backyard, you have no right whatsoever. But at the end of twenty years the law says 'you have been doing that so long that your neighbour must have granted you an easement. Therefore you have an easement'. This is, at least, overt fiction rather than any pretence about intention.

In order for prescription to take place, the right claimed must be the sort of right that can be an easement—back to *Re Ellenborough Park*[8] and its four conditions. It must be claimed by a fee simple owner against a fee simple owner. Moreover, it must be exercised openly, peacefully, and without permission. Walking across the neighbour's yard only at night, or breaking his gate in order to do so, will not do, and a claim will fail if he writes to give you his permission, or if he nods, smiles, and says 'go ahead' whenever he sees you. All these are inconsistent with the fiction that he has at some point actually granted an easement, and so will defeat a claim to prescription; the point used to be expressed by the pleasantly rhythmical Latin phrase *nec vi, nec clam, nec precario*. A further requirement is that the two parties involved—the person claiming the right and the owner whose land is to be the servient tenement—must both hold the land in fee simple. If the claimant is a leaseholder, he can only make the claim on behalf of his landlord (assuming the latter is the freeholder).

If these requirements are met, there are three procedures that can be used to make the claim, known as 'common law prescription', 'lost modern grant', and claims under the Prescription Act 1832.

Common law prescription works only if the claimed right has been exercised 'since time immemorial'; and the courts regard themselves as capable of remembering everything that has

---

[8] Note 3.

happened since Richard I came to the throne in 1189. Why this method is not officially obsolete is a mystery. If it is clear that the behaviour concerned cannot have gone on for so long - for example, if it involves a building of more recent construction - the claim will fail. Perhaps the only real use of common law prescription now is to explain why the courts invented the doctrine of 'lost modern grant'. This is the idea that, since 1189 is a bit distant now, if the claimant proves that he has been exercising the 'right' for twenty years, the court will find— despite clear evidence to the contrary—that he was granted the right claimed, at some point in the past, and must have lost it—there was a grant, at some point in modern times, but it has been lost. Evidence that no grant was made will make no difference at all, but evidence that the supposed grantor did not have capacity to grant it (eg because he was a child) will prevent a claim from succeeding.

In order to regularize this mess of fictions, the Prescription Act 1832 was enacted. It is even more badly drafted than the Land Registration Act 1925, and is not a pleasant read. It sets up three methods of claiming an easement: a claim for an easement of light; a claim for any other easement where the claimant has never been given permission; and a claim, again not for light, where the claimant was given oral (ie spoken not written) permission. The periods of use necessary for these three situations are respectively twenty years; twenty years; and forty years. There is provision in the Act for the use, on which the claimant relies, to have been interrupted for anything up to one year, so it may be that the claimant has only been using the pathway for nineteen years. What he must prove, however, is that his use of the pathway (or whatever), whether interrupted or not, has taken place in the *last* twenty years before he brings his action—whether that action is litigation in the courts or an application to the Land Registry for the entry of an easement. If he is relying on something more distant—something he used to do, and did for twenty years, but the neighbour has kept him out for the past two years—he will have to use 'lost modern grant'.

There are other details that distinguish the three methods and that need not detain us here. The point to be aware of is that there is indeed a lot of detail, and that much of the art of claiming easements by prescription lies in working out which method will fit the facts. This is a time-waster; and it bears little relationship to the purposes behind prescription. One of these is to confirm behaviour and arrangements that have suited people for long periods and which they have come to value and rely upon. Another is to ensure that land benefits from rights that are really essential for its use, whether for access or for the provision of services. Another is to avoid litigation over stale claims, where memories and evidence have faded: this is, as we shall see, one of the traditional justifications for the law of adverse possession.

Should prescription be retained as a method of acquiring easements, particularly where title is registered and guaranteed? Prescription has always been open to the criticism that it penalizes altruism or neighbourliness. Someone who has made no objection to next-door's car being parked on his bit of waste land perhaps does not deserve to have his land subjected to a legal right for his neighbour to use the parking space. On the other hand, prescription has some useful functions: hidden easements, particularly for drainage and other services, are vital to land use, and prescription can fill in the necessary rights when they have not been formally granted—but only after twenty years have passed.

The Law Commission concluded that prescription requires some dramatic tidying, but not abolition. It recommended that the three current methods be swept away and a single statutory scheme be substituted, whose requirements would be simpler but rather more strict than those of the current law.[9]

BRINGING EASEMENTS TO AN END

The surest way to end an easement is for the dominant owner to execute a release—a deed that gives up the easement—in favour of the servient owner. Application can then be made to remove the easement from the dominant owner's register of title (and, of

---

[9] The Commission recommended that it should no longer be possible to create profits à prendre otherwise than expressly; so they would no longer be able to be implied, nor created by prescription.

course, until that application is made, the easement remains registered and guaranteed).

It is possible to prove that an easement has been abandoned, but that involves proving that the servient owner intended to abandon it, which is remarkably difficult. Where, for example, a passageway behind a row of terraced housing has been blocked off by one or more of the households that are allowed to use it, by fences or sheds or the like, it may eventually be concluded that the easement is not wanted. 'Eventually' may take a long time. Twenty years' use of a pathway may generate a right of way, but twenty years' non-use is not sufficient to get rid of it (although, as we have seen, one year's non-use of an easement that is not obvious to inspection will make it unenforceable against a purchaser of the servient land).

There is no mechanism for the court or any other body to put an end to an easement, however obsolete, useless (to the dominant owner), or troublesome (to the servient owner) it may be.

The Law Commission has made a number of recommendations about the ending of easements. One would make the establishment of abandonment just a little easier: the establishment of a presumption of abandonment where an easement has been unused for twenty years—this would only be a presumption and could, of course, be rebutted. Another would make the express release of an easement a registrable disposition—that is, one that would not take effect at law until registered. That would eliminate the potential for mismatch between registration and the common law rules. Finally, the Commission recommended an extension of the jurisdiction of the Lands Chamber of the Upper Tribunal (formerly the Lands Tribunal), so as to enable it to modify or discharge easements, created post-reform, where they were obsolete, or where their loss could be compensated in money and their continued existence impeded a reasonable use of the land in the public interest. As we shall see, the Lands Chamber can currently do this for restrictive covenants, and it would be immensely useful to extend that jurisdiction to easements. In particular, it would reduce the ability for easements to be used to create 'ransom' demands when they impede development; currently the dominant owner can simply name his price.

The potential for the use of easements to demand ransom prices is particularly acute in the case of easements of light, which are a trap and an expense for developers. The Law Commission's report did not examine rights to light specifically, but the Commission has now commenced a separate project on such rights, building on its general recommendations in the 2011 report.

Enforceability of easements

So: once an easement has been created, does it remain enforceable once the servient land is sold? A sells part of his land to B, but keeps and lives on the rest. The transfer to B gives B a right to walk over A's back yard. If A subsequently sells his land to C, must C continue to give access?

Assuming A's land is registered: ideally, the burden of the easement will appear on A's register, because A and B will have created the easement expressly and completed the disposition by registration. Registration guarantees both validity and enforceability; there is no doubt that the easement will bind C because we know that a purchaser is bound by everything that appears on the register, and by overriding interests. But implication and prescription will create legal easements which will not appear on the register until someone claims or otherwise discovers them. Occasionally, legal easements created before registration of title to the servient land are not registered, by an oversight. Nevertheless these unregistered legal easements will normally bind C, because legal easements are, in most cases, overriding interests.

It is unfortunate that we have to say 'in most cases'. Paragraph 3 of Schedule 3 to the Land Registration Act 2002 is drafted so as to give some protection to the purchaser from rights that he could not have discovered—even though overriding interests bind a purchaser because of their status as such, and *not* because he knows about it (this should sound familiar from what we have said about paras 1 and 2 of the Schedule).[10] It provides that legal easements are overriding interests *unless* three conditions

---

[10] See Chapter 3, pp 51–2.

are all fulfilled, namely: the easement was not obvious on reasonably careful inspection; the purchaser did not actually know about it; and the claimant cannot show that the easement has been used in the last year. This means that an unseen, but daily used, drainage easement will bind a purchaser. So will an easement to pass over someone else's property via a fire-escape, rarely if ever used but clearly visible. But a right of access of which there is no visible clue, and which is used once every couple of years, can be lost when the servient land is sold.[11]

Moreover, equitable easements that are not recorded on the register of the servient land's title will not bind a purchaser. Most equitable easements are equitable precisely because they have not been completed by registration; some, however, are equitable because the grantor (the owner of the servient land) has only an equitable estate in land. The only way to preserve such an easement in case of sale is to record it on the register of the servient land; as an equitable easement it is not a registrable estate and so its validity is not guaranteed by registration, but its priority is preserved by the register.[12]

Finally, if title to the servient land is not registered, the enforceability of easements depends on the old rules: legal easements bind all the world. Before 1925 equitable easements bound a purchaser if he had notice of them; but since then, equitable easements have been registrable under the Land Charges Acts,[13] and so will be void against a purchaser if unregistered.

COVENANTS IN FREEHOLD LAND

A covenant is a promise in a deed. When A sells part of his land to B, the transfer imposes on A the obligation to let B walk across the back yard, as we have seen. It also imposes on both

---

[11] This account is incomplete because it does not discuss the transitional provisions for easements which were overriding interests under the Land Registration Act 1925 but do not qualify under the 2002 Act. The reader is referred to the Act itself, and to conventional textbooks.

[12] See Chapter 3, p 50.

[13] See Chapter 3, p 55.

A and B the duty to use the land only for residential purposes and not to run a business on it. This and other stipulations are common in sales of part, because seller and buyer are going to become neighbours and so have an interest (in the non-technical sense!) in the way the other uses the land. They are standard when an estate of freehold houses is built, each of which is to be under an obligation to all the others not to use the property for a business, and suchlike.

But while the right of way is created by a grant, made in the transfer to B, the right to control the use of the other's property is created by a promise given in the transfer. The grant is an easement. The promise is a covenant. The grant creates a property right. The promise may or may not create a property right for the person to whom it is made. The rules about the enforceability of covenants are much more unpleasant than those relating to easements. Easements and covenants are different animals that look the same—both give rise to obligations between landowners—but their genetics and behaviour are different. We have to look a little further at the characteristics of covenants, and the rules for their enforceability, before we see if we can bring easements and covenants together so as to create one species.

Characteristics of freehold covenants

Two parties are needed to make a covenant: the one who makes the promise and the one to whom it is made, or the promisor and the promisee, or the covenantor and covenantee. One has the burden of the promise and one has the benefit.

Two distinctions need to be borne in mind. First, covenants are said to be either positive or restrictive. Positive covenants are promises to do something: to keep a fence in good condition, for example, or to contribute to the cost of maintaining a shared driveway. Negative, or restrictive covenants are promises not to do something: not to use the land for business purposes, not to keep animals on the land, not to build on it, etc. Whether a covenant is positive or restrictive depends on its substance, not its wording. A promise not to allow the fence to fall down is positive; a promise to use the land for residential purposes only is negative. Substance may be easier to see if we ask whether or not keeping the promise involves expenditure or effort; if it does, it is positive.

Second, a covenant may 'touch and concern the land', or it may be merely personal. We met this in the context of leasehold covenants where the same distinction is relevant. A covenant touches and concerns the land if it has an effect on the value of the land, or changes the way one occupies it. Restrictions on its use are obvious examples.

Covenants are created expressly; they do not arise by implication and cannot be generated by time alone. So the space devoted to methods of creating easements is not needed here. Armed with the distinctions just discussed, we can look at enforceability.

Enforceability of freehold covenants

Oliver sold part of his land to Percy, who promised to maintain the fence dividing the two plots, and not to use his new property for business purposes. One covenant is positive, the other is negative; both touch and concern the land. Percy now sells the land to Quentin (or perhaps leases it or mortgages it; Quentin needs simply to be a purchaser in one of the many possible forms). Can Oliver enforce those promises against Quentin and subsequent owners? If not, they are now valueless. If he can, they are in some sense property rights because they are enforceable beyond the original parties to them.

The situation is more complicated if Oliver, too, has sold his land, because then we have to ask whether his purchaser, Raffles, is able to enforce the promises, even though they were not made to him. So whenever action is needed to enforce covenants, and the people involved are not those who made or received the promises, we have to ask: has the benefit of the covenant passed to the person who now wants to enforce it? And has the burden passed to the person against whom action is being taken?

None of this is necessary in the case of leasehold covenants. The passing of the benefit of covenants in leases, from the original landlord to his successor, is well-established by ancient rules; and the passing of the burden is managed by the doctrine of privity of estate. The current landlord and the current tenant are always liable to each other for the covenants made by landlord and tenant in the lease. As we have seen, the problem with leasehold covenants was that *too many* people may in the end be liable, and rules have had to be devised for getting people off the hook. Nor is there any problem about the passing of the benefit and burden of easements. Easements are indisputably property rights. The benefit of an easement sticks to land, in accordance with section 62 of the Law of Property Act 1925; a more visible expression of this is the noting of the benefit of an easement on the proprietorship register for an individual title. The burden of an easement—the fact of being a servient tenement—passes to a purchaser of land only in accordance with section 27 of the Land Registration Act 2002, if the title is registered, and there is no difficulty here if the easement is on the register or is an overriding interest. But covenants between freeholders are, in origin, just contractual promises. And while the contract lawyers have ways of getting the benefit of contractual promises to pass to other people, this cannot be done with obligations to keep promises. Contractual promises are personal obligations.

Again, equity rides to the rescue. Decisions in the courts of equity in the nineteenth century transformed covenants into something substantial enough to cling to the land, so that in some circumstances, but not all, subsequent buyers of the land must keep these promises even though they did not make them. The covenant can be enforced, and the usual remedies—damages or an injunction—are available. But equity's capacity to rescue the covenant was limited, indeed chopped in half, by one factor: the covenant must be negative. Positive covenants—those which, however worded, involve a promise to do something rather than to refrain from doing something— do not stick to freehold land. If you promise to maintain the fence between your property and mine, and then sell your land, I cannot make my new neighbour keep your promise.

That paragraph hides a hornet's nest of detail. It is not intended here to expound the detail sufficiently to enable the reader to operate the rules, only to explain enough detail to demonstrate what is wrong. To that end, two preliminary points are made, and then enough of the nightmare to alarm, but not enough to induce despair.

The first preliminary point is about method. In any action to enforce a covenant between freeholders, it is worth looking at the two sides and asking: does the defendant actually carry the burden of the covenant? And does the claimant have the benefit of it? If the answer to either of those questions is 'no', then the action will not succeed. The second point is an easy one: anyone who is a party to the original covenant will carry the burden, or bear the benefit, unless there has been a further agreement assigning the benefit to someone else, or explicitly releasing the burden.

(1) Does the defendant have the burden?

Looking, then, at the covenants made to Oliver a few paragraphs ago: if they are to be enforced, we have to ask if the defendant has the burden of them. If the defendant is Percy, the answer is obviously 'yes'; and it remains 'yes' even if Percy has sold the land, although there are few examples of this happening. Because freehold covenants do not involve the payment of rent, the liability of the original covenantor has never been the massive problem that it became for leasehold covenants.

If the defendant is Quentin, or another later owner, the answer bifurcates.

If the covenant is positive, the answer is 'no'. The covenant to maintain the fence cannot be enforced against anyone other than Percy. We shall see later that there are some indirect methods of achieving enforcement in some cases; but in general the burden of positive covenants does not pass. This is why flats must be leasehold or commonhold, because their interdependence is such that the observance of positive covenants is essential, in particular ones to repair, or to pay a maintenance charge to cover the upkeep of the common parts of the building and land. There has been some debate as to whether or not section 79 of the Law of Property Act 1925 makes the burden of

positive covenants pass in any event; the answer appears to be
that although the section reads as if it does, it was not intended
to do so (only to widen the original covenantor's liability), and
does not do so.

If the covenant is negative, the answer may be 'yes', if certain
conditions are fulfilled. This is because the landmark case *Tulk v
Moxhay*[14] decided that, under these conditions, the courts of
equity would enforce the burden of covenants against successors
in title; and although what was said in *Tulk v Moxhay* seemed to
apply to both positive and negative covenants, later cases discovered or decided that only negative ones had been intended.
Tulk was about the green patch in the middle of Leicester
Square, and the court's decision has kept it green (we should
give thanks when we picnic on it or queue for the cinema).
Later cases also attempted a rationale: it is said that once the
right, say, to build on land has been taken away from it, the land
will be passed on to others, shorn of those rights. The right to
build just is not in the bundle. This does not make sense, because
it is only under certain conditions that equity allows the burden
to pass, and where those conditions are not met the right stays in
the bundle. It makes more sense to say that the courts are
reluctant to pass to a purchaser the burden of a covenant that
involves expense, such as maintaining a road. But this does not
worry anyone in leasehold land. The issue has been addressed by
the House of Lords relatively recently, in *Rhone v Stephens*[15] and,
although it is difficult to find any logical basis for the distinction,
it was held that it has to stand, because of the chaos that would
be caused if the law were changed now by the courts. Careful
legislation, with some transitional provisions, would be another
matter.

The actual conditions for enforceability are: that the covenant
must touch and concern the land; that the covenant was
imposed in order to benefit land held by the original covenantee
(promisee); that the burden of the covenant must have been
intended to run with the land of the original covenantor (and
section 78 of the Law of Property Act 1925 ensures that this is

---

[14] (1848) 2 Ph 744.   [15] [1994] 2 AC 310, HL.

the case unless it is clear from the sale by Oliver to Percy that this
was not the intention); and that the covenant must be recorded
as a burden on the defendant's land (or, if the latter is unregistered, as a charge under the Land Charges Acts). For pre-1926
restrictive covenants, the latter condition is expressed as a requirement that the purchaser has notice of the covenant. As to
the second of those conditions, it is interesting to note that it is
very much like the requirement of a dominant tenement for
easements. Restrictive covenants can only be property rights if
they benefit land, not just a person. Thus if Oliver sold *all* his
land to Percy, Quentin and other later owners could not be
forced to observe Percy's covenants.

(2) Does the claimant have the benefit?

The rules on enforceability thus cut out a great many covenants
once land has changed hands; none of the positive covenants can
be enforced directly against successors in title to the covenantor.
But if the action is taken against Percy, or against Quentin and
for the restrictive covenant only, we have to ask if the claimant
actually has the benefit of the covenant.

If the claimant is Oliver, the answer is 'yes', obviously. He can
sue on the covenant forever—although it is not clear that he
would be awarded a remedy if the land was no longer his,
because in that case he would not have sustained any loss as a
result of the breach of covenant. Moreover, section 56 of the
Law of Property Act 1925 widens the field a little, making it
possible for the transfer from Oliver to Percy to join in others,
perhaps neighbours, as parties to the deed and as covenantees, so
that they too can enforce the covenant. Section 56 is a little like
section 79, mentioned above: its wording is obscure, and it can
easily be read as if it does rather more than this. But it seems
reasonably well-established that it does not.

If the claimant is Raffles, or any later owner of Oliver's land,
then there are two sets of rules, evolved by the two sets of courts
and maintained as alternative routes to enforcement even after
the courts united. Each route consists of a set of requirements,
which can be summarized as follows.

For the benefit of a covenant to run to a successor in title at law:

- the covenant must touch and concern the land;
- the benefit of the covenant must have been intended by the original parties to run with the land (and so the drafting of the covenant by Percy to Oliver must demonstrate this intent);
- the original covenantee (Oliver) must have had a legal estate in land; and
- the current claimant must have the same legal estate as had Oliver.

And for the benefit to run in equity, again the covenant must touch and concern the land, and then one of three things must have happened:

- the transfer from Oliver to Percy must have annexed the benefit to the land (again, this is done by wording in the transfer from Oliver to Percy, and only certain forms of words will do the trick); or
- the benefit must have been expressly assigned by Oliver to Raffles (again, special words are needed, attaching the benefit to a person rather than to land); or
- the deal between Oliver and Percy must have been part of a 'building scheme'—not, that is, just any new development, but one conforming to conditions set out by the courts.[16]

A wealth of detail attaches to each of these conditions, and a multitude of cases. There has been extensive litigation and academic debate as to whether or not section 78 of the Law of Property Act 1925 does the job, for the legal rules, of determining (in the absence of contrary intention) that the benefit of the covenant was intended to run and, for the equitable rules, of annexing the benefit to the land. It seems reasonably well-established that it does both these jobs.

Given two sets of rules for the passing of the benefit, which does one choose? It is not entirely clear whether or not it

---

[16] In *Elliston v Reacher* [1908] 2 Ch 374.

matters; but it would seem that if one is enforcing a restrictive covenant against a defendant who is not the original covenantor, the equitable rules for the passing of the benefit should be chosen. So they should if the claimant is seeking a specifically equitable remedy, in particular an injunction to order the defendant to do or not to do something. The proviso must be added that there is always a risk attached, because equitable remedies are discretionary and may, in theory and occasionally in practice, be refused if the claimant's conduct has been less than honourable.

Enough has been said, missing out swathes of detail, to establish that the rules about the enforceability of freehold covenants are unacceptably complicated. There should not be two sets of rules, one at law and one in equity, for the passing of the benefit and burden. A single set of much simpler rules would be a great improvement. The rules as they stand are the subject of so much uncertainty that a change, to clearer law, could not be said to damage any vested interests.

(3) Other methods

There are other ways, direct and indirect, of ensuring that covenants can be enforced.

Sometimes, an obligation is linked to a benefit. You pay to maintain a private road, and you get to use the road. In *Halsall v Brizell*[17] it was decided that one who accepts a benefit must also accept a burden linked to it. This sounds like a good way to enforce positive covenants, but it does not go very far. Some covenants, such as fencing, are not linked with a corresponding benefit. And subsequent cases have refined the rule; the link must be a very close one, so that observing the positive obligation is actually a condition of receiving the benefit; moreover, it must be a benefit that the person concerned can choose whether or not to accept. A road which is the only access to a house, for example, will not be maintained by this method.

Another method, very indirect and unreliable, is the chain of indemnity. Take Percy, who has promised to maintain a fence,

---

[17] [1957] Ch 169.

and is liable on that covenant forever. So when Percy sells, he may require his buyer, Quentin, to promise—by a covenant in the transfer deed—that *he* will observe positive covenants and will indemnify Percy (ie compensate Percy for any damages he has to pay) if they are broken. The covenant may be repeated with each sale, from Raffles to Selina to Tipsy, so that a chain of indemnities is created. The hope is that it will therefore ensure performance by the current owner, at the end of the chain, who knows she will be sued by her predecessors if she fails. Unfortunately a chain of indemnities does not ensure performance of the covenant, as it becomes worthless when one person in the chain dies or becomes bankrupt.

Another method of ensuring that a positive obligation sticks to land is for Oliver to impose a rentcharge on Percy, rather than requiring a covenant from him. A rentcharge is a monetary payment attached to freehold land—an unusual property right, mentioned only briefly in our introductory account of legal interests.[18] It can take the form of a maintenance payment, for a shared road for example. If it is not paid, the freehold is forfeited. Legal rentcharges are registrable estates, and if protected by registration they will bind a purchaser on the usual principles. Such obligations are very little used, perhaps because purchasers are unwilling to accept an obligation where breach carries such a Draconian penalty.

Finally, if there is any difficulty with the running of the benefit of the covenant, it may be that in some circumstances the Contracts (Rights of Third Parties) Act 1999 may help, in enabling a claimant who was not actually a party to a contract to sue on it; but as yet there are no decisions on the effect of that Act in this context.

BRINGING COVENANTS TO AN END

Covenants, like easements, may be released expressly; in effect, the person who has the benefit of it says 'I don't want this any more'. This rarely happens.

---

[18] See Chapter 3, p 43.

Many covenants are now extremely old, having been imposed in the nineteenth century when the industrial revolution was the motivation for land being sold off, by the landed gentry for new housing. At the time, it was a valuable form of private planning control. Now, the covenants may be meaningless—a promise not to build a house worth less than £200 is obviously pointless now—or it may be entirely unclear whether anyone has retained enough of the covenantee's original land to be able to enforce the covenant, or that it would benefit such a person to do so. Accordingly, section 84 of the Law of Property Act 1925 gives the Lands Chamber of the Upper Tribunal the power to modify or to discharge a restrictive covenant when it has become obsolete in one of these ways, or if the person entitled to the benefit of the covenant consents. The Lands Chamber deals with a steady stream of such applications; many more cannot be made because the age of the covenant, and changes in the ownership and use of land nearby, mean that it may have become impossible to work out which land now has the benefit of the covenant.

REFORM?

Need for reform

So: what is wrong with land obligations as the law stands? So much is unsatisfactory that it is hard to know where to begin. We have seen in the earlier parts of this chapter that the Law Commission in its 2011 report addressed a number of the obvious problems associated with easements and profits, in particular the fact that there are too many ways of creating them and not enough clear law about bringing them to an end.

That much is really a matter of tweaking, without implications for the structure of this area of land law. But the problems relating to freehold covenants are more fundamental. While easements and profits are interests in land, capable of taking effect at law and being registered, restrictive covenants are contractual rights that have been made to behave like property rights by means of an awkward blend of case law and statute. To the layman it is wholly unclear why the right to prevent his neighbour from building a wall in front of his window should operate in a different way from the right to prevent his neighbour from running a business on his (the neighbour's) property. The fact that one right is an easement and the other is the benefit of a restrictive covenant is largely a historical accident.

Moreover, the contractual character of covenants makes them unsuitable for use as property rights. As contractual commitments, they bind the covenantor for life, even when he has parted with the burdened land. The benefit of a restrictive covenant can only ever be an equitable interest in land, and so is not a registrable interest. That means that there is no public record of who holds the benefit of a restrictive covenant, and so it can be difficult if not impossible to work out whom to contact if the burdened owner wants to get the covenant discharged. There are too many sets of rules for their enforceability, and too much uncertainty within those rules.

Alongside these technical problems is the big practical issue: should the burden of positive covenants run with land? There are strong views both that it should, and that it should not.

In favour of positive obligations is the inconvenience, under the current law, of managing simple practical issues such as the maintenance of a shared boundary or drive. Such an arrangement is not sufficiently complicated to warrant the use of a leasehold or commonhold structure; but liability to carry out work cannot, as things stand, be tied to ownership of either property without the use of inappropriate or inefficient legal devices. Options include relying upon a chain of indemnity covenants or using an estate rentcharge (an ancient device that can be used to enforce a positive obligation on pain of forfeiture of the property—which is both complex and inappropriate).

On the other hand, there is the fear that if positive obligations can be tied to land, the passage of time may make that obligation burdensome—for example, if the nature of the property or even the price of materials changes—so that the land becomes too expensive to own and therefore unmarketable. There are also concerns that capricious obligations may be imposed, for example, to paint the fences pink. Part of the answer to those concerns is to observe that the market will itself control the nature of obligations, and that we do not find silly positive covenants, any more than silly negative ones, in leasehold property. The rest of the answer is that in permitting positive obligations—as a number of common law jurisdictions have already chosen to do—the law must devise ways of controlling the range and nature of obligations permitted, either by setting up a closed list of permissible obligations or, more flexibly, by transferring to positive covenants the concept of 'touch and concern', already discussed in the context of restrictive covenants. If positive obligations have to touch and concern the dominant land, a range of inappropriate or unduly onerous obligations (for example, to do work that would benefit the dominant owner but not his land) become impossible.

So the concerns about positive obligations are real, but there are ways of dealing with them.

Against that background, how should the law develop?

The Law Commission's early work and the significance of commonhold

There have been several reports and recommendations for reform of this area of the law from the 1960s onwards. The most significant have been those of the Law Commission.

The Commission's first approach to the problem was contained in a Working Paper in 1971.[19] The proposal there was that easements, covenants, and profits à prendre be brought within a unified scheme, and that they be known as land obligations, of a number of different types. The scheme distinguished neighbour obligations, where only two properties were involved, and development obligations used for a number of properties. Only certain types of obligation, corresponding to positive easements and to profits à prendre, would be capable of being created other than expressly, for example, by prescription.

It was some time before the Commission produced a report to follow that Working Paper. The recommendations made in

---

[19] Law Commission Working Paper No 36, 'Transfer of Land: Appurtenant Rights'.

the 1984 report[20] focused, again, on a unified scheme, but involving only obligations—negative and positive, both for developments and as between neighbours—without seeking to bring easements and profits into a reformed scheme.

Those recommendations were not implemented. Instead, the government chose to develop and implement commonhold—that is, a scheme for interdependent properties enabling them to be held as freehold without the use of a lease, and therefore without the landlord/tenant relationship, as discussed in Chapter 7. This is the concept known in some other jurisdictions as strata title. Where it is successfully implemented it resolves what we might call the large-scale problem of positive obligations, namely the impossibility as things stand of developing flats and other physically interdependent properties without using leases. But it does not solve the small-scale problem: how to manage the imposition of liability for straightforward burdens as between freehold neighbours, where there is insufficient interdependence for leasehold or commonhold to be appropriate. So while the need for the Commission's development obligations was met, there is as yet no answer to the need for neighbour obligations.

THE LAW COMMISSION'S 2011 REPORT

After the implementation of its 2001 report on land registration, the Law Commission was able, within the next few years, to turn its attention to some of the problems that its land registration work had revealed in the law of easements as well as to revert to the still-unsolved problem of freehold covenants.

In addressing the latter the Commission did not seek to deal with the large-scale problem of truly interdependent properties. There was no intention to revisit commonhold. Instead it looked both at the existing problems with restrictive covenants and at the need for simple positive obligations to be enforceable between neighbours. Following consultation the Commission took the view that the objections to the introduction of positive

---

[20] *Transfer of Land: The Law of Positive and Restrictive Covenants*, Law Com No 127.

covenants could be met but that, in the light of concerns about the possibilities for over-burdening land, care must be taken about the way in which positive obligations were introduced. And it was felt to be important not to replicate the contractual character of existing restrictive covenants. Not only are the rules of enforceability far too complex, but a *contractual* positive obligation must bind the original covenantor forever; that is rarely a practical problem for restrictive covenants but would be disastrous for positive obligations. It would replicate, for freehold land, the problem that the Landord and Tenant (Covenants) Act 1995 had to resolve for leases.[21]

The Commission's solution was therefore to recommend the introduction of a new legal interest in land: the land obligation. It could take the form either of a negative obligation— corresponding to current restrictive covenants—or to an obligation to do something on the burdened land, or on a boundary structure between the benefited and burdened land, or to make a payment to the dominant owner for work that *he* in turn performed under a land obligation. And the benefit of the land obligation must touch and concern the benefited land.[22]

That means that the land obligation, as a legal interest within the meaning of section 1(2) of the Law of Property Act 1925, is also a registrable interest pursuant to section 2 of the Land Registration Act 2002. So where title to the benefited land is registered there is a public record of that benefit. The right is a property right and not a contractual right, and so the liability of the burdened owner who first created the right ceases when he parts with the land, and it would be impossible to create new covenants in the old style because the draft Bill provides that land obligations take effect as such even if drafted as covenants. The 'touch and concern' requirement places a check on the range of obligations that can be imposed, as does the requirement that any obligation to do work must be on the burdened

---

[21] See Chapter 7, p 192.

[22] A way of achieving this is seen in clause 1 of the Law of Property Bill annexed to the 2011 report; the drafting of the clause, and the Commission's explanation of its operation in the report at paras 6.7 and following, are worth studying.

land or a boundary; so an obligation to work for the dominant owner on his land would not meet the criteria.

Most importantly, the enforceability of land obligations would mirror, for the most part, the rules for the enforceability of any other interest in land—albeit with special provision to ensure that those with very short-term interests in the burdened land would not be bound by positive obligations. The draft bill also addresses the enforceability of land obligations where the benefited or burdened land is sub-divided after the creation of the obligation, and the incidence of the burden as between landlord and tenant when the burdened land is let. The tortuous old rules for the enforceability of restrictive covenants have to retain a place in the land lawyer's armoury, however, because they will have to remain relevant for existing restrictive covenants—which of course would remain unchanged following the introduction of land obligations for the future.

Finally, the Commission recommended a redrafting of section 84 of the Law of Property Act 1925 so as to extend the role of the Lands Chamber of the Upper Tribunal. We have already mentioned the recommendation that it be possible to apply for the discharge or modification of easements and profits; it would also, of course, have to be the forum for applications to bring positive obligations to an end.

It was noted above that *Re Ellenborough Park* was a decision about the nature of legal interests in land, not really about easements as such.[23] The Law Commission's land obligations meet the *Ellenborough Park* criteria, subject to the same modifications as it recommended for easements.[24] The outcome of reform would be that easements, covenants, and appurtenant profits would stand side by side as interests in land with the same basic characteristics, although sufficiently different in detail to justify their being regarded as distinct interests rather than all bring grouped together under one label;[25] in particular, land

---

[23] At p 213.

[24] See p 213.

[25] Which is what the first edition of this book tried to do in suggesting the label 'land obligations' to refer to all three.

obligations would not be able to be created by prescription or implication, and have modified rules for enforceability.

So a brave new world is recommended. Whether it might become reality is not known at the time of writing this edition; the government's response should be known in the summer of 2012.

BIBLIOGRAPHY

E. Cooke, 'To re-state or not to re-state? Old wine, new wineskins, old covenants, new ideas' [2009] 73 *The Conveyancer* 448.

S. French, 'Towards a modern law of servitudes: re-weaving the ancient strands' [1982] 55 *Southern California Law Review* 1261.

N. Gravells, 'Enforcement of Positive Covenants Affecting Freehold Land' (1994) 110 *Law Quarterly Review* 346.

Law Commission *Transfer of Land: The Law of Positive and Restrictive Covenants* (Law Com No 127) (London, HMSO, 1984).

Law Commission *Making land work: easements, covenants and profits à prendre* (Law Com No327) (London, The Stationery Office, 2011).

P. O'Connor, 'Careful what you wish for: positive freehold covenants' [2011] 75 *The Conveyancer* 191.

9

WHATEVER HAPPENED TO RELATIVITY OF TITLE?

This chapter concerns relativity of title, which used to be an important concept, but is no longer. We need to explore why this is. Closely linked with relativity is the law relating to adverse possession; again, this used to be central to land law, but is no longer. Yet the study of the law of adverse possession remains, as it has always been, a uniquely useful way of re-examining concepts fundamental to land law; and it has also become, very recently, a fascinating illustration of the interplay between common law concepts and the developing jurisprudence of European human rights.

RELATIVITY AND LIMITATION

To get the idea of relativity of title, remember what was said in Chapter 3 about deeds. Where title is unregistered, ownership of land is proved by producing a stack of deeds, which when read through from the top down tells the story of the ownership of that land. Apart from being on paper rather than oral, this is conceptually no different from peasant folk proving title to land by reciting a genealogy: this land is mine because I inherited it from my father, who had it from his father, etc. The idea being expressed is: 'the land is mine, not by virtue of one single indisputable transaction, but because I live here and I [and my predecessors] have been here longer than anyone else'. What is being asserted is not an absolute title, but a relative one: the best available right to possess the land.

Why did English land law develop so as to depend upon proof of relative rather than absolute title? After all, in the early Middle Ages it was still possible to prove a right to hold land by pointing to a Crown grant, whether documented or by appealing to witnesses and memories. The answer to this question lies

in medieval court processes. Of the numerous ways of
recovering land in the Middle Ages, two procedures seem to
have steered the substance of this part of the law. One was the
'writ of right' (a writ was a document summoning the parties to
court)—the *breve de recto tenendo*. Such a writ required proof of
the best possible entitlement to the land—something like absolute title—and it was tried by battle. It was not therefore to be
undertaken lightly. Even when trial by battle became obsolete,
the writ remained procedurally and evidentially inconvenient.
The other way of doing it was to use the 'assize of novel
disseisin'. This was tried by producing witnesses before a jury;
and it was relatively quick and easy, and safer for those of a
nervous disposition. What had to be proved was simply that you
were in possession of the land before your opponent, who was
supposed to be a recent trespasser, hence the 'novel'. Accordingly, the action in trespass came to be used always in preference
to the writ of right, as a general way of asserting title to land, and
English law did not bother to develop any other way of proving
title absolutely. Thus it has been said that all an English landowner can ever prove is a relative title—an entitlement that is
better than that of whoever is disputing it—rather than an
absolute title indisputable by anyone at all.

The trouble with relative title, of course, is that, logically,
proof is never complete. The weakness of a title going back 100
years might be that someone else could prove a chain of title
going back 150 years, and so on. Surely the system requires us to
prove ownership all the way back to 1066, or as far back as we
can get? It does not, and the reason it does not is the concept of
the limitation of actions. There is a policy that court proceedings
should be brought reasonably promptly, so that evidence does
not go stale and so that people can be reasonably confident that
what they hold will not be challenged after a while. This applies
as much to the law of obligations as to the law of property. You
can sue for a breach of contract up to six years after a breach, and
after that there is nothing you can do about it. And so it goes for
land as well. If someone else sets up home in your house or starts
grazing horses in your spare field, you cannot put off forever the
day on which you take court proceedings to throw him out.
The principle of limitation of actions as it operates in land law

means that, at the end of the limitation period—twelve years—you will not only be unable to take action to recover your land but you will actually lose your title to the land.

The logical outcome of this is that when proving ownership of land, where title is unregistered (where title is registered, the law is now different, as we shall discuss), all one really has to do is to prove that one has been in possession of the land for longer than the limitation period: the last twelve years. And this puts a convenient limit on the size of the heap of deeds that one has to keep.

In practice, in unregistered land the requirements for proof of title take one a little further back than that, for the avoidance of doubt and in order to ensure that good quality evidence of title is available. The stack of deeds is supposed to start with a document at least fifteen years old (thus a little longer than the limitation period). That document must be a 'good root of title', namely one which gives comprehensive information about the land, and must be a transaction for value rather than a transmission after death. Thus the landowner whose family acquired a farm, or perhaps a stately home 200 years ago, would keep at the bottom of his heap of deeds the conveyance to his ancestor 200 years ago, plus all the documents transmitting the land down the generations since then, plus any documents dealing with the land in the meantime: mortgages, leases, grants of easements, records of sales of part of the land, etc. Jones, selling his ordinary suburban house, bought and sold every few years, would simply trace title back to the last conveyance more than fifteen years ago. That small stack of deeds says: 'this land is mine because I bought it from Bloggs ten years ago, and he bought it from Biggs twenty years ago. Since you can see that I am in possession of the land, there is no chance that it has been acquired by a squatter in the course of the last twenty years. So you can safely buy it from me.' Notice the importance of possession in that analysis: the claim is not watertight without it because if Jones is not in possession of the land someone else might be, and might have been, for all we know, for more than twelve years because Bloggs may not have bought a good title from Biggs.

Suppose someone else—Sam the squatter—*did* take possession of the land, or of some of it, nineteen years ago. The land is now his. How does that work?

SQUATTER'S TITLE

Let us embroider the story a little; and for the sake of understanding how adverse possession and relativity of title *have* operated, let us assume that all the titles in it are unregistered despite the fact that, in real life, compulsory registration would have changed that.

Bloggs bought the land from Biggs in 1980. It is not an ordinary house, but a large farm and Bloggs was not a careful farmer. In 1981 his neighbour Sam, who had been trespassing by grazing his goats on an unfenced area belonging to Biggs and then to Bloggs for some time, put up a fence around that area, separating it from Bloggs' land and joining it on to his own. The goats grazed on quietly. In 1990 Bloggs sold to Jones, who did not notice the discrepancy between the land on the plan and the fencing on the ground. Jones now wants to sell; and *his* purchaser has noticed that Jones is not in possession of the goat field. Investigations are made. It turns out that Sam can prove the date on which he put the fence up, and can show (from a mixture of documentation, photographs, and the evidence of his wife and the neighbours) that he has been in possession of the field ever since. If he can also show that he intended to possess the land and to exclude others, including the 'true' owner, so far as was practicable, then he has proved, first, that Jones ceased to be owner of the land seven years ago, at the point when Sam clocked up his twelve years' possession.[1] Second, the evidence Sam has collected is equally proof that he is the owner of the goat field. He can produce that evidence to the Land Registry and his title can be registered, on a voluntary basis. He is not obliged to register, but a purchaser is unlikely to accept his title unless it is acceptable to the Registry.

The detail of what a squatter must prove in order to grow a title to the land in this way has been evolved over the years in the courts. The courts have analysed possession as having both a physical element—the squatter must, as a matter of fact, be in possession of the land—and a mental element—he must actually intend to be there and to use the land as his own, and to keep

---

[1] Limitation Act 1980, s 17.

others out so far as practicable, and his actions must make that clear. Mending a fence around an area in order to keep livestock in it will not necessarily do this; fencing an area and padlocking the gate will. He does not have to show that he intended to become the owner, nor that he meant to steal it, nor that he thought the land was his, nor that he would not have been unwilling to pay rent for the land if asked. There is no need for him to have actively evicted Bloggs, nor for his activities on the land to have been interfering with Bloggs or Jones. But he must not be there with permission; permission makes him a licensee, and a licensee cannot be in adverse possession. This means that one easy way to defeat a claim by a squatter is to give him permission to stay.

Before 1833, successive limitation statutes required that the squatter's possession be *adverse*, in the sense that it must be inconsistent with the way the paper owner intended to use the land. The Real Property Limitation Act 1833 dropped that requirement. The courts revived it in *Leigh v Jack*[2] in 1879, holding that if a squatter was using land for which the paper owner had no current use, and was not actually interfering with anything the owner wanted to do, he was not in adverse possession and the limitation period could not run against the owner. That decision was not clearly overruled until 1990.[3] Notice that a consequence of these developments is that it is possible for a landowner to lose land inadvertently, by carelessness about the activities of a trespasser during a period when he had no use for the land but intended to develop it in the future. This may, in some contexts, sounds like a draconian penalty for understandable slackness. Yet if we move away from fields of goats and into an urban context, the limitation of actions can be said to have a social and redistributive function in the context of squatting, in empty property, by those who have no home. Adverse possession in such circumstances may be seen as sensible, or as opportunistic, or as theft; now and then there are calls for it to be criminalized. It is not obvious that the use of a an empty building for shelter is wrong; and while an

---

[2] (1879) 5 Ex D 264.
[3] *Buckinghamshire County Council v Moran* [1990] Ch 623.

owner's neglect should not readily lead to his losing his entire property, it is not obvious that giving the squatter a good title after twelve years' tolerance or ignorance by the landowner is particularly harsh.

Reverting to matters of title: the squatter's title arises, not from the ending of the entitlement of the paper owner of the land after twelve years, but from his own possession. It works like this. At the point just before Sam takes possession of the field (it is not clear when that is, but it happens, at the latest, when he puts the fence up), Bloggs has a legal fee simple estate in it. Just after Sam takes possession, so has Sam, purely because he has possession of the land.[4] There are two fees simple in the land at this point, and for the next twelve years. Someone who has taken possession of land has a fee simple in it because of the status of possession in legal proceedings. If all that is needed to remove another person from land is proof that you were in possession of it before he was, then possession is a strong right, and so, over time, possession itself came to be regarded as an estate in land, provided the possessor is not on the land by permission. And the law allows this estate to be transmitted to one's heirs, so that it can be called a 'fee'.[5] If Sam dies after five years' possession, his heir (by his will or intestacy) will take over that five years' credit, as it were, and can carry on squatting. There is no particular restriction on its duration, so it is a fee simple. By section 1 of the Law of Property Act 1925, it qualifies as a legal fee simple.

So for the first twelve years of Sam's possession there are two legal owners of the land; but one owner has a stronger right than the other. Both Bloggs and Sam have the right to keep others out of the field. But while Bloggs has the right to remove Sam too (he could take down the fence and chase off the goats or, if that does not work, he can sue in trespass), Sam has the right to eject anyone who enters the land against Sam's will *except* Bloggs. Bloggs still has the best available right to possession of the land; but in legal proceedings between Sam and another, later trespasser, Sam will win, because he has a better right to

---

[4] *Asher v Whitlock* (1865) LR 1 QB 1, Exch Ch.
[5] Chapter 2, p 21.

possession—he has been there longer—than anyone else except Bloggs. Title is thus relative. What matters in any given set of proceedings is having a better title than one's opponent, not being the 'true' owner of land. If this all sounds medieval, it is. But it has been fiercely defended by lawyers because it has the virtue of pragmatism. It enables the purchaser of land to start from the assumption that whoever has possession of land is supposed to be there, and it ties ownership of land to the truth about what is happening on the ground.

Sam's squatter's title is therefore not one that he has taken from Bloggs or Jones. His title is acquired by possession. It is always a fee simple title, even if Bloggs and Jones happen to be leaseholders rather than freeholders.[6] If that is the case, their right to the land ceases at the expiry of the limitation period just as it does if they are freeholders. Suppose they held, successively, a 99-year lease granted by Fred the freeholder in 1951. In 2050, their lease would have ended anyway. Sam has by then been enjoying a fee simple for a number of years. But when the 1951 lease ends, Fred becomes entitled once again to take possession of the land. And from that point onwards, Sam can be evicted by Fred for twelve years, because Fred has the right to sue in trespass until the limitation period expires against him, as it did decades ago against the successive leaseholders.

The law of adverse possession is particularly useful in the context of mistakes about boundaries. I build a garage at the edge of my land. I make a mistake about the boundary, so that the garage encroaches onto your garden by about 20cm. Neither you nor I notice. I have physical possession of that 20cm; I certainly intend to use the land as my own, it being part of my garage. For twelve years, if you notice what has happened you can make me move the garage. After twelve years the mistake does not matter because the law of adverse possession has brought ownership into line with possession and I am now the sole owner of the 20cm strip. If anyone notices the discrepancy between the land and the plans, we can check the date when the garage was built and we can redraw the plans. This avoids

---

[6] *Fairweather v St Marylebone Property Co Ltd* [1963] AC 510.

litigation and ensures that documentary title can easily be brought into line with what is happening on the ground.

That, then, is the background; and that is still the law in the rapidly reducing number of instances of unregistered title. But the Land Registration Act 2002 dramatically reduced the circumstances in which title can be acquired by possession where title to the land is registered. This will now be so very rare that it is no longer realistic to say that title is in any sense relative in registered land.

THE REVOLUTION: ADVERSE POSSESSION AND REGISTERED LAND

In a number of jurisdictions, acquisition of title by adverse possession is not possible when title is registered. Indeed, it was not possible under the early English registration statutes in the nineteenth century. The limitation of actions is not needed as a way of avoiding trials of very old disputes with stale evidence if the only evidence of title needed is the register itself. But the Land Registration Act 1925 allowed it, because of its usefulness in dealing with boundaries. Experience with the early registration statutes, where boundaries had to be determined precisely, indicated that it would be much easier to leave boundaries rather loosely indicated on Land Registry plans, and to allow adverse possession to operate to resolve difficulties when they arose.

Working out the mechanics of adverse possession when title is registered is not straightforward. Suppose, in our example above, Biggs' title was registered. Bloggs would have become the registered proprietor and his title would have included the goat field. What happened when Sam achieved twelve years' adverse possession so that Bloggs ceased to be the owner of the goat field? He did not, of course, notice this happening (neither did Sam, unless he was unusually well-informed), and no change was made to the register. Bloggs remained the registered proprietor of the goat field and that means, as we have observed,[7] that

---

[7] Chapter 3, pp 65 ff.

he still held the legal title to that land, even though adverse possession is supposed to have taken away his title. The solution to this problem adopted by the Land Registration Act 1925 is to say that from the point when the limitation period expires, Bloggs holds the registered title upon trust for Sam. If Sam eventually registers his squatter's title, Bloggs' legal title to the goat field will disappear. The same analysis works for the boundary mistake, where eventually the Land Registry plans for the two titles will be amended.

This meant that the Land Registration Act 1925 did not truly abolish relativity of title. It substituted a registered title for a deeds-based title. But it did not eliminate the possibility of a concurrent and unregistered fee simple by adverse possession, growing quietly in the background, maturing after twelve years into one that defeats the ownership of the registered proprietor. Proof of possession, as well as reference to the register, remained an essential part of the proof of title.[8]

The use of a trust to manage the discrepancy between paper ownership and the truth of ownership on the ground is ingenious, but uncomfortable. Sam is supposed to have a legal title from the point at which he takes adverse possession; is it converted to an equitable one when the trust takes effect? If Bloggs owns the land jointly with his wife would Sam's interest be overreached when Mr and Mrs Bloggs sold the land? If so, would Bloggs hold the sale proceeds on trust for Sam? In any event, the imposition of a trust is unnecessary, because Sam's interest was an overriding interest[9] and would bind a purchaser just as could other legal, unregistered interests such as an easement or a short lease.

---

[8] Just a few cases may still be decided under the Land Registration Act 1925, where it is claimed that title was actually acquired by a squatter before 2003 and remains valid because of the transitional provisions of the Land Registration Act 2002.

[9] The 1925 Act included an overriding interest: 'rights acquired or in the course of acquisition under the Limitation Acts'. This meant that Sam's years of adverse possession still counted in his favour when Bloggs became owner; and that once he became absolutely entitled as against Bloggs, his ownership remained enforceable against purchasers, even if he was not in actual occupation of the land. That overriding interest is not found in the 2002 Act.

At a more general level, the idea of having more than one fee simple in registered land was upsetting to land registration theory. Can there be more than one registered freehold estate, as in the case where Biggs and Bloggs were leaseholders and they have lost their titles but their landlord has not? The practice of different Land Registry offices differed in such cases.[10] And what, at a higher level still, about the idea of the guarantee of title? If registration means that one's title is guaranteed, does it make sense to have the possibility of losing it to a squatter?

The answer to that last question is actually 'yes', if land has been abandoned, and for boundary problems. But in other respects adverse possession is not relevant to registered land because it is not needed as a way of controlling the proof of title. All the business about restricting the age of deeds one needs to keep and produce in order to show title is irrelevant when title is seen simply by looking at the register. So much of the need for adverse possession is gone, even though some of the practical justification remains.

ADVERSE POSSESSION AFTER THE LAND REGISTRATION ACT 2002: TITLE BY REGISTRATION

Section 96 of the Land Registration Act 2002 abolished the limitation period for registered titles. It did so because the Law Commission was persuaded by the technical conveyancing point just mentioned, by the argument about guarantee, by the fact that limitation is not needed to prevent stale evidence of title, and by one further issue: the need to encourage voluntary registration. One of the aims of the Land Registration Act 2002 was to get rid of unregistered title and ensure that all land gets on to the register. As we have seen,[11] land is forced on to the register when it is sold or mortgaged, when ownership changes because of a change of trustees, or when it is transmitted

---

[10] In *Spectrum Investment Co v Holmes* [1981] 1 WLR 221 the squatter was given a leasehold title, becoming a tenant under the lease that the dispossessed leaseholder had held, but with a different title number.

[11] Chapter 3, p 48.

on death. Some land never goes through these processes, because it is held on a family trust, for example, or owned by a university or a local authority. One way of persuading such entities to register their land voluntarily is to make registration attractive: and so by providing that there is no limitation period with respect to registered titles—ie there is no restriction on how long one can delay before evicting a trespasser—the Land Registration Act 2002 has made registered titles squatter-proof. Subtract fifteen years from the figures in the story of Sam, Jones, Biggs, and Bloggs, but assume again that Biggs' title was registered. Now, at the point when Sam has been in possession of the land for twelve years, the Land Registration Act 2002 is in force. There is no limitation period for registered titles, Bloggs does not automatically lose to Sam, and Sam has no right to registration.

This means that proof of title has been divorced from proof of possession just as surely as the Land Registration Act 1925 divorced it from deeds. All that is needed to show ownership of land is the Land Register. And that is why it no longer makes sense, except for those areas of land whose title is not yet registered, to say that title to land in England and Wales is relative. Legal ownership is by registration alone. Although, technically, a squatter can still be growing a fee simple by adverse possession, that fee simple will never, by itself, mature into true ownership and so it is not a significant interest. There are some very limited circumstances, to be discussed below, where Sam can become the registered proprietor of the land; but adverse possession alone is never sufficient. In those limited cases, the title Sam acquires on registration is the title that the dispossessed proprietor lost. It is a takeover; if Bloggs was a leaseholder, Sam will take over the lease so far as it relates to the field. The squatter's fee simple, acquired by adverse possession, disappears.

Now that, in the vast majority of cases, the squatter's interest in the land can no longer turn into true/sole ownership, it may be that we shall in time cease to regard it as a fee simple (since most land law concepts have been defined by reference to their practical effects). So it would be a short step to a legislative redefinition of the squatter's interest during the qualifying period. All the rigmarole about his ability to evict later trespassers is scarcely necessary; he need not be regarded as having a property right during this period. Limitation starts to look much more like the prescription of easements.

So that is what has happened to relativity of title. But there is more to say about adverse possession, and about its surviving role.

ADVERSE POSSESSION AND HUMAN RIGHTS

The statutes of limitation can be said to deprive landowners of their property without compensation. English law has never regarded them in this light; we have always viewed them as a necessary rule of litigation and a component in conveyancing practice. As we have seen, the necessity for the limitation of actions to recover land is considerably weaker once title is registered. And alongside the growing appreciation of the inappropriateness of limitation in registered title there has been a new awareness of the human rights difficulties inherent in the principle.

JA Pye (Oxford) Ltd v Graham[12] was a landmark decisions on adverse possession. It concerned farmland, specifically land used by JA Pye (Oxford) Ltd, to whom it did not belong, for grazing horses; the company had had a grazing licence, which had expired and had not been renewed. The land was not currently useful to its registered proprietor, but was intended to be developed in the future; the registered proprietor was a property developer and the land, with its development value, was extremely valuable. It would have been very easy for the owner to turn the squatter off the land; JA Pye (Oxford) Ltd was inoffensively taking advantage of the owner's failure to object to his presence, and would have left if asked. Eventually, however, the company realized the strength of its position and claimed a title by adverse possession, before the coming into force of the Land Registration Act 2002.

Pye (Oxford) Ltd lost its land after appeals as far as the House of Lords. The decision was seen as an uncomfortable one, in that

---

[12] [2002] UKHL 30.

the loss of so much land was an excessive penalty for the owner's laziness. But human rights considerations were dismissed by the Court of Appeal on the basis that the Limitation Act 1980 does not take away the owner's land, but simply forbids him access to the courts to recover it. This is quite simply incorrect, because of the fact that the owner's title is also extinguished; but in the House of Lords, surprisingly, the company conceded that human rights arguments were not relevant because the dispossession took place before the coming into force of the Human Rights Act 1998.

Pye then made a claim in the European Court of Human Rights on the basis that the United Kingdom government, by maintaining the limitation of actions to recover land, had deprived it of its possessions, otherwise than in the public interest and without compensation, contrary to Article 1 of the First Protocol to the European Convention on Human Rights. So the parties were different: Pye had lost its land already, and the defendant was the government, on the basis that the legislation caused the deprivation of Pye's possessions.

The government's argument against the Article 8 point was that there was no deprivation, because the Limitation Acts are part of the conditions of landholding in this jurisdiction. It is a given that if you allow a trespasser on to your land and fail to take action for twelve years, your title is lost and his is confirmed. The European Court's view was that ownership simply cannot be qualified in that way. In so holding, the Court showed its very European concept of land ownership. The government's position was much more in tune with the common law concept of ownership as a bundle of rights, and perhaps still not fully divorced from the feudal idea of landholding as a privilege exercised upon conditions. The government's argument was fatally weakened by the fact that it had already legislated to reform adverse possession in registered land. The European Court's judgment appears to have been very much influenced by the changes made in the Land Registration Act 2002, as if the issue had already been decided by the government against itself. It was unmoved by the argument that Pye was responsible for its own loss—and Pye had indeed been very careless, given that the squatter had on more than one occasion requested a grazing agreement and would have paid rent if asked. It seems that whatever the extent of the landowner's inadvertence or carelessness, the Court regarded the Limitation Acts as the cause of the loss.

The European Court declared that the loss of Pye's land was not in the public interest, in view of the fact that its title was registered. The Court expressed approval of the changes made in the 2002 Act—as had the English judges in *Pye v Graham*—and so gave the impression that the human rights problem in the 1925 statute has in fact been solved for the future.

The European Court's decision left the government with a potentially serious liability for compensation in the event of future claims brought under the 1925 Act. Worse, the decision was set to cause serious upheaval in Ireland and Northern Ireland, whose title registration statutes are modelled on the English 1925 statute and allow the acquisition of title by adverse possession, and where inheritance issues are quite commonly resolved on the basis that land is not transferred on death, the family keeps on farming, and everything sorts itself out eventually by virtue of possession.

The government appealed the decision in *Pye* to the Grand Chamber of the European Court of Human Rights.[13] It succeeded, by a 10:7 majority; it was held that, rather than being a deprivation of possessions, the law of adverse possession amounted only to a control of use. As such, it served a legitimate aim in the public interest, and was a proportionate means of achieving that aim. Accordingly, there was no violation of Article 1 of the First Protocol to the Convention. The majority noted that in other European jurisdictions there was no question of compensation being part of an adverse possession regime. It regarded the high value of the land (around £2.5 million) as irrelevant since, if adverse possession is to work at all, it must do so regardless of value.

A relief, certainly, for the government and for land law in a common law system; a surprise too, perhaps. Is it the end of the story? The decision of the Grand Chamber is not binding

---

[13] *JA Pye (Oxford) Ltd v UK* (2007) 46 EHRR 1083.

authority so far as the United Kingdom courts are concerned; they are required simply to 'have regard' to the European Court's decisions. The Grand Chamber's decision, restoring as it does our legal orthodoxy, must be of the highest persuasive authority and it is unlikely that it will be questioned. But it is not impossible. We know now, as we did not know in the immediate aftermath of the Grand Chamber decision, that the European Court of Human Rights does not always regard a statutory regime as compliant in its entirety and in all circumstances. The saga, whose latest chapter is *Manchester City Council v Pinnock*,[14] reminds us that, by analogy, it may be dangerous for us simply to say: our law of adverse possession is human rights compliant. There must still be possibilities for challenge, perhaps even under the new regime of the Land Registration Act 2002, as noted below.

THE RESIDUAL LAW OF ADVERSE POSSESSION

Adverse possession remains a live concept, for two principal reasons.

First, and most obviously, it is alive and well where title is not registered. Landowners whose titles are not registered may still lose them to squatters.

The next episode in the story of a squatter on unregistered land is likely to be either that the problem is discovered on sale, as it was in our story of Bloggs, Jones, and Sam, or that the squatter applies for registration of his title. In either case, the outcome is likely to be that the squatter's title is registered, with or without litigation. If Sam simply applies for registration, independently of any transaction, Jones will not even know about the registration. It may be years before he discovers that his deeds are no longer proof of ownership of that particular part of his land.

An alternative outcome for the story of Sam the squatter in *unregistered* land is that Jones, or a purchaser from Jones, applies

---

[14] [2010] UKSC 45; see Chapter 7.

for registration of title to the land. We have said little about first registration, apart from the fact that it is triggered by certain transactions, and that it is also available on a voluntary basis—owners might register because they have lost their deeds, or with the intention of making their land squatter-proof, as discussed above. Section 11 of, and Schedule 1 to, the Land Registration Act 2002 set out the interests that will bind the land on first registration, and for the most part the intention is to replicate whatever was the position just before registration. But section 11(4) states that, on first registration, the land is subject to any interests on the register, any interests listed in Schedule 1, and any interests acquired under the Limitation Act 1980 *of which the registered proprietor has notice* (emphasis added). Schedule 1 is a list of interests that override first registration; contrast Schedule 3, which is the list of interests, already repeatedly discussed here, which override registered dispositions. There are some interesting differences between the two lists, but one element they have in common is paragraph 2. The details in the two paragraphs 2 are different; but the effect is that if Sam is in actual occupation of the land still, his interest survives registration. He can, when forced to do so, by a challenge from the newly registered proprietor, or on his own initiative, apply to have the register altered so that he becomes the registered proprietor. But it is possible that after clocking up his twelve years, Sam left. He holds an unregistered fee simple in that land, nevertheless. There was some concern in Parliament while the 2002 Act was being debated about squatters who acquire title and then abandon the land. So the effect of the provisions of section 11(4) is that if Sam is not in actual occupation, Jones' newly registered estate will only be subject to Sam's interest if Jones has notice of him. Constructive notice is presumably included.

Accordingly, an unregistered title can be lost to an adverse possessor without the dispossessed proprietor knowing anything about it. The squatter can get his title registered, ditto. But if the dispossessed proprietor happens to apply voluntarily for first registration, not knowing that he has lost his title already to a squatter who, however, is not currently occupying the land, the dispossessed proprietor will actually regain his title, and the squatter will lose what he gained. This is far-fetched, but possible. It demonstrates the potency of registration. It also demonstrates an alarming tendency for ownership to be lost, without the owner knowing. The potential for a human rights challenge is obvious, and the counter to that challenge is the public interest in not allowing unregistered title to be lost to a squatter who then abandons the land but retains title to it. It is arguable that for the sake of certainty and marketability (not to mention individual desert) in such a case paper title should prevail, and that it certainly should do so once registered.

The second reason why adverse possession remains a live concept is that it still plays a restricted role in registered title, as follows. For one thing, there may still be cases where title to land was registered under the 1925 Act and was lost to a squatter before the Land Registration Act 2002 came into force in October 2003. Transitional provisions were designed to ensure that there should be no difficulty in the squatter applying now for his title to be registered.

The 2002 Act, of course, makes things very different. It accepts the possibility of Sam and his adverse possession of the goat field. It states that there is no limitation period with respect to registered title, so that there is no point at which Jones loses his title automatically by operation of law. But there are two ways in which Sam can acquire land by adverse possession nevertheless. The Act provides that after 10 years' adverse possession, Sam can apply for registration as the proprietor of Jones' registered title (not, notice, for registration of *Sam's* title acquired by adverse possession). When he does so, the registrar will inform Jones. If Jones responds within 65 working days, stating that he objects to Sam's registration, then Sam will not be registered as proprietor. Jones then has a further two years to evict Sam. If Jones does not reply to the notice, or if Jones fails to get rid of Sam in the next two years, then Sam has a right to apply to be registered, and to take over Jones' title to the goat field.

So the first way in which Sam can acquire title to the field is if the land has been abandoned by Jones—demonstrated by his not replying to the registrar's notice, or not bothering to follow up the notice by evicting Sam. One of the concerns that arose in the discussions that followed the first European Court decision in *JA Pye (Oxford) Ltd v UK* was that the new legislation might be found not to be compliant with the European Convention on Human Rights in a case where that 65-day period was inadequate and in fact gave the registered proprietor no safeguard; for example, where he was ill, or the notice for some reason did not reach him. That concern has now abated, but it may not be wholly without foundation.

The Act provides that even if Jones makes objection Sam can be registered if he falls within one of three exceptions. Two of them actually have nothing to do with adverse possession; they occur when Sam is entitled to the land because he has an equity arising from an estoppel,[15] or otherwise, for example under a registered proprietor's will. The point about both of these is that adverse possession is irrelevant; Sam could have applied to the court to be registered as proprietor of the land. But the law gives him a little reward for having also been in adverse possession of the land for ten years: it enables him to use the procedure appropriate to adverse possession, namely an application to the Land Registry Adjudicator,[16] instead of having to use the court system. The Adjudicator is cheaper and quicker.

But the third exception is about adverse possession; it is the case where there is a genuine mistake about boundaries, as in the example of my garage, given above. This is therefore the second way in which Sam can acquire title by adverse possession.

So the draftsman of the 2002 Act did cater for two instances of practical need for adverse possession, namely abandoned land, and boundary problems. But the law of adverse possession can no longer simply redistribute land from those who do not bother to those who have a use for it.

EVALUATION

An initial concern about the 2002 Act was that it might not have left sufficient room for adverse possession. The Act fails to allow it as a resolution for boundary disputes where there has been no mistake. I might have deliberately encroached on your land to

---

[15] Chapter 4, p 96 ff.   [16] Land Registration Act 2002, s 107.

build my garage: even there, there is something to be said for a limit to the length of time in which my garage is at risk of legal proceedings. If it has stood happily on the land for fifty years without the neighbour minding, and then I apply to have the Land Registry plan brought into line with possession on the ground, it may not be right to have to litigate about states of mind at this distance. But the adverse possession provisions of the Land Registration Act 2002 help only the virtuous squatter, who is saving land from abandonment, or who genuinely got the boundary wrong when he built his garage.

On a more general level, there was some doubt as to whether or not the law had been improved by the abolition of the limitation period for registered titles. It has certainly had some of its desired effect, in that since the Act came into force a number of local authorities have registered their titles. The register has been made more powerful. The uneasiness that remained before the decision in *Pye* was the divorcing of title from possession. There is a risk that at some stage too much land will be rendered unusable, even if not actually abandoned, by the non-application of the limitation period, or that legal ownership may be out of synch with physical possession to an uncomfortable extent. This has happened in other jurisdictions; it is not unimaginable that there may have to be a re-think.

Following the first European Court decision in *Pye*, concern was expressed in the opposite direction. The worry was that despite the fact that the decision was limited to the interaction of the law of adverse possession with the provisions of the Land Registration Act 1925, nevertheless the provisions for registration of a squatter in the limited circumstances that the 2002 Act allows might themselves be violations of the registered proprietor's human rights. The Act might not have gone far enough in eliminating adverse possession.

Those two trains of thought could not stand together, and the first edition of this book—written shortly before the Grand Chamber's decision—ended on a note of considerable uncertainty. The Grand Chamber's decision has resolved that uncertainty insofar as it can be resolved in a human rights environment where, it seems, no statutory regime can conclusively be said always to be human rights compliant.

There remains, therefore, the other concern: that the 2002 Act has cut back the law of adverse possession to a level at which its utility is severely reduced. Relief about *Pye* should not blind us to the challenge that the 2002 Act has produced and whose full effects may not be felt for some years.

BIBLIOGRAPHY

N. Cobb and L. Fox, 'Living outside the system? The (im)morality of urban squatting after the Land Registration Act 2002' (2007) 27 *Legal Studies* 236.

E. Cooke, 'A postscript to *Pye*' (2008) 59(2) *Northern Ireland Legal Quarterly* 140.

M. Dockray, 'Why do we need adverse possession?' [1985] 49 *The Conveyancer and Property Lawyer* 272.

Law Commission and HM Land Registry, *Land Registration for the Twenty-First Century; a conveyancing revolution*, (Law Com No 271) (London, The Stationery Office, 2001) Part XIV, pp 299 ff.

A. W. B. Simpson, *A History of the Land Law* (Oxford, Clarendon Press, 2nd edn, 1986) Ch II.

INDEX